THE NATIONAL ARMY MUSEUM BOOK OF

THE TURKISH FRONT

THE NATIONAL ARMY MUSEUM BOOK OF

THE TURKISH FRONT
1914–1918

THE CAMPAIGNS AT GALLIPOLI,
IN MESOPOTAMIA AND IN PALESTINE

Field Marshal Lord Carver

GCB, CBE, DSO, MC

PAN BOOKS

in association with

The National Army Museum

First published 2003 by Sidgwick & Jackson

This edition published 2004 Pan Books
an imprint of Pan Macmillan Ltd
Pan Macmillan, 20 New Wharf Road, London N1 9RR
Basingstoke and Oxford
Associated companies throughout the world
www.panmacmillan.com

ISBN 0 330 49108 3

3 5 7 9 8 6 4 2

A CIP catalogue record for this book is available from
the British Library.

Typeset by SetSystems Ltd, Saffron Walden, Essex
Printed and bound in Great Britain by
Mackays of Chatham plc, Chatham, Kent

Foreword

The death of Field Marshal Lord Carver on 9 December 2001 marked the passing of one of the distinguished soldiers of the twentieth century. His achievements in the course of a long and exceptional career were recognized in his lifetime and will no doubt receive further attention from commentators in the future. At the National Army Museum, however, he was also respected as a military historian. In 1999 he wrote the *National Army Museum Book of the Boer War* and in 2001, shortly before his death, he completed the typescript of this, his last work. It is to be hoped that its posthumous publication serves, in a small way, as a memorial to him.

When the commissioning of this book was first mooted, the Field Marshal, a noted exponent of desert warfare during the Second World War, was the obvious choice to write it. As ever, the authoritative nature of his writing has fully justified the decision. It is worth observing too that, for him, the events he has described were immediate history. He was born the day before the first Gallipoli landings took place and as a cadet at the Royal Military College, Sandhurst in the early 1930s one of his set texts was Colonel Archibald Wavell's recently published *The Palestine Campaigns*.

But if the campaigns against the Turks could be studied by Michael Carver in the early 1930s for their strategic and tactical lessons, what of their significance in the first decade of the twenty-first century? One only has to reflect upon media coverage to discover the answer. By defeating the Turks and dismembering the Ottoman Empire, the British resolved the age-old Eastern Question of what to do with the 'Sick Man of Europe'; but in so doing they inadvertently initiated a problem which is proving just as difficult to resolve: the Arab–Israeli conflict. The British also created out of Mesopotamia an independent Iraq. With the 'war against terrorism' currently in the forefront of politicians' minds, the issue of 1915 of whether or not to march on Baghdad has a resonance today for many in the West.

In this book Lord Carver made extensive use of the Museum's Indian Army archive and it is worth recalling that the National Army Museum,

established by Royal Charter in 1960, developed from the Indian Army
Memorial Room at the Royal Military Academy, Sandhurst. The promotion
of an understanding of the army of British India and its achievements has
always been one of the National Army Museum's prime concerns. A fighting
force that bore the brunt of the war in Mesopotamia and which contributed
significantly at Gallipoli, as well as in Egypt and Palestine, has long deserved
greater recognition. It is appropriate, therefore, that the book's jacket and
cover design incorporates the Indian Army Meritorious Service Medal and
its Ribbon.

Although Field Marshal Lord Carver was unable to complete a list of
acknowledgements before his death, he would have wished to thank Dr
Alastair Massie, Head of the Museum's Department of Archives, Photographs, Film and Sound, who liaised with him on this book throughout its
gestation and has willingly completed several outstanding tasks, not least in
relation to selecting and captioning the illustrations. Gratitude is also due to
William Armstrong and Ingrid Connell of Pan Macmillan, whose support
of this volume is gladly and publicly recognized.

Ian G. Robertson
Director, National Army Museum
June 2002

Preface

The war that Britain fought against the Ottoman Empire (or Turkey, as it was usually called at the time) as part of the First World War against the Central Powers, basically Germany and the Austro-Hungarian Empire, has generally been treated and chronicled as three separate campaigns: at the Dardanelles (or Gallipoli), in Mesopotamia (modern Iraq), and in Palestine. Although separate in several ways, they were interlinked and affected each other, and this book pulls them all together. Much has been written about Gallipoli, much less about the other two, and hardly anything treating them as one, as this book does. Its main aim is not to provide any new historical evidence or aspect, but to portray what it was like to serve in those campaigns. Half of what follows consists of extracts from letters, diaries or other papers of participants, held in the archives of the National Army Museum. All the originators were citizens of the United Kingdom, and although the armies in which they served relied heavily on soldiers from other parts of the British Empire, notably Australia, New Zealand and India, there are no contributions from them. Nor are there any from the French, who made a significant difference at Gallipoli, or from the Russians, who were fighting Turkey from their territory at the same time. There are several contributions from British soldiers serving in the Indian Army.

Many of the participants served in more than one of the three campaigns. After Gallipoli, the 13th and 29th British Infantry Divisions served in Mesopotamia, and the 10th, 53rd and 54th Infantry and the 2nd Yeomanry Divisions, and some Australian and New Zealand mounted troops, served in Palestine. The 3rd and 7th Indian Infantry Divisions served in Egypt before being sent to Mesopotamia, and then returned to fight in Palestine in 1918.

Casualties were high in all three campaigns, both in action and from disease, and the sufferings of the soldiers in some respects were starker than on the Western Front. Prisoners of war were treated harshly, although officers, from the accounts in the archives, were treated much better than the other ranks, of whom the Indians suffered particularly severely. There were many examples of great courage and endurance, particularly in the ANZAC sector at Gallipoli, and some instances of a significant lack of those qualities. Heights of incompetence at the higher level were seen at Suvla Bay and in some actions in Mesopotamia. The accounts in the pages that follow provide a stark reminder of what the soldiers endured.

Contents

List of Illustrations

All are from the National Army Museum's collection. The number after the description is the negative number.

Section One: Gallipoli

Section Two: Mesopotamia

Maps

OTTOMAN EMPIRE, 1914

RUSSIA

AUSTRIA-HUNGARY

CRIMEA

ROMANIA

Belgrade

Bucharest

Sevastopol

BOSNIA
(AUSTRIA-
HUNGARY)

Danube

BLACK

BULGARIA

Sofia

SERBIA

ITALY

ALBANIA

Constantinople

Salonika

Gallipoli

Ankara

GREECE

Smyrna

Athens

Rhodes

CYPRUS

CRETE

M E D I T E R R A N E A N   S E A

Benghazi

Sollum

Alexandria

Mersa
Matruh

LIBYA
(ITALY)

Cairo

Suez

Siwa

EGYPT

Nile

RUSSIA

SEA

CASPIAN SEA

GEORGIA

ARMENIA

KARABAGH

Erzerum

AZERBAIJAN

TURKEY

P

Mosul

LURISTAN

Euphrates

Tigris

Alexandretta

Aleppo

SYRIA

Homs

Tripoli

Baghdad

Beirut

MESOPOTAMIA   Kut

Damascus

Basra

Amman

Jerusalem

Gaza

KUWAIT   *PERSIAN GULF*

ARABIA

Aqaba

RED SEA

███ Ottoman Empire

▨ Areas occupied by Britain

0   100   200 miles
0   100   200   300 kilometres

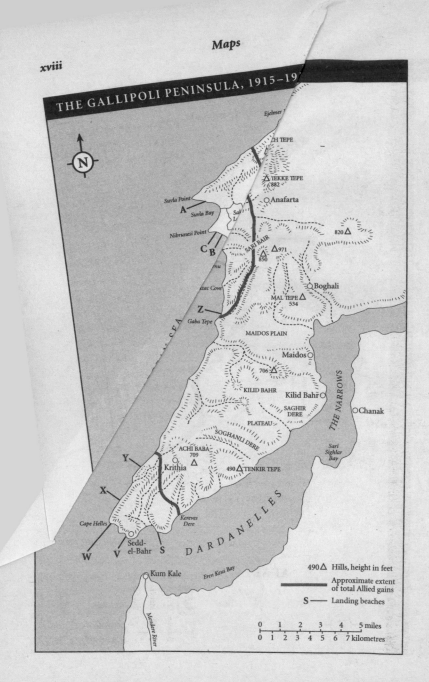

THE GALLIPOLI PENINSULA, 1915–19

Ejelmer

CH TEPE

△ TEKKE TEPE
882

○ **Anafarta**

Suvla Point

A

Suvla Bay

Nibrunesi Point

820 △

SARI BAIR

C

B

△ 971
850 △

○ **Boghali**

zac Cove

MAL TEPE △
534

Z

Gaba Tepe

MAIDOS PLAIN

○ **Maidos**

706 △

KILID BAHR

○ Kilid Bahr

SAGHIR
DERE

○ Chanak

PLATEAU

SOGHANLI DERE

THE NARROWS

Sari
Sighlar
Bay

Y

ACHI BABA
709
△

Krithia

490 △ TENKIR TEPE

X

Cape Helles

Kereves
Dere

W   V   S

Sedd-
el-Bahr

DARDANELLES

○ Kum Kale

Eren Keui Bay

Menдere River

490 △ Hills, height in feet

Approximate extent
of total Allied gains

S — Landing beaches

0   1   2   3   4   5 miles

0 1 2 3 4 5 6 7 kilometres

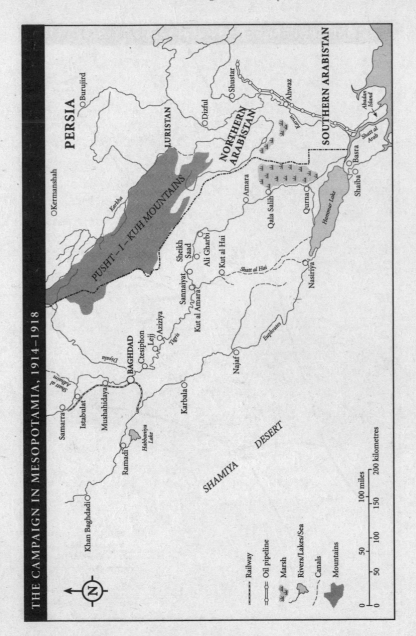

THE CAMPAIGN IN MESOPOTAMIA, 1914–1918

PERSIA

Burujird

Kermanshah

LURISTAN

Dizful

Shustar

Ahwaz

NORTHERN ARABISTAN

SOUTHERN ARABISTAN

Karkha

Abadan Island

Shatt al Arab

PUSHT–I–KUH MOUNTAINS

Amara

Qala Salih

Basra

Shaiba

Qurna

Hammar Lake

Sheikh Saad

Ali Gharbi

Kut al Hai

Sannaiyat

Shatt al Hai

Nasiriya

Kut al Amara

Aziziya

Lejj

Ctesiphon

Tigris

BAGHDAD

Najaf

Euphrates

Shatt al Adhim

Samarra

Istabulat

Mushahidaya

Karbala

Ramadi

Diyala

Habbaniya Lake

SHAMIYA DESERT

Khan Baghdadi

Railway

Oil pipeline

Marsh

Rivers/Lakes/Sea

Canals

Mountains

100 miles

200 kilometres

50   100   150

0   50   100

0   50

N

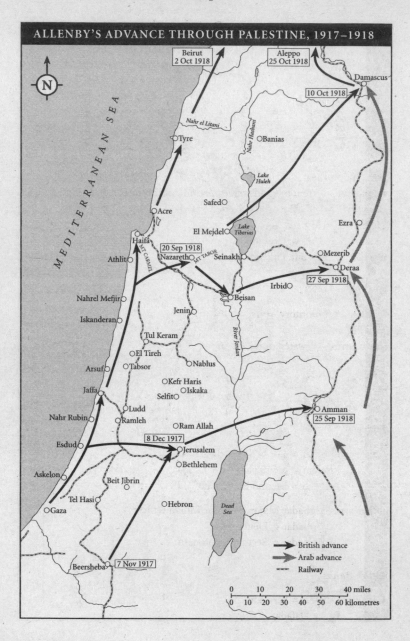

ALLENBY'S ADVANCE THROUGH PALESTINE, 1917–1918

Beirut
2 Oct 1918

Aleppo
25 Oct 1918

Damascus

10 Oct 1918

Nahr el Litani

Banias

Nahr Hasbani

Tyre

Lake
Huleh

Safed

Ezra

Acre

El Mejdel

Lake Tiberias

Mezerib

Haifa

20 Sep 1918

Deraa

Athlit

Nazareth

MT TABOR

Seinakh

27 Sep 1918

Irbid

Beisan

Nahrel Mefjir

Jenin

River Jordan

Iskanderan

Tul Keram

El Tireh

Arsuf

Tabsor

Nablus

Jaffa

Kefr Haris

Iskaka

Selfit

Amman
25 Sep 1918

Ludd

Nahr Rubin

Ramleh

Ram Allah

Esdud

8 Dec 1917

Jerusalem

Bethlehem

Askelon

Beit Jibrin

Tel Hasi

Hebron

*Dead
Sea*

Gaza

Beersheba   7 Nov 1917

British advance
Arab advance
Railway

| 0 | 10 | 20 | 30 | 40 miles |

| 0 | 10 | 20 | 30 | 40 | 50 | 60 kilometres |

MEDITERRANEAN SEA

MT CARMEL

Glossary

Urdu

atta flour, meal
bundobust system or mode of regulation, arrangement
chupatty baked cake of unleavened bread
maidan open space, square
nullah dried-up watercourse, ravine
resai or razai quilt, coverlet

Arabic

khashm promontory, spur
tel hill, mound
wadi dried-up watercourse, ravine

Indian Army ranks

Officers

Cavalry: Risaldar Major = Senior Indian Officer
        Risaldar = Lieutenant
        Jemadar = Second Lieutenant

Other arms: Subadar Major = Senior Indian Officer
        Subadar = Lieutenant
        Jemadar = Second Lieutenant

Other Ranks

Cavalry: Dafadar = Sergeant
        Lance Dafadar = Corporal

Acting Lance Dafadar = Lance-Corporal
Sowar = Trooper

Other arms: Havildar = Sergeant
Naik = Corporal
Lance-Naik = Lance-Corporal
Sepoy, Rifleman, Sapper, Gunner = Private

1

The Turkish Question

It was not inevitable that Britain and her allies should have found themselves in 1914 at war with Turkey as well as with Germany. In and since the Crimean War (1854–6), Britain's policy had consistently been to preserve the crumbling structure of the Ottoman Empire in order to prevent others, especially Russia, from absorbing any part of it and particularly from occupying the entrance (or exit, depending in which way one approached it) of the Black Sea at the Bosporus, which itself was controlled further south by the Dardanelles, the two together usually being referred to as 'the Straits'. The opening of the Suez Canal in 1869 had accentuated the interest of Britain and France in the Near East, and was followed by Britain's occupation of Egypt, officially part of the Ottoman Empire, in 1882, while protesting that it was a temporary measure until the newly installed Khedive Tewfik had put his financial house in order, under the guidance of Major Evelyn Baring, later Lord Cromer. While the attention of Britain and France was focused on the Nile valley, Germany began to develop an interest and influence in Turkey and to establish a presence there. In 1882 a German, Colonel Koehler, was appointed deputy chief of the Turkish General Staff and Inspector-General of Education, succeeded on his death the following year by Lieutenant Colonel von der Goltz, who became a Turkish Field Marshal, commander of their First Army, and died in Baghdad after the Turkish capture of Kut in 1916. In 1883 a direct rail link between Berlin and Constantinople was completed, and, in Asiatic Turkey, the Deutsche Bank was granted the right to extend to Ankara the existing line from the Bosporus to Izmit. In 1893 this right was extended to a line from there south to Konya, rights to further extensions being granted at intervals as far as the Persian Gulf. By 1914, however, construction had not penetrated the mountains of eastern Turkey. It was still short of Baghdad by 365 miles. Although there was some British opposition to the 'Berlin to Baghdad' railway, it did not come from the government.

At that time the expansion of Russia's empire eastward towards India caused great concern, especially in India where Lord Curzon became Viceroy in 1899, and the view taken was that the railway and German influence generally would strengthen Turkey and help her both to face her traditional Russian enemy and to keep under control subversive elements within the Ottoman Empire who might cause trouble to British investors. More ominous, as it was to prove, was the growing influence of Germany in the Turkish army, strongly encouraged by the forceful and aggressive German Ambassador to the Sublime Porte, Baron Marschall von Biberstein, who was to remain in post from 1897 to 1912. He received full support from Kaiser Wilhelm II, who had succeeded to the Prussian and German Imperial thrones in 1888 and dismissed, in 1890, his Chancellor Bismarck, one of whose principal pillars of policy had been to maintain good relations with Russia.

The virtual dismantlement of Turkish rule in the Balkans, fixed by the Congress of Berlin in 1878, was followed in 1898 by a war with Greece as a result of which Turkey was forced to remove her troops from Crete and some Aegean islands and withdraw from almost all of Thessaly. Five years later Macedonia rebelled against Turkish rule. These signs of the disintegration of the Ottoman Empire increased the dissatisfaction within Turkey, among not only the non-Turkish population but also the growing body of young men who had been influenced by a Western European education. In 1869 a Committee of Union and Progress had been founded by a group of students at the military college of medicine, and it extended itself through a network of cells within similar colleges, later to be dubbed the Young Turk movement. A number of its members, several of whom were army officers, including Mustafa Kemal, the future Atatürk, were serving in Salonika, where censorship and police control of subversive movements was less strict than in Constantinople. Their leaders were Enver and Djemal Pashas, both army officers, and Talaat Bey, a postal official. Provoked by the news of an Anglo-Russian Entente sealed by King Edward VII's meeting with the Tsar in June 1908, they spearheaded a revolt in Salonika at the beginning of July. This was followed by a military coup in April 1909 in which the Young Turks forced the deposition of the Sultan and his replacement by his brother Reshad, a mild character, who took the title of Mehmed V.

Others had begun to try and take advantage of this disturbed state of affairs. In October 1908 Bulgaria declared independence and a few days later the Austro-Hungarian Empire declared the annexation of Bosnia-Herzegovina, which it had administered since 1878. Russia, the basis of whose interest in the area was that she had no ocean port in Europe that was not frozen during the winter, demanded that she should be free to move her warships through the Straits, while Britain insisted that this must be accompanied by the right of others to do the same in the opposite direction. In September 1911 Italy invaded Libya and occupied the Dodecanese Islands in the eastern Mediterranean. While the various powers were thus engaged, Serbia and Bulgaria formed an alliance designed to rid Serbia of Turks and throw the Austro-Hungarians out of Bosnia-Herzegovina. Italy's war ended in October, Libya being transferred to her, while she hung on to the Dodecanese in breach of the peace terms. Bulgaria, Serbia, Montenegro and Greece then declared war against Turkey, hoping to expel her totally from their countries. Russia, anxious that the Bulgarians might reach Constantinople, stepped in to broker a peace, the Turks having successfully held the Bulgars before Adrianople. A conference to settle matters was held in London in May 1913. Turkish rule in Europe was confined to a small part of Turkish Thrace, excluding Adrianople. Greece acquired the rest of Thrace including Salonika, while Serbia held on to Macedonia, previously part of the original Bulgaria, in order to have access to that port. Greece absorbed Crete, already virtually free of Turkish rule, and the other Aegean islands, and Albania was created out of slices of Serbia and Macedonia. This was followed by the Second Balkan War in which the victors fought each other over the spoils.

These humiliations inflicted on the Ottoman Empire incensed the Young Turks. Enver and his colleagues decided on drastic action and, on 23 January 1913, seized control and effectively brought constitutional government to an end. The two Balkan Wars increased their resentment against the Europeans generally and especially those powers which were occupying areas that had formed part of the Empire. They were also disappointed that their new friends the Germans had not provided them with any material support. However, they recognized that they must have some foreign help if they were to avoid future such humiliations (and if possible recoup some of their losses), to be able to borrow the money with which to modernize their country, especially its communications, and to have the security in which to do so. Although Russia was their hereditary enemy, Talaat favoured an approach to her; Djemal, Navy Minister, to France; Enver, War Minister, to Germany; and Djavid, Finance Minister, to Britain. The last had been encouraged by Winston Churchill, who had visited Constantinople in 1909 as President of the Board of Trade, and in 1911, when he was First Lord of the Admiralty, an official approach was made to Britain for a permanent treaty. Churchill was in favour but the Foreign Secretary, Sir Edward Grey, turned it down, warning the Turks that they should not do anything to disturb their friendship with the great naval power 'by reverting to the oppressive methods of the old regime or seeking to disturb the British status quo as it now exists'. Accordingly, in 1913, a German military mission of seventy officers, headed by General Otto Liman von Sanders, arrived at Constantinople to reorganize and train the army.

At its head the Sultan was nominally Commander-in-Chief, but real power rested in the hands of Enver, Minister for War, heading the Superior War Council, of which von der Goltz was Vice-President. The army was divided into three elements: the Active Army (Nizam), the Active Reserve (Hitiyal) and the Territorial (Mustahfiz), totalling 150–200,000 men, forming thirty-six divisions, capable of being raised to 800,000 on mobilization, adding another nine full-strength divisions. Operationally it was divided into four 'Inspectorates' and one additional command, as follows:

  I. Thrace, Western Asia Minor and Anatolia: five corps (I–V), each of one cavalry brigade and three infantry divisions;
 II. Kurdistan: three corps (IX–XI) of the same composition;
III. Cilicia and Syria: two corps (VI, VIII), each of one cavalry brigade and two infantry divisions;
 IV. Mesopotamia: two corps (XII, XIII), each of two infantry divisions, XII having one cavalry brigade, XIII one cavalry regiment;
In the Hejaz and Yemen (South-West Arabia): one corps (VII) of two infantry divisions.

Liman von Sanders himself was appointed commander of I Corps at Constantinople, to which Russia objected, complaining that it was the equivalent of stationing a German garrison there. In response the Turks changed the name of his appointment to Inspector-General and made him a Field Marshal in their army. While the Germans trained and reorganized the army, Britain was doing the same for the Turkish navy, Rear Admiral Arthur Limpus heading the naval mission.

When the Serbian nationalist Gavrilo Princip shot Archduke Franz Ferdinand in Sarajevo on 28 June 1914, the Germans were therefore well established in Turkey, especially in their links with the army. On 28 July, the day on which Austria declared war on Serbia, Churchill took action which had a decisive effect on Britain's relations with Turkey. Two of the new *Dreadnought* class of battleship had been built for the Turkish navy in British shipyards on the Tyne. The money to pay for the ships, the *Sultan Osman I* and the *Reshadieh*, had been raised by public subscription in the hope that they would make possible the restoration of the Aegean and Dodecanese islands lost to Greece and Italy. The former had been completed but both were waiting until a dock large enough to hold them had been finished at Constantinople. On 27 July, the day before the Austrian declaration of war on Serbia, Admiral Limpus set sail with the Turkish navy from Constantinople to meet the *Sultan Osman I* and escort her to a lavish welcome at Constantinople. On the 28th Churchill raised the possibility of requisitioning them before they could leave the Tyne, the *Sultan Osman I* showing signs of being about to do so. In spite of doubts about its legality, the Cabinet on 31 July approved their seizure, and that an offer should be made to Turkey to pay for them. No actual action was taken nor was the Turkish government formally informed until 3 August, the day before war was declared on Germany.

But from at least 29 July, Enver and his colleagues had realized what Churchill intended. On 22 July Enver had approached Wangenheim, the German Ambassador, for an alliance, but had been turned down, the Germans thinking that Turkey had nothing of value to offer them; but two days later Kaiser Wilhelm II ordered that it be reconsidered, and on 28 July Enver, Talaat and Prince Said Halim, Grand Vizier and Foreign Minister, without the knowledge of Djemal or Djavid, began negotiating a secret defensive treaty by which Germany undertook to defend Ottoman territory if it were threatened, while Turkey undertook to remain neutral unless Germany was forced into war by the obligations of her treaty with Austria. In any case Turkey would not fight on Germany's side unless Bulgaria did also. The treaty was signed on 1 August, and it is very probable that Germany was persuaded to change her mind by an offer by Enver to sell her the two battleships, which he by then knew were going to be requisitioned by Britain. The following day Turkey's mobilization was ordered and an announcement made that she would remain neutral.

The incident which forced a decision about Anglo-Turkish relations was that of two German warships, the *Goeben*, a 23,000 ton battlecruiser, and her escort, the 4,500 ton light cruiser *Breslau*, under the command of Admiral Souchon, whose wartime task was to attack ships transporting troops from North Africa to France. They had been in the Mediterranean, ready for that, since 1912, and were at Haifa when the Admiral heard the news of Sarajevo. He immediately sailed for Pola, the Austrian base in the Adriatic. At the end of the month he left and by 2 August was coaling at Messina in Sicily, from where he sailed to attack Algerian ports. While engaged in this on 3 August, he was ordered to Constantinople and returned to Messina, from where he slipped away, reaching the Dardanelles on 10 August, while the British and French fleets were expecting him to make for the Straits of Gibraltar. Under pressure from the German mission at Constantinople, Enver gave the order to let them through the Dardanelles, which had been mined on 2 August.

Their presence off the Golden Horn over the next two months exerted a strong influence both on those who favoured Germany and on those who did not. In an attempt to regulate their presence, the Turkish government declared that they had bought them to replace the ships Britain had commandeered. Britain's chances of countering this German influence were weakened by the absence of our ambassador, Sir Louis Mallet, on leave. He did not return until 18 August. Four days later Britain, France and Russia offered to guarantee Turkey's independence and integrity if the German crews were dismissed and the Straits reopened to merchant shipping: if this were rejected, they would be regarded as enemy ships and fired on if encountered. As no response was made to this offer, the British naval mission was withdrawn on 27 September. However, the Turks still hesitated to commit themselves to join Germany in the war. Their stalling tactics infuriated Berlin, and strong pressure was brought to bear on Ambassador Wangenheim. Enver had always been in favour, but almost all of his colleagues in the Committee of Union and Progress preferred neutrality. Enver's argument was strengthened by German victories: her rapid advance into France and especially her crushing defeat of the Russians at Tannenberg and the Masurian Lakes. Not only did the threat from Russia appear to have been significantly reduced, but there was a possibility that Germany might win the war in a matter of months. If Turkey did not join in, the chance of recovering some of the lost territory with the help of the victor might be missed. By 10 October Enver had won over his principal colleagues on condition that Germany paid two million Turkish pounds for the support of the Turkish armed forces. This was paid in two instalments on 12 and 17 October. Talaat and Halil Bey then proposed to keep the money but stay neutral. Without telling his colleagues Enver conspired with Wangenheim and Admiral Souchon that the latter, with the *Goeben* and *Breslau*, escorted by the Turkish navy, should attack Russian ships in the Black Sea, but claim that the latter had fired first and that Souchon had been forced to fire in self-defence. However, on his own initiative, Souchon bombarded the ports of Odessa, Sebastopol and Feodosia on 27 October with the intention, in his own words, 'to force the Turks even against their will to spread the war.' Three days later the British, French and Russian ambassadors left, Turkey declaring war on 31 October, Russia following suit on 4 November, Britain and France next day.

As Turkey joined the war the Young Turk triumvirate broke up, Talaat remaining in Constantinople, while Enver set off to face the Russians in the Caucasus and Djemal went to be Governor and Commander-in-Chief in Syria, which included Palestine. Britain's immediate concern was to ensure that the Suez Canal remained free from interference and that the Anglo-Persian Oil Company's installations at Abadan at the head of the Persian Gulf were secure.

The British garrison in Egypt was small: only four infantry battalions, one cavalry regiment, one horse artillery and one mountain artillery battery, and one field company of the Royal Engineers. Its commander was Major General Sir Julian Byng, who was replaced in September 1914 by Major General Sir John Maxwell. Lord Kitchener, the Consul-General, left to become Secretary of State for War and was succeeded, with the title of High Commissioner, by Sir Arthur McMahon. This garrison had to be prepared not only to defend the canal, but also to deal with any subversive movement against the British presence, whether from Egyptian nationalists or provoked by Turkey. Egypt was nominally under the suzerainty of the Ottoman Sultan, to whom an annual tribute was paid by the Khedive, Abbas Hilmi. He was anti-British, and, having been in Constantinople in August, stayed there. When Britain declared war on

Turkey on 5 November, martial law was declared and a promise made
that Britain would ensure the defence of Egypt, whose people would not
be required to take part. On 18 December Egypt was declared a British
Protectorate and Abbas Hilmi deposed, his place being taken by his
uncle Prince Hussein. Cyprus was annexed at the same time.

Under the war plans of the War Office in London, the all-regular
garrison was due to join divisions being mobilized in Britain and be
replaced by two infantry divisions and a cavalry brigade of the Indian
Army. Kitchener now changed this, the Indian Army formations being
ordered to France and a Territorial Army division, the 42nd (East
Lancashire), despatched from England. The latter reached Egypt at the
end of September, a brigade of the 3rd Indian Division having meanwhile
been held there on its way to France. Before the end of the year the 42nd
was joined by the 10th and 11th Indian Divisions.

By that time a threat to the canal had developed. The Sinai desert to
the east had been lightly patrolled by camel-mounted Arab police. When
they were withdrawn, Turkish troops immediately occupied El Arish, on
the coast a hundred miles east of Port Said, and Nekhl, in the desert
sixty-five miles east of Suez on the track to Aqaba. Djemal Pasha's
Fourth Army had two corps, VIth in southern Turkey and northern
Syria, and VIIIth in southern Syria and Palestine, with its headquarters
at Damascus. The latter was commanded by another Djemal, known as
Djemal Kutchuk, whose chief of staff was the Bavarian Colonel Kress
von Kressenstein. The corps totalled some 65,000 men with 100 guns.
By the middle of January 1915 he had concentrated round Beersheba
some 20,000 men, including one Arab division, the 25th, with nine field
artillery batteries and one of 5.9in howitzers. As mobile troops, he had
one cavalry regiment, some camel companies and some mounted Bedouin. 10,000 camels formed his supply train. He had another division
ready to follow up if this force succeeded in seizing a crossing of the
canal.

To face this threat, Maxwell had a total of 70,000 troops in Egypt by
January, including the 10th and 11th Indian Infantry Divisions; but the
42nd Division, some Yeomanry regiments and Australian and New
Zealand units, all destined to move on to France, were in the process of
training and receiving equipment. They were held in the Delta round
Cairo. Available for the defence of the canal were the two Indian infantry
divisions, the Imperial Service Cavalry Brigade and an Indian camel

corps, supported by Indian mountain artillery and some from the Egyptian army, in all some 30,000 men. The weakness in artillery was partly compensated for by the presence of British and French warships in the canal. A detachment of the Royal Flying Corps and some French naval seaplanes provided a form of reconnaissance. Major General A. Wilson, commander of the 10th Indian Division, was placed in overall command of the troops of both divisions, who manned posts on both banks of the canal. The most important area was that of Ismailia, in the centre, the terminus of the Sweet Water Canal, the only source of fresh water, brought from the Nile. Although there was a railway from there both to Port Said and to Suez, there was no road and movement between posts depended on launches in the canal, which were in short supply.

The Turks began their advance from Beersheba in mid-January, taking ten days to cross Sinai, marching by night. On 26 and 27 January light attacks were made on posts at Kantara in the north and Kubri, seven miles north of Suez, in the south. These were clearly diversions. Before dawn on 3 February a major attack was launched at Tussum, at the southern end of Lake Timsah, six miles south-east of Ismailia. The few who managed to cross the canal were killed or captured and further daylight attacks in the same general area also failed. Djemal Pasha, who was present, ordered a withdrawal back to Beersheba, having lost about 1,400 men, half of them as prisoners of war. British casualties totalled some 150. The Imperial Service Cavalry Brigade crossed to the east bank, keeping contact with the withdrawal, but making no serious attempt to harass it. It is difficult to see what the Turks had expected to achieve – possibly an uprising of the Egyptians against the British. They had made no preparations to cause serious damage to the canal itself. No further attacks on the canal were made during the rest of 1915.

The Gulf

Britain's interest in the Persian Gulf stemmed from a trade agreement between the East India Company and the Shah of Persia. In trading in the area, significantly for pearls from Bahrein, the Company had established good relations with the two powerful sheikdoms at the Gulf's head, that of Kuwait on the west side of the Shatt-al-Arab, the estuary of the joined Tigris and Euphrates, and that of Muhammerah to the east of it. Both sheikhs resented interference by their respective overlords, Kuwait of the Ottoman Sultan, Muhammerah of the Shah. The government of India, which succeeded the East India Company, developed this relationship and the Royal Navy patrolled the Gulf to support it and to suppress piracy. In 1901 William D'Arcy, a British citizen of Irish descent who had made a fortune in gold in Australia, obtained a concession from the Shah to drill for and exploit oil resources in south-west Persia, and in 1908 he struck it near Ahwaz on the River Karun, nearly a hundred miles upstream from its junction with the Shatt-al-Arab in the territory of the Sheikh of Muhammerah. This was the foundation of the Anglo-Persian Oil Company, later British Petroleum. A pipeline was laid from Ahwaz to the island of Abadan on the Shatt, where storage tanks and a distillery were built. By 1914 it had become a major source of oil, and the Admiralty, anticipating a change from coal to oil for their warships, persuaded the British government to buy a controlling share in the company. The possibility of war with Turkey posed a clear threat. In addition two German cruisers, the *Emden* and *Königsberg*, were somewhere in the Indian Ocean and it was feared that they might make for Basra. Suspicions were aroused by strong Turkish protests at the presence of British warships in the Gulf and their passage up the Shatt, although no objections had ever been raised before, if they kept to the eastern side of the channel. On 28 September 1914 a Royal Navy sloop, HMS *Espiegle*, waiting for high tide to clear the bar, entered the Shatt, followed by the armed merchantman *Dalhousie*, while the sloop *Odin* stayed to patrol the entrance. *Espiegle* sailed up to the Sheikh's capital at Muhammerah, at the mouth of the Karun, while the *Dalhousie* stopped at Abadan. The Turkish Governor of Basra, Subhi Bey, demanded their departure by 21 October, threatening to blockade them there if they did not comply. Meanwhile he planned to block the waterway above the Karun. Two days later, under small-arms fire, *Espiegle* dropped down to Abadan.

Meanwhile telegrams were exchanged between London and Delhi about action to secure the oil installations. The Viceroy, Lord Hardinge, was not keen to do anything: he was sensitive to the fear that, if the Ottoman Empire sided with Germany, he would face serious trouble from his large Muslim population and also possibly from the tribes on the North-West Frontier. Although the Indian Army numbered 160,000 and the British army in India 75,000, they were trained and equipped only for mountain warfare or internal security. However, the reforms introduced by Kitchener, when he was Commander-in-Chief from 1902 to 1905, had at least organized them into operational formations. London insisted that 'a demonstration' should be made by sending a brigade of Lieutenant General Sir Arthur Barrett's 6th (Poona) Division to Abadan. Accordingly Brigadier General W. S. Delamain's 16th Brigade, with four infantry battalions, one British (2nd Dorsets) and three Indian (20th Punjabis, 104th Wellesley's Rifles and 117th Mahrattas), with two mountain batteries, each of four 10pdr guns, and a company of Bengal Sappers & Miners, sailed from Bombay on 16 October in five transports, escorted by the battleship HMS *Ocean*, unaware of their destination. A week later they anchored off Bahrein awaiting events, some of the troops being trained in rowing the ships' boats in case of an opposed landing. Brigadier General Delamain had been told that his task would be to occupy Abadan in order to protect the oil refinery, the tanks and the pipeline. How he was to effect the last from Abadan was not clear. If hostilities with Turkey erupted, he was to occupy Basra, in which case the rest of the 6th Division would be despatched to back him up.

When news of the *Goeben* and *Breslau*'s bombardment of Russian ports in the Black Sea was received, the force, known as Indian Expeditionary Force 'D', sailed for the Shatt, arriving at the bar on 3 November and spending two days there while the channel was swept for mines. On 6 November, leaving *Ocean* behind, as she drew too much water to cross the bar, the Turkish fort at Fao was silenced by the sloop *Odin* and occupied by *Ocean*'s Royal Marines, as its defenders fled, while Delamain sailed up to Abadan, choosing to land three miles above the refinery and nine below Muhammerah. As there were no barges or tugs and no landing stages, and the current ran strongly, it was a tricky operation, taking two days to get the men, their equipment and their 650 mules ashore. There they were attacked on 11 November by some 400 Turks, who were easily repulsed. A few days later the rest of the 6th Division began to arrive, with no better means of disembarkation than Delamain had had. On the 15th, having been ordered by Barrett to reconnoitre for a move towards Basra, Delamain sent forward three battalions, which successfully engaged a small Turkish force. Four days later Barrett decided to attack what he believed to be the main Turkish position just above Muhammerah, deploying Major General C. I. Fry's 18th Brigade and two squadrons of the 33rd Light Cavalry to join

Delamain in the advance. As they moved off on 19 November, a heavy rainstorm broke out and the whole area became a sea of mud. They soon came up against the old fort of Zain, which they proceeded to attack. Turkish fire was fortunately inaccurate, and, with the support of one battery (10th Battery Royal Field Artillery) of 18pdrs, the fort was captured and the Turks withdrew to Basra, having suffered, it was believed, some 1,000 casualties, while Barrett's force had lost 353, including four sapper officers, the loss of whom was sorely felt on account of the lack of any craft to help movement in this watery maze, and of bridging equipment.

Subhi Bey now decided to implement his plan to block the waterway below Muhammerah, but one of the sinking ships swung in the tide, leaving a channel clear. *Espiegle* steamed up to inspect it, driving off the Turkish gunboat *Marmarris* and silencing guns which were covering the block, whose defenders fled. Informed by local Arabs that the way was now clear to Basra, Wellesley's Rifles and the Mahrattas were embarked in *Espiegle* and *Odin* and sailed unopposed into Basra on 21 November.

While Barrett built up his force there and a British administration was established under a Political Officer, Sir Percy Cox, who was to have a long association with the country thereafter, *Espiegle* and *Odin* continued upstream to find out where the Turks had got to, reaching Qurna, forty miles up at the point where the Tigris and Euphrates join. It was traditionally the site of the Garden of Eden. The ships met *Marmarris* again and came under fire from guns on shore a few miles below Qurna, returning to Basra after dark. On 3 December they sailed upstream again with the Wellesley's Rifles and Mahrattas and, in a merchant ship, two companies of the 2nd Norfolks from 18th Brigade, with some sappers and two field guns, escorted by three armed launches. They were landed on the east bank three miles below Qurna and began to advance over flat open ground towards a thick plantation of date palms on the east bank of the Tigris opposite Qurna. While the ships bombarded the village of Muzereh on the near side of the plantation, the infantry fought their way forward through it to the Tigris bank. Having no means of crossing, they were withdrawn back to their landing place, Turkish troops returning to Muzereh. In the next few days the rest of 18th Brigade was brought up and another attack was launched, strongly supported by fire from the ships. Again they reached the Tigris and again withdrew, this time leaving a rearguard to prevent the Turks returning. A third attempt on 8 December was made on the initiative of the Royal Navy and the two battalions that had become associated with them. While Captain Hayes-Sadler led his ships past the confluence and up the Tigris beyond Qurna, Wellesley's Rifles and the Mahrattas, moving widely round to the north of Muzereh, reached the Tigris bank a mile north of the plantation. An Indian sepoy, followed by an officer, swam across the wide fast-flowing river with a light line, with which the two then pulled across a hawser to which a boat was then linked to form a ferry by which the battalions crossed. Cut off by them and bombarded by the ships, Subhi Bey surrendered with 42 officers and 1,000 men, having lost nearly as many in the fighting round Muzereh. British and Indian Army casualties were 27 killed and 292 wounded, the navy losing 2 killed and 10 wounded.

Barrett had thus eliminated most of the Turkish 38th Division, and Basra and Abadan appeared secure; but the administrative infrastructure to support his force, if it were to be engaged in further operations, was hopelessly inadequate. Soldiers left to garrison Qurna expressed the view that Adam and Eve were fortunate to have been expelled from the Garden!

2

Gallipoli: The Landings

Ten days after the *Goeben* and *Breslau* had passed through the Dardanelles Straits, the Greek Prime Minister, Eleutherios Venizelos, offered to
join Britain, France and Russia in the war against Germany, and, two
days after that, it was revealed that Russia had asked him whether Greece
was prepared to land an army on the Gallipoli peninsula in conjunction
with a Russian attack on the Dardanelles. On 31 August Churchill
discussed the possibility of an attack on Turkey with Kitchener and
wrote next day to the Chief of the Imperial General Staff, Lieutenant
General Sir James Wolfe Murray, suggesting that the War Office and
Admiralty should together work out a plan to seize the peninsula, using
a Greek army, in order to open the Straits to enable a British fleet to
enter the Sea of Marmara. The advice of the Director of Military
Operations and Intelligence, Major General Charles Callwell, was that an
attack on the peninsula would need 60,000 troops to overcome the
Turkish garrison, estimated at 27,000, and would be a difficult operation.
On 4 September the Greek government were told that, if Turkey joined
Germany and Austria-Hungary, Greece would be welcomed into the
Entente and that Britain would cooperate in an attack by her on the
peninsula. They had prepared a plan which involved 60,000 men landing
on the west coast south of Gaba Tepe and advancing from there to the
southern tip at Cape Helles, after which they would systematically clear
the Turkish troops from the western shore of the Straits so that clearance
of mines could start. A minor landing would be made on the east side
of the entrance at Kum Kale. At a later stage 30,000 men would be
landed near Bulair to cut the neck of the peninsula. A condition of
participation was that they should be protected by Allied forces from an
attack by Bulgaria, which at that time was still neutral although clearly
sympathizing with Germany.

After Turkey's declaration of war on 31 October and her completion
of mining in the Straits on 2 November, the Royal Navy's Eastern

Mediterranean Squadron, commanded by Vice Admiral Sackville Carden, blockading the entrance, bombarded the Turkish forts on either side, at Sedd-el-Bahr and Kum Kale. This led the Turks, on German advice, to increase their defences, one of the most significant measures being the deployment of mobile guns to give covering fire to the minefields. At the end of the month the newly formed War Council in London considered a strategy for removing or reducing a Turkish threat to the Suez Canal. Churchill's proposal for an attack on the peninsula was rejected as impractical. A decision on his alternative of a feint there to distract attention from a landing near Alexandretta (modern İskenderun) to cut Turkish communications with Syria and Mesopotamia, originally favoured by Kitchener, was deferred. These matters were considered again in the New Year, 1915. The influential Cabinet Secretary, Lieutenant Colonel Maurice Hankey, favoured a threat to Constantinople which he thought would remove Turkey from the war and bring hesitant countries on her western borders to the side of the Entente. Lloyd George, Chancellor of the Exchequer, took a different view. He wished to turn to the defensive on the Western Front and concentrate against the Austrians in the Balkans, limiting action against Turkey to the Alexandretta proposal. Matters were brought to a head by a Russian demand that her allies should do something to relieve the pressure which Enver was developing against them in the Caucasus. Kitchener and Churchill agreed that something should be done and that a naval demonstration at the Dardanelles 'might have some effect in stopping reinforcements going east'. In fact, by the time that this was decided, the Russians had turned the tide against Enver.

Admiral of the Fleet Sir John ('Jacky') Fisher, the First Sea Lord, agreed. He proposed that 75,000 regular and Indian soldiers in France should be relieved by Territorial Army ones and, ostensibly sent to Egypt, should land on the Asiatic side of the Straits, south of Kum Kale, while the Greeks landed on the peninsula, the Bulgarians attacked Adrianople and the Russians, Romanians and Serbs attacked the Austro-Hungarians. Meanwhile a squadron of old British battleships would force their way through the Straits, a plan as unrealistic as his previous proposal for landings in the Baltic. Kitchener refused to withdraw troops from France, whose government would have raised objections, and by then the Greeks had become unenthusiastic. The cooperation of Romania and Bulgaria was a pipe dream. Churchill latched on to Fisher's proposal to use old battleships and signalled Carden: 'Do you consider the forcing of the Straits by ships alone a practicable operation? . . . Importance of result would justify severe loss.' Carden replied: 'I do not consider Dardanelles can be rushed. They might be forced with a large number of ships.' Pressed for a plan, Carden came back with one for a methodical step-by-step advance through the Straits, gradually reducing its defences with the fire of the ships' guns. He stressed that aerial reconnaissance was necessary, that ammunition expenditure would be heavy and that he needed more ships. The War Council having approved in principle on 13 January, Carden was ordered to prepare for it urgently, being promised reinforcements including the brand-new battleship *Queen Elizabeth* with her 15in guns, the operation forming part of her final sea trials and gun calibration. But Fisher was beginning to have doubts, both about attempting it without any support on land and because of the effect losses might have on the navy's battleship strength. On 25 January he expressed his doubts in writing to the Prime Minister, Herbert Asquith, who thought that he was merely trying to revert to his Baltic project. When the War Council met three days later to give final approval to Carden's plan, he threatened to resign, but was persuaded by Kitchener not to, a final decision being deferred until later in the day after Churchill and Kitchener had successfully twisted his arm. On 5 February Carden was given a formal order to start his operation, if possible, ten days later, but qualified by the phrase: 'It is not expected or desired that the operation should be hurried to the extent of taking large risks or courting heavy losses.'

Four days later it became known that Bulgaria was about to join the Central Powers, and the War Council discussed how to help Serbia, Kitchener offering to send the last unused regular division, the 29th, to Salonika. This was not agreed, but his offer revealed that it was available for the eastern Mediterranean. The navy were pressing for troops to secure the shore and the Turkish forts as they destroyed them, and Churchill had already ordered two Royal Marine battalions from the Royal Naval Division* to be sent there for that purpose. On 16 February

---

* The division had been formed on the outbreak of war from the Royal Marine Light Infantry battalions and two brigades of naval reservists who had been called up but for whom there were no ships. It had been sent, in vain, to try to defend Antwerp in October 1914.

the War Council decided to despatch the 29th Division to the island of Lemnos, which had been taken by Greece from Turkey in 1912 and was forty miles west of Cape Helles. Two days later Churchill ordered the rest of the Royal Naval Division to be sent there also. They were to be joined there by a division of French and North African troops, known as the Corps Expéditionnaire d'Orient, commanded by General Albert d'Amade. These divisions were to support naval operations by small-scale landing parties and garrisoning defences which the navy had taken or destroyed. They were not intended as an assault force.

On 19 February Carden's ships opened fire at long range on the two forts covering the entrance, Sedd-el-Bahr on the west and Kum Kale on the east shore, but did not succeed in reducing them by the end of the day. Bad weather prevented further operations for three days, during which the Turks were able to repair the damage inflicted; but by the end of 25 February the outer forts had been silenced and abandoned, and the entrance between them swept of mines.

Meanwhile Kitchener had changed his mind, cancelling the move of the 29th Division on 19 February and, on 20 February, ordering Lieutenant General Sir John Maxwell in Egypt to send as many Australian and New Zealand units as he could to the Gulf of Mudros at Lemnos. One Australian brigade, the 3rd, was ready to leave three days later, the rest having to wait for shipping to arrive from elsewhere. They were to be commanded by Lieutenant General Sir William Birdwood of the Indian Army, well known to Kitchener, who ordered him to Mudros to see Carden and report his personal assessment of the likelihood of success of the navy's operations and on whether or not troops would be needed to land on the peninsula to attack the forts from the rear. Birdwood met Carden on 2 March, reporting two days later to Kitchener by telegram that, if troops became involved, their role could not be limited (as Kitchener had envisaged) to merely garrisoning defences taken by the navy. A large force would be needed, of which, as Carden agreed, the main part should land round Cape Helles, while a diversionary landing should be made at Bulair, near the neck. He rejected landing on the Asiatic coast. In a later telegram he gave his opinion that the navy could not succeed in forcing the Straits on their own. By then two companies of the Plymouth Battalion of the Royal Marine Light Infantry had tried to land to occupy the ruined forts of Sedd-el-Bahr and Kum Kale, but had had to withdraw from both after losing 20 killed, 24 wounded and 4 missing. Attempts to reduce the Intermediate Defences in the ten-mile-long stretch up to Kephez Point were proceeding very slowly. Minesweeping was carried out by converted trawlers, which lacked the power to work against the strong current, and had to move upstream and sweep down it. This meant they were doubly vulnerable to the mobile Turkish artillery sited to cover the minefields, and they abandoned daylight sweeping. Churchill was becoming impatient and told Carden to take greater risks. Birdwood's advice and the expected arrival of the French so-called corps persuaded Kitchener to send the 29th Division after all and, to Birdwood's disappointment, to appoint a more senior general in command. He chose another old friend from the Boer War, General Sir Ian Hamilton. The decision having been made on 11 March, Hamilton was summoned next day and told by Kitchener: 'We are sending a military force to support the Fleet at the Dardanelles and you are to have command.' With no more detailed orders or advice from the General Staff, he was bundled off on the 13th from Charing Cross station to embark on a light cruiser at Marseilles, arriving at Tenedos to meet Carden on the 17th.

Carden, however, had succumbed to strain, and his second-in-command, Vice Admiral John De Robeck,* had taken his place. He had planned a further attempt to clear a passage through the Straits, which started the following day, 18 March. The fleet was divided into three lines, the more modern battleships forming Line A, the French ones B and the older British ones C. Line A would move into Erin Keui Bay, east of Kum Kale, which had already been swept clear of mines: from there they would bombard, at a range of 14,000 yards, the forts on either side of the Narrows, Kilid Bahr and Chanak: under cover of this fire, Line B would pass through to fire at the same targets at a range of 8,000 yards. Line C would act as a reserve to guard the flanks and replace Line B. Two hours after A had begun its bombardment, minesweeping would start to clear a passage beyond the 8,000 yard range, up to which, by the morning of the 18th, the area had been reported clear. Bombardment was to continue at a lower scale during the night and an attempt made

---

* Rear Admiral De Robeck was junior to Rear Admiral Wemyss, who was governor of Lemnos, but who proposed that De Robeck should succeed Carden as acting vice admiral.

next morning, having finally silenced the forts, to pass through the Narrows.

Line A entered the Straits at 10.30 a.m. on the 18th and began their bombardment an hour later under fire from Turkish mobile artillery, which did not greatly trouble them, receiving no serious return fire from the forts. Soon after midday De Robeck ordered Line B forward. As the French ships came within a range of 10,000 yards of the forts, they came under heavy fire from them and the mobile batteries. At 13.45, as this fire seemed to be slackening, De Robeck ordered the minesweepers forward and the ships of C to replace the French, one of which, the *Bouvet*, hit a mine a quarter of an hour later and sank quickly with an almost total loss of life. The minesweepers now came under intense fire and were forced to withdraw, De Robeck being unaware that they had exploded three mines in front of Line A, an area believed to be clear. In fact a Turkish minesweeper, the *Nousret*, had undetected laid a line of twenty mines off the shore in Erin Keui Bay on the night of 7/8 March. At 16.11 the battlecruiser *Inflexible*, on the right of Line A, hit one which caused severe damage to her bow. Three minutes later the battleship *Irresistible* struck one which disabled her so that she lost power and steering, coming under heavy fire from the shore. HMS *Ocean*, sent to take her in tow, also hit a mine and was severely damaged by gunfire and abandoned. Both sank after their crews had been rescued. De Robeck, believing that these were mines floated down on the current, withdrew the rest of the fleet, *Inflexible* making her way to Tenedos where she ran aground, and the French battleship *Gaulois*, also hit, doing the same on another island. Uncertain of the origin of these mines, De Robeck suspended the operation on 19 March, but, when bad weather intervened next day, cancelled it altogether. He and his second-in-command, Rear Admiral R. E. Wemyss, were now convinced that they could not make another attempt unless the army occupied at least the western shore. This conclusion, hotly contested by Commodore Roger Keyes, De Robeck's chief of staff, was confirmed in a formal meeting between De Robeck and Hamilton on 22 March and reported to London where it led to fierce argument between Churchill, backed by Asquith and Kitchener, who wanted De Robeck to try again, believing that the Turks had run out of ammunition and that panic reigned in Constantinople; but all three Sea Lords in the Admiralty, Fisher, Wilson and Jackson, supported 'the man on the spot'. Asquith refused to overrule the admirals and Churchill, after trying to persuade De Robeck to change his mind, had to accept Asquith's decision, reluctantly, because he realized that it involved a significant delay before another attempt could be made to force the Straits, during which the Turks would be able to strengthen their defences, which they did.

On 24 March, Enver appointed the German General Liman von Sanders to command a newly formed Fifth Army, responsible for the defence of the Dardanelles region. At that time the strength of the Turkish forces in the area, most of them scattered along the shorelines, was more or less the same as those Britain and France were in the process of assembling at Mudros; but in the next four weeks they were to be significantly strengthened and reorganized. Liman von Sanders concentrated them into three zones and improved communications between them, so that he could move formations from one zone to another. In the northern zone he deployed one division round Bulair and another on the mainland north of the peninsula neck: two more were stationed on the Asiatic coast at and to the south of Kum Kale: the central zone of the peninsula was to be the responsibility of the 9th Division, commanded by Khalil Sami Bey, the 19th, commanded by Mustafa Kemal Bey, being held in reserve round Boghali, six miles north of the Narrows. The 9th Division's three regiments (each of three battalions) held sectors as follows: the northerly 27th from Aghyl Dere to Semerly Tepe, the southerly 26th from there to Cape Helles, while the 25th was in reserve on the Kilid Bahr plateau which overlooked the Straits on either side of the Narrows.

Neither Hamilton nor anyone in London seems to have seriously considered whether or not the forces which, haphazardly, had been ordered to assemble at Mudros would be strong enough to overcome these defences. They were certainly not prepared or organized in any way for an amphibious assault against a well-defended and rugged hilly peninsula. To get them into some sort of state to undertake the operation, those already at Mudros, the Royal Naval Division and the French Corps Expéditionnaire d'Orient, had to be moved to Egypt, where the transports carrying the 29th Division were diverted. There the Australian and New Zealand forces were organized into two divisions, the 1st Australian, commanded by Major General William Bridges, and the New Zealand and Australian Division, commanded by Major General Sir Alexander Godley, the two forming the Australian and New Zealand

Army Corps (ANZAC), commanded by Birdwood. The 29th Division was commanded by Major General Aylmer Hunter-Weston, who had already commanded a brigade in France. Hamilton did ask Maxwell to spare him one Indian brigade, preferably Gurkha, but did not press his request until the eve of his return to Mudros, when Maxwell replied that he 'would do his best' provided that he could be given some naval seaplanes in exchange. He never told Hamilton that on 6 April he had received a telegram from Kitchener telling him to 'supply any troops in Egypt that can be spared, or even selected officers or men, that Sir Ian Hamilton may want, for Gallipoli ... This telegram should be communicated by you to Sir Ian Hamilton.'

The latter and his staff (without the administrative and logistic staff, who had only arrived from Britain a few days before) returned to Mudros on 10 April and, with De Robeck's staff, finalized the plan three days later. The principal objective was to be the Kilid Bahr plateau. The main assault was to be made by 29th Division at and on either side of Cape Helles. Their objective, which it was hoped they would reach by the end of the first day, was the Achi Baba ridge six miles inland. A secondary landing was to be made by the ANZAC Corps on the beaches north of Gaba Tepe, which was twelve miles north of Cape Helles, their objective being the ridge of Mal Tepe, five miles inland, just south of Boghali. The French were to follow 29th Division, landing round Helles, but initially would land one regiment near Kum Kale to prevent guns from there firing into the rear of the Helles landings. The Royal Naval Division was to make a diversionary simulated landing near Bulair. Assaulting troops were to be transferred offshore into rowing boats towed by steam pinnaces or picket boats, the leading waves from warships, the subsequent ones from transports. The only specialist landing craft was a converted collier, the *River Clyde*, which was to be driven ashore, the soldiers emerging from four holes cut in the sides onto lighters brought alongside by a steam hopper, from which they would reach dry land. The landings would be strongly supported by naval gunfire, De Robeck's fleet having been reinforced by four more old battleships, bringing its strength to eighteen battleships, twelve cruisers and twenty-nine destroyers, formed into two squadrons, the 1st commanded by Wemyss, supporting the Helles landings, and the 2nd by Rear Admiral Cecil Thursby, supporting the ANZAC landing.

The landings were planned for 23 April, the ANZACs before dawn and the Helles assault after it; but bad weather caused a two-day postponement. It was during this period that Lieutenant Rupert Brooke, in Lieutenant Commander Bernard Freyberg's company of the Hood Battalion in the Royal Naval Division, contracted blood poisoning from an insect bite on his lip. He died in a French hospital ship and was buried on the 23rd on the island of Skyros near to which the SS *Grantully Castle*, carrying the battalion, was anchored. They sailed to take part in the operation four hours later.

The postponement affected the ANZAC landing. In order to achieve surprise, it had been planned that the final approach to the point at which troops would be transferred from warships to boats should take place after the moon had set: on 25 April this was not until 03.00, leaving only an hour before first light. In that hour, owing to a midshipman's well-intentioned use of his initiative, the right-hand tow of the leading wave altered course to the north, forcing those to the left of it further north also and causing the parallel tows to get mixed up with each other. The outcome was that the three assaulting battalions of the 3rd Australian Brigade, 9th on the right, 10th in the centre and 11th on the left, landed around the promontory of Ari Burnu, the 11th to the north of it, where they found the exits from the beach steep and difficult to negotiate, and the 9th and 10th mixed up together just south of the promontory on a narrower front than intended. The 12th, landing later, was meant to concentrate in reserve, but its men, distributed among different ships, on landing rushed enthusiastically inland behind those who had already pushed ahead from the beaches. In spite of these mishaps, the brigade commander, Colonel Ewen Sinclair-Maclagan, when he himself landed at 05.00, was moderately satisfied with his position. Surprise had undoubtedly been obtained, his leading troops had established themselves on the high ground about a mile inland and casualties had not been heavy. It had been planned that Colonel James M'Cay's 2nd Australian Brigade, the next to land, would advance to the left of the 3rd, directed towards Battleship Hill and Chunuk Bair, and beyond that to Koja Chemen Tepe and the Kilid Bahr plateau; but, as 3rd Brigade had landed further north than intended, Sinclair-Maclagan suggested that the 2nd should come in on his right to secure the southern half of 400 Plateau, which was unoccupied and in the direction from which he expected a Turkish counter-attack. M'Cay agreed, but the first of his troops, landing well north of Ari Burnu, came under heavy fire and suffered many casualties. The remainder landed at Anzac Cove, south of Ari Burnu. With the change in their orders, they became disorganized, eventually sorting themselves out on the edge of the southern half of 400 Plateau. It is not surprising that when the divisional commander, Major General Bridges, landed at 07.30, he found it difficult to obtain a clear picture of who was where and what was happening. In fact the 11th and 12th Battalions of 3rd Brigade were making steady progress towards Chunuk Bair, reaching Battleship Hill at 09.00, against Turkish rearguards which made full use of the rugged, scrub-covered terrain. Thereafter, however, resistance stiffened, largely due to the personal intervention of Mustafa Kemal.

When Khalil Sami, commander of the Turkish 9th Division, received news at 05.30 of the landing, he thought at first that it was a feint to distract attention from a principal landing near Bulair. He therefore ordered only two battalions of his 27th Regiment to the area to reinforce the one manning the coast defences near Gaba Tepe. By chance Mustafa Kemal had ordered his division's 57th Regiment to parade at that time for a field day. When Khalil Sami learned that the Australians were heading for Chunuk Bair, he asked Kemal to send one of his battalions there. Realizing the urgency of preventing the enemy from reaching the Kilid Bahr plateau, Mustafa Kemal ordered the whole of the 57th to move immediately to Chunuk Bair with himself at their head, and the rest of his division, the 72nd and 77th Arab Regiments, to follow. The 57th began to come into action about 10.00 against the 11th and 12th Australian Battalions on Battleship Hill and Baby 700 to the south of it. At the same time the 27th Regiment began to attack the 3rd Brigade's positions on Second Ridge, the western side of 400 Plateau. When the 1st Australian Brigade began to land at about 10.30 it was directed to that area, but Sinclair-Maclagan realized that a more serious situation was developing on his left. Major General Sir Alexander Godley's New Zealand and Australian Division was not due to land until after all of the 1st Australian Division's brigades had done so, but most of his New Zealand Brigade had in fact landed and Bridges received Birdwood's permission to use them to reinforce his left, although one of its units, the Auckland Battalion, had become dispersed all along the line, as had been the battalions of 1st Australian Brigade as they came ashore. A fierce battle raged round Baby 700 for the rest of the day, by the end of which the Australians and New Zealanders had been forced back to the western edge of the high ground at the Nek and Russell's Top. The 4th Australian Brigade, as it landed late in the day, sent its 15th and 16th Battalions to join the New Zealanders at Pope's Hill, linking the left of the line to the right on 400 Plateau, where isolated positions had been withdrawn to the western edge. Hardly any artillery had been landed, leaving the infantry dependent for supporting fire on the navy. As there was persistent doubt as to where the forward troops were, this could seldom be safely and effectively used. Australian and New Zealand casualties had reached a total of some 2,000: their collection and evacuation proved slow and difficult, not least because provision for dealing with this number, with the beaches under shellfire, had not been anticipated. There were only two British hospital ships in the force, one supporting the ANZAC landing, and both were soon full.

By the end of the day Bridges had doubts about persisting with the ANZAC effort round Gaba Tepe. He did not believe that the corps could now reach its objective and thought it would be better employed in reinforcing the Helles landings. At 21.15 he referred his doubts to Birdwood, who had been ashore earlier and returned to his headquarters ship, HMS *Queen*, and now came ashore again to discuss it with Bridges. Having done so, he decided to refer it to Hamilton, signalling to Thursby in the *Queen* to transmit it. The latter was horrified and was about to come ashore himself to discuss it, when the *Queen Elizabeth* approached and he decided to go aboard and discuss it with Hamilton and De Robeck. He gave them his personal opinion that it was impracticable to evacuate the forces ashore overnight. After discussion with those present, Hamilton dictated an order to Birdwood to 'stick it out', telling him 'to dig, dig, dig until you are safe', which Thursby personally took to Birdwood ashore.

While these dramatic events were unfolding round Gaba Tepe, the Royal Naval Division was executing its diversion at Bulair. Ships of the 3rd Squadron bombarded the shore of the Gulf of Saros intermittently all day from 05.30 onwards. To give the impression of a landing, shortly before dark, boats from the transports were lowered and towed by trawlers towards the shore, returning under cover of darkness. One platoon from the Hood Battalion was to land, light flares and fire their rifles before being withdrawn; but Freyberg suggested that, to avoid the risk of casualties among them, he, as a strong swimmer, should alone swim ashore and light flares, which was agreed. During the night he was towed in a rowing boat to within three miles of the shore, being rowed for another mile from there before he began to swim. Having swum for an hour and a half, he found the shore undefended and lit three flares before starting to swim back, being picked up by his ship's cutter at 03.00 after another long swim. The plan for 29th Division's landings was more complicated. The main assault was to be delivered on either side of Cape Helles, headed by Brigadier General Steuart Hare's 86th Brigade, landing at V Beach to the east, W to the west and X two miles further north, on the west coast. Once he had secured these, Brigadier General Henry Napier's 88th Brigade would land on V Beach and the two together advance to link up with two subsidiary landings carried out by battalions of Brigadier General William Marshall's 87th Brigade under direct command of Divisional Headquarters, one at Y Beach, two miles north of X, and one at S Beach on the east coast on the far side of Morto Bay one and a half miles north-east of the fort and village of Sedd-el-Bahr. When 86th and 88th Brigades had advanced to a line joining these two beaches, 87th Brigade, having landed two more battalions, would pass through 88th Brigade, picking up its units which had landed earlier, and thrust forward up to the high ground of Achi Baba, which it was expected to secure by the end of the day. The landing at Y was Hamilton's idea, not popular with Hunter-Weston. The latter would exercise command of his division from Rear Admiral Wemyss' flagship, HMS *Euryalus*.

The first landing was at Y Beach at 04.45 without any preliminary bombardment, the 1st King's Own Scottish Borderers and one company of the 2nd South Wales Borderers on the left and the Plymouth Battalion of the Royal Marine Light Infantry on the right, the commanding officer of which, Lieutenant Colonel Geoffrey Matthews, was supposed to be in overall command, although the commanding officer of the KOSB, Lieutenant Colonel Archibald Koe, does not appear to have paid much attention to that. The orders which Matthews had received, which had only been verbal, were to threaten a Turkish withdrawal, capture a gun believed to be in the area, attract Turkish attention away from the other landings and make contact with the force landed at X Beach to his right. Although they were faced by a steep 150 foot high cliff, it was not defended, and by 06.20 the whole force was on top, described by Commodore Roger Keyes, who saw them as the *Queen Elizabeth* passed by at that time, as 'a large body of troops sitting about on the cliffs,

smoking and quite unconcerned'. Half an hour later Matthews saw a
Turkish company making its way south out of range of his rifles, but did
nothing about it. Later in the morning he and his adjutant made a
personal reconnaissance to within 500 yards of the village of Krithia, one
and a half miles inland, and found it deserted; but merely returned.
About midday the KOSB, independently, sent a helio message to the
troops that had landed at X Beach, asking if they should do something
to join up and telling them they, the KOSB, were staying where they
were, expecting to join up with the others when they advanced. No reply
was received and no further attempt at contact made.

The other subsidiary landing, at S Beach, was made by the 2nd South
Wales Borderers with three of their four companies. Two of them were
to land at the north-east corner of Morto Bay, while the third landed
round the corner to scale the cliff and attack a gun position known as
De Tott's Battery. They were in boats towed by trawlers which, owing to
lack of power, had difficulty in making headway against the current in
the Straits. The naval bombardment was due to start at the same time
everywhere, 05.30, but Wemyss held it for half an hour; but unwilling to
delay the main assault any further, opened up at 06.00, when the SWB
were ninety minutes away from their release point. The De Tott's Battery
company met no opposition on landing and soon secured their objective,
which effectively removed opposition to the landing of the other companies in the bay. By 08.30 they were securely in position, having
suffered a total of 63 casualties.

The defence of Morto Bay had been entrusted to one platoon of
Colonel Mahmut's 3rd Battalion of the 26th Turkish Regiment. He
had one company defending V and one W Beach. The rest of his
battalion was in reserve north of Krithia. There were therefore only
twelve Turkish soldiers watching X Beach when it was subjected to an
exceptionally effective bombardment by HMS *Implacable*, which came
closer inshore to deliver it than did the ships at other beaches. The 2nd
Royal Fusiliers therefore landed unopposed. Their task was to turn right
and secure Hill 114, make contact with the 1st Lancashire Fusiliers,
who would have landed on W Beach, and then 'form an outpost line'
north and inland of X Beach to cover the left flank of the expected
advance. On their way to Hill 114 they were attacked, probably by the
Turkish company which the Marines on Y Beach had seen passing
across their front, but managed to beat them off and continued towards

their objective. Meanwhile the landings at V and W Beaches were running into trouble. They were the obvious places to land, both from their location at the tip of the peninsula and also because the beaches were comparatively wide and their exits easier to negotiate than those on the west coast. However, they were funnel-shaped and flanked by 150 foot high cliffs: the fact that they were the best places for a landing was as obvious to the Turks as it was to Hamilton and his staff. Each was defended by a company, covering with machine-gun fire barbed-wire obstacles at and above the waterline, among which mines had been laid. The naval bombardment did little harm to these fixed defences. It had kicked up such clouds of dust that observation of fall of shot had been almost totally obscured, and the Turks manning the defences withdrew while it was in progress, returning to their posts in the pause between its lifting to targets further inland and the arrival of the first boats. The leading battalion at W was the 1st Lancashire Fusiliers. Their tasks were, on the right, to take Hill 138, and link up with the 1st Royal Munster Fusiliers who would have landed on V Beach. Their boats came under intense fire before they had reached the shore and many men jumped into the water, whether ordered to do so or not, their rifles getting wet and clogged with sand. Only two of the twenty-four boats in the first wave reached the shore, many of the men in the others being drowned. Those who reached land faced a thick barbed-wire entanglement. Brigadier General Hare was in the second wave and directed his boat to the left of the bay, where, beyond the wire, he hoped to be able to land under the lee of the cliff and climb up it. He and his party succeeded in this and other Fusiliers on the left side of the landing joined him there. Unfortunately he was then badly wounded, a loss which was to have serious effects on the direction of operations. The two staff officers accompanying him, Major Thomas Frankland and Captain Mynors Farmar, took control, returning to the beach and organizing a move inland from the right-hand side towards Hill 138. By 08.00 the Turks had withdrawn and the Fusiliers linked their two thrusts to form a line covering W Beach, but could do little more, having lost eleven officers and 350 men killed or wounded. Unfortunately Frankland was killed as he tried to make contact with V Beach, where the situation was grim.

Captain C. A. Milward was a staff captain at the headquarters of 29th Division on board the cruiser HMS *Euryalus*. His diary records:

Went on deck about 5 a.m. in the dim light of dawn. Found a dead calm sea, and the ship just moving. Gallipoli just visible in the dim morning mists and the Lancashire Fusiliers already seated in the tows of cutters and pinnaces alongside. All was deadly still and silent, the engines of our ship hardly made a sound. One couldn't help pitying the men sitting there in their boats, feeling as nervous as one feels just before a polo match. It was indeed a hush before the storm. There lay the Peninsula with not a sign of life on it, but the Turks were there all right in their trenches watching our every movement.

At 4.30 a.m. we all went on the Bridge and the Bombardment began. We were now close into Cape Tekke, the extreme end of the Peninsula. The sight now was wonderful – never to be forgotten. A beautiful sunny morning, a glassy sea, on one side the Peninsula, and Asia Minor, apparently uninhabited, being pounded to bits, and in every other direction ships and ships and ships – British battleships round Helles, all the best of the pre-Dreadnought era, cruisers, destroyers, French Battleships off the Asiatic Coast, like top-heavy walnuts, all bumps and excrescences, the five-funnelled Russian cruiser, the 'Askold', 'The Packet of Woodbines', and, in the background, the newest and mightiest, yet so symmetrical, as to look quite small and low – 'Queen Bess', one funnelled and one-masted with her eight 15-inch guns. All these ships had their allotted areas to bombard, some the coastline, some searching up the valley behind and some dropping their 12 and 15-inch shell which burst with mighty columns of smoke on Krithia and on the summit of Achi Baba. The 'Implacable' slowly steamed towards the shore, belching smoke from every gun available, a magnificent sight.

The boats had disappeared in the smoke of the bombardment. Suddenly a heavy rifle fire broke out and we heard the dreaded rattle of machine gun fire. We felt that all was up and feared disaster. Such a thing as the possibility of a landing effected against heavy machine gun fire never entered one's head. Presently boats were seen returning out of the smoke and I said: 'They are coming back'. The smoke however then cleared away and we realised that the boats were returning empty. Each boat was slowly propelled by the sole survivor of its crew, himself wounded, feebly swinging his oar. And then we looked and all along the water's edge, below the wire entanglement, there was a row of dead men. We could see the splash of the bullets as the Turks fired at them. Presently out of this row of dead, some ten men sprang up and slowly and calmly proceeded to climb over the barbed wire. Two actually got across and lay down in the sand-hills beyond. The rest fell on the top of the barbed wire and lay there – 83 of the Lancashire Fusiliers out of these men were buried on the beach that night. Meanwhile several tows from the 'Euryalus' had been landed under the cliffs to the right and left of the beach. We saw the men being collected in large numbers to the left, and after a time these were led up the cliffs. 'This attack was a science'. The Turks spotted this and some came charging forward to drive our men into the sea. To keep the men cool, the Brigade Major, 86th Brigade, Frankland, seized a man's rifle and set an example by bowling over two leading Turks. Not long afterwards he was killed while reconnoitring towards V Beach. The Brigadier General Hare had already been badly wounded. Presently the Lancashire Fusiliers began to advance over the edge of the cliff in fine style, by section rushes. We could see the Turks in trenches behind firing hard and bowling a good many over. I pointed out this trench to the Naval Officers and after some time a few 9.2 shells were dropped on to the trench in enfilade and these effectually cleared the Turk out. The Fusiliers were then able to advance. The Beach and its approaches were now clear, and we were able to land a Royal Naval Division Beach Party, who quickly cleared away the wire entanglement, and commenced a road off it. A Mountain Battery and two 18-pounder guns were put ashore. No words can sufficiently praise the Lancashire Fusiliers.

The characteristics of V Beach were similar to those of W, but more men were due to be landed there. The 1st Royal Dublin Fusiliers, with three companies, was to form the first wave, due to land at 06.00. Half an hour later the rest of the battalion, with the 1st Royal Munster Fusiliers and two companies of the 2nd Hampshires, were to land from the *River Clyde*. Their tasks were, on the right, to capture the village of Sedd-el-Bahr and link up with the 2nd South Wales Borderers at De Tott's Battery; on the left, to join hands with the Lancashire Fusiliers on Hill 138. The first wave was delayed by the current of the Straits, and the *River Clyde* steamed in a circle waiting for the boats to get ahead. But when the delayed bombardment opened up at 06.00, the boats carrying the Dublins were still behind the *River Clyde*, whose Captain, Commander Unwin, decided he could delay no longer and drove his ship ashore slightly ahead of and to the right of them. Unfortunately the steam hopper, with its towed lighters, which was meant to form a gangway between the bows and the shore, swung sideways. Commander Unwin himself, with Able Seaman Williams, entered the water and gallantly managed to pull the lighters into position between the ship and the shore, but Williams was wounded and Unwin had to let go, so that the lighters drifted away. Meanwhile both the exits from the ship and the boats to the left of it came under intense fire. A series of attempts to disembark the Munsters and the Hampshires from the ship only led to piles of dead and wounded, and by 09.00 the two commanding officers, Lieutenant Colonel Henry Tizard of the Munsters and Lieutenant Colonel Herbert Carrington-Smith of the Hampshires, who was in overall command, decided to make no further attempt. Only 300 out of the 700 men of the Royal Dublin Fusiliers from the boats had managed to get ashore, but they could get no further forward than a bank about ten yards inland.

Captain Milward's diary takes up the tale:

Twice a Naval Lieutenant (Morse) managed to get away in a pinnace from the 'Clyde' to tell us how they stood and his tale was not inspiriting. The Dublin Fusiliers who been sent ashore in boats had been killed to a man or drowned. The boats had been wrecked and the crews killed.

So great was the depression that we had great difficulty in dissuading General Hunter Weston from going himself to V Beach to lead the men in the attack. We pointed out that with the large number of troops now landed at W Beach we could afford almost to ignore Seddul Bahr by attacking their position there from the West and taking them in flank. From the first, landing parties of the Lancashire Fusiliers had worked their way to the right under the cliffs and had established a signalling station at Helles Lighthouse. Half a Company from there had advanced as far as the barbed wire of Hill 138 and had been seen lying there ever since, unable to go forward or come back. They had hoisted their red screen to point out their position to the Naval gunners. Combined with these at about 3 o'clock a general attack on Hill 138 was commenced. This was made by the Worcesters and the Essex and from the Bridge of the 'Euryalus' we watched these two fine battalions feeling their way forward in extended lines over the lip of W beach. They went where the sorely tried Lancashire Fusiliers had been established since morning and up the glacis-like slope towards the crest of the hill.

The Turks had not been idle and a good many bullets had even fallen on board our ship. Many times during the morning had I climbed up the fighting tops to try to discover some movement of the enemy, beyond the near ridge. Eagerly did we now watch the advance of the infantry and in suspense did we await again a sudden outburst of fire which would mow down these men and send the others reeling back down the hillside. Intent, with every muscle taut, the first man crept up to the Turkish trenches, looked over and jumped in. The wonderful shooting of H.M.S. 'Swiftsure', dropping her 12 inch shells 10 yards over our men's heads, had been too much for the Turkish nerves and they had evacuated these trenches at the western end of the hill. We found them full of broken and twisted rifles. The Worcesters now proceeded to work along below the hill to tackle the eastern end and the Redoubt where all the barbed wire was. Again we looked on in suspense. We saw two brave men move forward and stand on the sky-line cutting the wire 'as though they were merely snipping grapes from a vine'.

Captain David French was with the 1st Royal Dublin Fusiliers at V Beach and wrote this account:

As we approached the shore shrapnel began to burst over the boats but caused no damage. About 6.30 am we were quite close to the beach in a little bay. The R. Clyde had grounded before it was intended & a hot rifle fire was poured into her from the Turkish trenches. As soon as the 'tows' got into shallow water the picquet boats, which had taken charge of us again, cast off & the bluejackets commenced to row. You can imagine how slowly we progressed – 6 men pulling a heavy boat with about 30 soldiers – each carrying over 60 lbs kit & ammunition on his body –!! At this moment the warships ceased cannonading – and a most appalling fire – machine gun, rifle & pom-pom was opened on us from the enemy, while concealed howitzer batteries from inland added to our discomfort with shrapnel. I was in the last boat of my tow and did not realize they had started at my boat until one of the men close to me fell back – shot. I realized immediately that having practically wiped out the other three boats ahead they were now concentrating their fire on us. I jumped out at once in the sea (up to my chest) yelling to

the men to make a rush for it & to follow me. But the poor devils –
packed like sardines in a tin & carrying this damnable weight on
their backs – could scarcely clamber over the sides of the boat and
only two reached the shore un-hit while the boat just ahead of mine
suffered as much – the same number escaping from that. The only
other officer in my boat never even got ashore being hit by five
bullets. A picquet boat most heroically came right in close & towed
the boat back to the battle-ship 'Albion' which was now anchored
about 800 yds. from the beach.

I had to run about 100–150 yds in the water and being the first
away from the cutter escaped the fire a bit to start with. But as soon
as a few followed me the water around seemed to be alive – the
bullets striking the sea all round us. Heaven alone knows how I got
thro' – a perfect hail of bullets. The beach sloped very gradually –
fortunately. When I was about 50 yds. from the waters edge I felt
one bullet go through the pack on my back & then thought I had got
through safely when they put one through my left arm. The fellows
in the regt. had told me I was getting too fat to run but those who
saw me go through that bit of water changed their opinions later – I
ran like h---ll!!!!! On reaching the shore I made for a bit of cover and
found one sergeant who bound up my wound. I then ran along the
beach to join another officer and in doing so had to pass the mouth
of a nullah. Three bullets whizzed past & needless to say I did not
expose myself for some minutes. It *was* hot!

I could find only 30 or 40 men intact & we commenced to dig
ourselves into the low cliff. Why the Turks with their vast preparations did not level this bank of earth down I cannot imagine. Had
they done so not one of us would have escaped. While the tows were
being pulled into the shore the Munsters began to disembark from
the R. Clyde & they, too, suffered terribly. I was about 50 yds from
where she grounded & as the men ran ashore they were 'mown'
down. I counted 42 killed in one platoon not a single man escaping.
And still they came down the gangways. It was an awful sight but
they were a real brave lot. After a few minutes it became even harder
for them to get ashore. After passing down the gangways & across
the lighters under a heavy fire they had to run along about 25 yds of
jagged rocks – each side of the ridge now being covered with bodies.

Well, we lay there all day & at night the remainder of the troops
dis-embarked from the R. Clyde which originally brought along with

her 2000 troops. Never shall I forget that night. Heavy fire incessantly. Drizzling with rain. Wounded groaning on all sides, &, surrounded by dead I admit I thought it was all up. I had only about 20 men with me left behind at that part of the beach.

By now Brigadier General Henry Napier's 88th Brigade was due to start landing on V Beach, but Hunter-Weston had diverted its leading battalion, the 1st Essex, to W Beach to support the Lancashire Fusiliers' attack on Hill 138, but had not changed the destination of the rest of the brigade. Napier himself, with the 4th Worcesters, approached the port side of the River Clyde and tried to reach land over the lighters, while the rest of the Hampshires beached their boats on the starboard side. Most of the Worcesters became casualties or got no further than the lighters, where Napier and his staff officer were killed: 35 men of the Hampshires got ashore, but no further than the bank. At 10.21 Hamilton, who had seen V Beach for himself from the Queen Elizabeth at 08.30, told Hunter-Weston and Wemyss to send no more men there. Meanwhile the Essex, having landed at W Beach, failed to gain Hill 138, owing to enfilading fire from Hill 114, which the Lancashire Fusiliers had still not taken. By this time Hamilton wished to exploit the apparent success of the landing at Y Beach and, at 09.21, asked Hunter-Weston if he would like more troops sent there. Having received no reply, he repeated the signal at 10.00, demanding an acknowledgement. Unaware of the real situation at V Beach, and after consulting Wemyss, Hunter-Weston replied at 10.35, declining the offer. Meanwhile the French, although several hours late in starting, partly because of the current, had captured Kum Kale by 11.15 and held it for the rest of the day against Turkish counterattacks; and the rest of 88th Brigade, which had been stopped from going to V Beach, were landed to join the Essex at W, Colonel Owen Wolley Dod, the senior staff officer at Headquarters 29th Division, being sent to replace Napier in command. He organized a successful attack by the 4th Worcesters on Hill 138, only to discover that there was another higher hill beyond it, not shown on his map, called Guezji Baba. This was also taken by the Worcesters, but they found themselves under fire from Hill 141, north of Sedd-el-Bahr. Hunter-Weston then ordered an attack on it, but there was a long delay in passing the order on and darkness prevented its implementation. By then the Worcesters had reached the cliffs overlooking the western side of V Beach.

While these bloody battles were being fought, the troops at Y Beach
were doing nothing. Although Lieutenant Colonel Koe's message to X
Beach had been forwarded to Headquarters 29th Division and repeated
nearly two hours later, no reply had been received, Hunter-Weston being
under the impression that the Royal Fusiliers at X Beach were already in
touch with the KOSB. This appears to have been due to an error in a
signal which reported that they were in touch with the Border Regiment,
whose 1st battalion had also landed at X Beach. By then the KOSB and
the RMLI at Y Beach had been withdrawn into a smaller perimeter,
unaware of events further south and still expecting to see the rest of the
division advancing to join them. It was late in the afternoon before it
was realized that they might find themselves isolated under Turkish
attack and preparations for defence were made in the hard ground. At
17.30 the attack came from a battalion of the Turkish 25th Regiment
and was repulsed with the help of naval gunfire. When Brigadier General
Marshall at X Beach heard the sound of battle at Y, he asked Hunter-
Weston if he should send some troops to help, thus weakening his own
defences. Divisional Headquarters took two hours to answer, telling him
not to. Turkish attacks at Y continued through the night, Matthews
sending repeated signals reporting the seriousness of his position, to
none of which did 29th Division reply or initiate action. As dawn broke
at 05.30 Matthews repeated his request for reinforcement and ammunition and again got no response. When naval gunfire support resumed
at 06.00 some shells fell short, causing heavy casualties to a company of
the RMLI on the left flank, and some of them began to withdraw to the
beach. Half an hour later boats were seen to be evacuating casualties
from the KOSB's sector and the two events started a rumour that a
withdrawal had been ordered. Matthews was in fact considering a move
south to join X Beach, but Koe ruled it out. Matthews then signalled
Hunter-Weston that, unless he received reinforcement and ammunition,
he would have to withdraw to the beach. Still no answer. The only
reserve troops were the French. At 06.25 Hunter-Weston asked for a
French regiment to be landed on W Beach to capture Hill 141, which
would open up V Beach. It did not reach Hamilton until 08.15. An hour
earlier Hamilton had offered him a whole French brigade; but five
minutes later first heard of the desperate situation at Y. He therefore
told General d'Amade to send a brigade to X Beach, from which to go
to Y's help; but at 08.11 Hunter-Weston accepted Hamilton's original

offer and, as a result of the usual muddle and bad staff work, it was to W Beach that the French brigade was sent, to Hamilton's dismay. Meanwhile losses on both sides at Y were mounting and the unauthorized withdrawal to the beaches continued until, at 09.30, it was accepted as inevitable and total evacuation was completed by mid-afternoon.

By this time the situation at V Beach had improved. In the dark the few soldiers remaining on the *River Clyde* were able to disembark. Lieutenant Colonel Carrington-Smith had been killed during the afternoon, command devolving on Tizard of the Munsters who remained on board, understandably reluctant to separate himself from his communications having seen what had happened to commanders who had gone ashore. Effective command of the troops ashore at V Beach was exercised by two lieutenant colonels who were acting as liaison officers from Hamilton's staff, Weir de Lancey Williams and Charles Doughty Wylie, and Major Arthur Beckwith of the Hampshires. Together they organized an attack which cleared Sedd-el-Bahr and after that, early in the afternoon, Hill 141 in the attack in which Doughty Wylie was killed. Tizard then at last came ashore. By now the Turks were withdrawing. Tizard's men linked up with some of the South Wales Borderers in Morto Bay, and the Worcesters, advancing from W Beach, joined hands with them west of Hill 141 at 16.00. There was now a continuous line from Morto Bay on the right to X Beach on the left, but the company of the South Wales Borderers at De Tott's Battery was still isolated.

Although it was clear that the Turks were withdrawing, Hunter-Weston was in no mood to take any risk by pursuing them. He ordered his division to dig in where they were, adding: 'There must be no retiring. Every man must die at his post rather than retire.' He decided to wait until the French Général de Brigade Vandenberg's Brigade Metropolitaine had reinforced him before even attempting to link up with the SWB at De Tott's Battery. The French brigade was to be deployed on his right, taking over Hill 141 and relieving all the troops in Morto Bay. A combination of their late arrival and a shortage of boats held them up, and it was not until 04.00 that General d'Amade reached Hill 141 and contacted Tizard, whom Hunter-Weston promptly relieved of his command. Hunter-Weston himself remained on board *Euryalus*, appointing Brigadier General Marshall, commander of 87th Brigade, overall commander ashore. Hunter-Weston had hoped to begin a general advance at midday on the 27th with the French on the right, 88th

Brigade in the centre and the 87th on the left, what was left of 86th Brigade forming his reserve. Although reconnaissance patrols reported that the Turks had withdrawn, he postponed H-hour to 16.00. Having suffered 1,900 casualties in the two days of fighting at Helles, the Turkish 25th and 26th Regiments had in fact pulled back to a line running from the west coast just north of Y Beach, south of Krithia to the Kereves Dere, a mile north of De Tott's Battery. Hunter-Weston's planned advance did not reach as far as that, being limited to a quarter of a mile north of De Tott's Battery on the right and the mouth of Gully Ravine, halfway between X and Y Beaches, on the left. This was reached without difficulty, except on the west flank where 87th Brigade was 500 yards short of its objective. The South Wales Borderers, having been relieved by the French, marched across the peninsula overnight to join their other company, passing unharmed between the British and Turkish front lines.

Hunter-Weston planned a major effort to take him to his first main objective, the high ground of Achi Baba, for the following day, 28 April. He was conscious of the weakness of his infantry, both from casualties and from lack of rest and shortage of food and water, and of the weakness in the fire support for them: only twenty-eight pieces of artillery had been landed and the flat trajectory of the naval guns meant that their fire could not be used for close support, a short way ahead of the attacking troops. He therefore set his objectives short of Achi Baba itself. 87th Brigade was to advance on both sides of Gully Ravine to a small hill, Yazy Tepe, to the west of the high ground. On their right 88th Brigade would capture Krithia and then face east: the French would advance one mile to the Kereves Dere and swing their left flank round to keep contact with 88th Brigade's right flank. The final line would then run almost due north–south as a start line for a subsequent attack on Achi Baba from the west. It was a complicated plan, made more difficult to implement by the rough stream beds ('dere' in Turkish) running south from Achi Baba. H-hour was set for 08.00, but orders did not leave divisional headquarters until 22.00 on the 27th, battalions not receiving theirs until shortly before the attack was due to start.

On the right the French met heavy fire from the Kereves Dere and were forced back to their start line, holding up the advance of 88th Brigade's right flank. This delayed the rest of the brigade, which got within a mile of Krithia before coming up against the Turkish defences, where the attack petered out into a series of isolated attempts to get forward. On the left 87th Brigade advanced for three miles astride Gully Ravine, but then were also brought to a halt by the Turkish defence. Hunter-Weston had now come ashore, but still left Marshall acting as an operational deputy. The latter then used 86th Brigade both to take ammunition up to the 88th, who were running short of it, and to launch an attack between the 88th and the 87th to the west of Krithia. At the same time, in the early afternoon, the latter tried again to advance, but, as they drew level with Y Beach, were forced back as they were counter-attacked by the Turks, who had been reinforced during the day by eight battalions. A further attempt by the French to advance was also driven back, exposing the right flank of 88th Brigade, the battalions of which, from right to left, began also to withdraw to conform. The whole attack ground to a halt. At 17.15 Marshall proposed to hold that position until dark and then dig in slightly behind it, to which Hunter-Weston agreed at 18.00. This brought the Helles landings to a close, 29th Division having lost 187 officers and 4,266 men, of whom 36 and 1,850 were from 86th Brigade, the Royal Dublin Fusiliers being reduced to a lieutenant and 374 men.

In the ANZAC sector the night of 25/26 April was spent in digging in and filling gaps in the line with companies from the New Zealand and Australian Division as they came ashore. Under cover of naval gunfire on the 26th, the line was gradually reorganized so that companies could join their own battalions, battalions their own brigades, and brigades their own division, a boundary between the two being set by Birdwood with the New Zealand and Australian Division in the north and the 1st Australian in the south. It ran inland from the centre of Z (later called Brighton) Beach along Bolton's Ridge and Second Ridge, on the west side of Plateau 400, to Courtney's Post. The Australian Division had an amalgamated 1st and 3rd Brigade on the left and 2nd Brigade on the right: the New Zealand and Australian Division had Colonel John Monash's 4th Australian Brigade on the right and Colonel Francis Johnston's New Zealand Brigade on the left. This reorganization was helped by the arrival of four battalions from the Royal Naval Division over the next two days, the Portsmouth, Chatham and Deal Battalions of the RMLI and the Nelson Battalion from the 1st Naval Brigade. They came into the line on the northern half of 400 Plateau between the two divisions.

Mustafa Kemal was also being reinforced. With the arrival of two more regiments, he launched attacks all along the line, but concentrating on Baby 700, on 27 April; but they were held by a combination of resolute defence, counter-attacks and naval gunfire. By this time casualties since landing totalled 179 officers and 4,752 men. Kemal launched a further attack on 1 May before dawn, the main effort being made against the marines, who held it successfully. Birdwood was himself planning an attack on that day, but Bridges protested that his division was not yet in a fit state to take part. Godley was willing, however, and on 2 May launched three battalions, two Australian and one New Zealand (the Otago), on Baby 700 after dark. It was a complicated plan, involving preparatory moves over difficult ground. The Otago battalion arrived at the start line half an hour late, by which time the Australians had already been held up by the Turks, who then concentrated their fire on the New Zealanders, inflicting heavy casualties. Godley then brought in his reserve, the battalions from the Royal Naval Division who had a short time before been relieved by Australians from the 1st Division. They launched a further attack before dawn on 3 May, but it also failed at high cost. A picture of what that cost was in human terms is provided by a letter written from Alexandria on 8 May by Captain Lawrence Wedderburn, a medical officer aboard HM Transport *Caledonia*, acting as an ambulance ship:

> I have been trying to bring myself to write of what I've seen but I can't. It's too horrible. Our numbers on board rose at one time to 915. One day we were ordered to transfer them all to B11. I took it upon me to say that my cases would suffer in being moved again: and asked if we might proceed to Alexandria, as we were short of provisions and medical stores. This was granted. Our slight cases were taken off, and we got on more serious cases from other ships, making up 825. I also got another M.O. and two orderlies. The former an Australian (is my senior, which is a pity: and doesn't do much work). We set off doing our best for them but horribly understaffed; only twenty R.A.M.C. orderlies, and badly equipped. I have had twenty three deaths on board, eight after leaving Gallipoli. We arrived here last night and have got rid of 130 cases, the worst ones, and proceed to Malta tomorrow, with the rest. Then back to Gallipoli. I am very tired, but we'll get a rest after Malta for a day or two. I could have done far more operative surgery, if I had had time:

but we had to let a lot slip in order to benefit as many as possible, and it was sickening seeing men die, when one could have helped them if one had had time & physical energy. I had two amputations through the middle thigh – one on a turk, for gangrene – he is living still; the other a stretcher bearer – he died of shock. We have many minor amputations, and experience of bullet and shell wounds in every conceivable part of the body. It is all terribly sad and wearing. The Tommies are splendid – great fellows, but it is all too sad. I had a lot of the 5th Royal Scots, officers and men. Great fellows too. Can you imagine 250 wounded coming along side at one time? And only four M.O.'s to look after them! More arriving at all hours of the night – probably they had been lying out for hours – or days – without food. They go to sleep at once, and we let them sleep if possible. The cabins of a ship are not convenient for carrying in bad cases: and latterly I rigged up cots in the music and smoking saloons. The ships Company are great friends and help all they can, and here everybody is anxious to give us all we ask when it is too late.

One of those evacuated to the *Caledonia* was Captain David French. He described his experience:

I superintended the wounded being taken off that afternoon [the day after the landing] & then was sent off to the 'Caledonia' – a hospital receiving ship. The wounded had a ghastly time – none of the Dublins being attended to – except with field dressings – by a medical man for 36 hours. Any doctor who approached the shore was immediately knocked out, & eventually orders were given to them that they were on no account to land until 'V' beach was 'safe'. We ran terribly short of water as each of us carried 3 days iron rations – a service waterbottle filled or a beer-bottle of lime juice & water (in the pack) only. Luckily I took a considerable quantity of morphia ashore which greatly alleviated the sufferings of those – in some cases smashed to pieces. P. kindly sent me weekly a bott. of Liq. Brandy after leaving England & I had one of these with me !!!! All Tuesday [the landings had been on Sunday], Wed., & Thurs. I watched the operations room from the hospital 'Sicilia' before sailing for Egypt. On arrival there we were told we could not be landed as every hospital was full – four ships having gone before us.

The arrangements were scandalous: they had absolutely under-estimated the probable number of casualties by a very large margin.

The French had made *no* arrangements for the wounded & relied on us. The 'Aragon' – not converted into a hospital ship – took 700 wounded to Alexandria with 2 doctors, & my servant, who came in her, said the stench below decks owing to wounds getting septic was so appalling that even he – a Tommy – could not venture below!!! And this sort of thing went on for days – several ships being as bad.

The action in the ANZAC sector on 3 May brought to a close the landing phase, which had already ended at Helles.

3

Gallipoli: Butting the Brick Wall

While further attacks at Helles were suspended, the force there was being strengthened bit by bit. More artillery, supplies and transport were landed and the force was strengthened by the arrival of the headquarters and five battalions of the Royal Naval Division, under Major General Archibald Paris, and the French Brigade Coloniale from Kum Kale, the two French brigades forming a division commanded by Major General Masnou. Other reinforcements were on their way: Brigadier General Vaughan Cox's 29th Indian Brigade and Major General William Douglas's 42nd (East Lancashire) Division from Egypt, and a second French division from Marseilles, commanded by Major General Maurice Bailloud. Although the increase in artillery was especially welcome, there was a general shortage of ammunition and only shrapnel was available for the British 18pdr field guns: for high explosive shell the Royal Artillery relied on the 4.5in howitzer, of which there were only eight. The navy was also running low and had to preserve stocks to meet the unlikely eventuality that they got through the Straits and had to engage the Turkish navy in the Sea of Marmara, and then threaten Constantinople. The French artillery was better equipped and supplied.

Meanwhile Liman von Sanders was also being reinforced with three divisions, which allowed him to move more troops down to the south of the peninsula, forming two groups, one under Essad Pasha opposite the ANZAC sector, the other, under the German Colonel von Sodenstern, facing the Helles front. On 30 April Enver ordered von Sanders to deliver a major attack there, which was launched during the night of 1/2 May. The main effort was made against the French, who were reinforced by the Worcesters from 88th Brigade and three battalions from the Royal Naval Division which was in reserve. The temporarily amalgamated Dublin and Munster Fusiliers were also strongly attacked south of Krithia. All these attacks were successfully held. An attempt by the French to counter-attack and gain ground was only partially successful.

They suffered 2,000 casualties and the British 700, while the Turks lost heavily.

Hamilton, who had transferred his headquarters from the *Queen Elizabeth* to the transport *Arcadian*, from which a cable was run ashore, now decided to stay on the defensive in the ANZAC sector and told Birdwood to transfer two brigades to Helles, where they would be joined by the one New Zealand and two Australian field batteries which had not yet landed. In the 29th Division, 86th Brigade was disbanded, to be replaced by 29th Indian Brigade on its arrival. The amalgamated Dublin and Munster Fusiliers went to 87th Brigade and the Lancashire and Royal Fusiliers, who had also been temporarily amalgamated, to the 88th. The first brigade of 42nd Division to land, the 125th, would also join 29th Division on arrival. The 2nd Naval Brigade, commanded by Commodore Oliver Backhouse, consisting of the Anson, Hood and Howe Battalions, was placed under command of the French Division, which placed its Brigade Coloniale under Backhouse's overall command. Major General Paris, with the headquarters of the Royal Naval Division, was to form a Composite Division from his two remaining battalions, Plymouth and Drake, and the two transferred ANZAC brigades, the New Zealand and 2nd Australian. This reorganization was to be completed by 6 May when Hamilton planned to make his next attack to take Achi Baba.

He favoured a night attack, but Hunter-Weston and d'Amade insisted on a conventional daylight one, to be preceded by an artillery programme, which would be limited by the shortage of ammunition and by the lack of any definite intelligence about the Turkish defences. Little patrolling had been done and aerial reconnaissance was confined to two flights a day by the one naval aircraft which carried a camera. The 29th Indian Brigade had arrived on 1 May, but Cox decided that the four Muslim companies of its two Punjabi battalions should not be called upon to fight their co-religionists: the battalions were to be replaced by Gurkhas, but they had not yet arrived. The 125th Brigade, for whom it would be their first taste of action, did not land until the afternoon of 5 May, and the two transferred ANZAC brigades before dawn on the 6th. The plan was similar to that of the previous attempt. In the first phase the whole line would advance for about a mile, which, on the right, would take the French over the Kereves Dere to the high ground beyond. 29th Division would then swing its left flank round, capture Krithia and

then face east, with its left flank at Yazy Tepe, turning from there back
to the west coast. In the final stage, 87th and 88th Brigades would attack
Achi Baba from the west and south-west. On the Turkish side, von
Sodenstern, who had been slightly wounded, had been replaced by
another German, Weber Pasha. He had 20,000 troops disposed in well-
dug defences, protected, on the German model, by concealed outposts,
manned with machine guns.

The preparatory bombardment in this Second Battle of Krithia
opened at 10.30, and, when the infantry began to move forward at 11.00,
it soon became clear that it had not been effective. As before, the French
started late, and, when they did, the Brigade Métropolitaine met heavy
fire on the near side of the Kereves Dere. The Brigade Coloniale advanced
cautiously on its left and a gap began to develop between it and the 2nd
Naval Brigade, who came under intense fire as they tried to fill it. By the
end of the day the advance on the French Division's front was no more
than 400 yards. 88th Brigade in the centre had made little greater
progress, and by 16.00 began to dig in, still short of Krithia. The raw
125th Brigade, having landed at W Beach on the previous afternoon, had
to march overnight to its assembly area near the head of Gully Ravine,
which it did not reach until 02.00. Owing to a mistaken order, it did not
start its attack until 11.30, and, after advancing 400 yards to its first
objective, was held up by Turkish machine guns, which naval gunfire
was unable to subdue. By the end of the day, therefore, the general
attack had not even reached the main Turkish positions. Casualties had
not been heavy, and Hamilton ordered the operation to continue next
day, two more brigades, one from the 2nd French Division and the
127th from the 42nd, having landed. H-hour was set for 10.00, preceded
by only a quarter of an hour's artillery programme. The day saw a feeble
repetition of the previous day's attack, with even less ground gained; but
Hamilton was determined to press on 'with the utmost possible vigour',
and ordered that a further attack should be launched at 10.30 on 8 May.

125th Brigade had suffered a bloody nose in the Gully Ravine and
was withdrawn into reserve, being replaced by 87th Brigade, while the
New Zealand Brigade joined 29th Division in the central sector. The
plan was that the French would limit themselves to an attempt to cross
the Kereves Dere, while the New Zealand Brigade passed through the
88th to capture Krithia, while 87th Brigade, on its left, took Gully Spur
on the west side of the Ravine. Hunter-Weston issued a warning order

shortly before midnight on 7 May, but formal written orders did not
leave his headquarters until two hours before the attack was due to start
at 10.30, again preceded by only a quarter of an hour's artillery
preparation. Again the attack petered out after the advance varied from
none at all to 200 yards. Hamilton had now come ashore at W Beach
and set up his headquarters on Hill 114. At 16.00 he ordered that yet
another effort should be made, starting at 17.30 and making use of
brigades, including the 2nd Australian, which had not yet been involved.
Again it would be preceded by only a quarter of an hour's bombardment,
but using more guns than before. Some gains were made, but none of
more than 600 yards; but the cost had been high: 6,500 casualties, of
which 1,000 were in the 2nd Australian Brigade – half its strength.

Captain Milward's diary for 8 May read:

> At 3.p.m. the whole force was ordered to attack. A heavy bombard-
> ment for ½ hour preceded it, but it was a hurried affair. Bombard-
> ment of naval and field guns was tremendous. (The sea is still full of
> warships and transports). Unfortunately on left S.W.Bs.* mistook the
> order and did a charge when it was really left to their own initiative
> and those damned machine guns again knocked out 2 companies. In
> the centre the New Zealanders and Australians were pushed in to go
> through the poor attenuated 29th Division – with the latter in
> support. They carried out the charge magnificently. It was a wonder-
> ful sight. We saw it all, looking up the broad valley towards Krithia
> from our Hill 138 above our camp. One seldom sees such a view of
> a battle these days – magnificent but rather horrible.
>
> The left we couldn't see, but in the left centre we saw the New
> Zealanders advance to the left of and out of the fir wood. They
> charged with dash and lost little, 10 men in the advance, but they left
> behind them to the left rear a Turkish machine gun hidden in the
> thick gorse and this did great damage. Up the open valley in the
> centre we saw the Australians advance under a heavy shrapnel fire
> quite calmly, doubling forward and they gained ground about 400
> yards ahead. They met with a white flag incident and took no
> prisoners in consequence. The general of the Brigade and his two
> staff officers were both hit. They have a fine spirit, but lack the
> subterfuges of the Regulars in the attack. On the right the French did

---

* South Wales Borderers.

really well and progressed about 800 yards. I could see a Turkish counter-attack coming down along the ridge on to the French under the tremendous fire of the French 75s. The few survivors came along down the hill on to the French trench, when all the latter rose up and annihilated them.

The attack ceased for want of new troops about 7 p.m. We had gained about 400 yds, but are still a mile from Krithia and still further from the Hill 472 behind it and Achi Baba, which is our objective. We must get on on the left before we can take this.

Lieutenant H. D. O'Hara, one of the few survivors of the Dublin Fusiliers from V Beach, on 15 May wrote to his fellow officer, Captain David French:

Riccard arrived last night with a small draft and told us where you were, so I am sending you a line in the hopes that it may find you somewhere. I hope your wound is getting better. You were reported as very cheerful – is there any chance of your coming back – for your own sake I hope not – this is absolute hell this show with precious little chance of coming out alive. The total British casualties (excluding French) from the first fortnight were just short of 20,000. The New Zealanders got an awful dusting about a week ago and suffered about 3,000 casualties – they are simply splendid fellows with any amount of pluck and dash. I dare say you have heard how we have joined up with the Munsters as a composite battalion, officially known as the 'Dubsters' – it is far from being a satisfactory arrangement and we hope to split up as soon as we get some more officers – we now have Riccard, Taylor, Stirling, Floyd and self. I commanded the regiment for exactly 2 days before we got Floyd back, he was with the transport.

I am now continuing 2 days later and we are once more the Dublins having separated from the Munsters. We had desperate heavy fighting for the first fortnight after landing, hardly a night's rest but we have now been resting away in reserve since 8th. You will be glad to hear the men have done splendidly and Hunter Weston gave out that the Dublins and Munsters were the two regiments that had done best of all. It is terribly sad losing all our officers. I don't know whether Grove and Molesworth are at Malta – they were both wounded on the 28th. The day of the big retreat – a most awful show that was – the whole division simply took to their heels and ran – if the Turks had followed us up we would have been driven into the sea I think.

We had a desperate night attack on May 1/2 – the Turks attacked with the bayonet with a force computed at some 40,000 from 10.30 at night till dawn next morning, and ourselves and the Munsters were in the part of the line where they came thickest – we were some 350 strong and fired nearly 150,000 rounds – there was practically no barbed wire out and they actually got into the machine gun trench where Sgt. Emery was at handgrips with two of them but we were re-inforced by the Royals and drove them out. When dawn broke they were only about 500 yards away running like hell and we had a fine time as we simply poured volley after volley into them – their casualties must have been simply colossal – there were over 300 dead just in front of our trenches. The fighting has now developed into trench warfare just the same as in France and the staff think it will be some months before we get to the top of Achi Baba which is not very comforting – we have not even got the village of Krithia yet. I have put a cross up over Grimshaw's grave but I can't find where the Colonel* is buried – perhaps you may know – all the rest are in the same grave except the poor old Major† and Corbet and Kennedy is having a big cross made. The French have got 'V' beach now but there is a small cemetery railed off. I hope poor old Crozier gets better – he behaved splendidly in the attack on the hill 141 on the 26th and I sent in his name for gallantry and also Grimshaw's who simply threw away his life by standing up and screaming in the way he always used to do – there was no need for it at all and we could ill spare him, but he was a real brave man and no mistake. I am hoping Crozier will get a D.S.O. as I wrote as strongly as I could when I sent in my report. You will be sorry to hear that S.M. [Sergeant-Major] O'Mahony was killed on the 8th – put his head over the parapet for a second and was shot through the mouth.

Be sure and write soon – you are about the only one of my pals in the regiment left now with the Major and Corbet and Bernard all down – it is very sad indeed – anyhow I don't expect to survive long

---

* Lieutenant Colonel R. A. Rooth.
† Fetherstonhaugh.

myself* – a Captain on the staff here said the first fortnight was
incomparably worse than Mons or La Bassee, so you see we have had
a rough time.

Hamilton had to admit at least a temporary defeat. He was keenly
aware that Kitchener would be unwilling to send him more troops, and,
in reporting the situation, he said that his troops had done all they could
'against semi-permanent works, and they are not able to carry them.
More and more munitions will be needed to do so.' In reply Kitchener
asked him what operations would be needed to continue the attack in
cooperation with the navy. Hamilton answered that no major operation
would be possible in the near future, but that he hoped, with minor
operations at Helles, to improve the position in preparation for an
offensive, which would need a corps of two fresh divisions. On 10 May
Kitchener told him that the 52nd (Lowland) Division would be sent out
immediately.

Signals had also been passing between De Robeck and the Admiralty.
His irrepressible chief of staff, Roger Keyes, supported by some other
senior naval officers, urged De Robeck to make a renewed attempt to
force their way through the Straits, arguing that many of the guns which
had been covering the minefields had been moved to face the army on
land. De Robeck himself had serious doubts and referred the matter to
the Admiralty, which led to a serious rift between Churchill and Fisher.
The former was all in favour. Fisher, already disillusioned with the
campaign, worried about his battleship strength. As Italy joined the
Entente, she had been promised naval support in the Adriatic; but more
serious was the intelligence that at least one German submarine, the
U21, had passed through the Straits of Gibraltar, heading for the eastern
Mediterranean, where the Royal Navy's most modern battleship, the
Queen Elizabeth, was off the Dardanelles.

Fisher, having discussed it with Hankey, registered his disapproval
with the Prime Minister, Asquith, before sending Churchill a memorandum starkly refusing to have anything to do with the project and

---

* He died on a hospital ship on 29 August 1915, from wounds received shortly after the
  battalion had been moved to the Suvla sector. He was at that time the only officer of
  the battalion who had landed on V Beach and not become a casualty. He was twenty-
  three, had been awarded the DSO, and was buried at Gibraltar.

threatening resignation if it went ahead. Churchill pulled out all the stops in reply, writing:

> We are now committed to one of the greatest amphibious enterprises of history. You are absolutely committed. Comradeship, resource, firmness, patience, all in the highest degree will be needed to carry the matter through to victory. A great army hanging on by its eyelids to a rocky beach, and confronted with the armed power of the Turkish Empire under German military guidance: the whole *surplus* fleet of Britain – every scrap that can be spared – bound to that army and its fortunes as long as the struggle may drag out: the apparition of the long-feared submarine – our many needs and obligations – the measureless advantages – probably decisive on the whole war – to be gained by success. Surely here is a combination & a situation wh requires from us every conceivable exertion & contrivance wh we can think of. I beg you to lend your whole aid and goodwill, & ultimately then success is certain.

But Fisher was adamant, even when Churchill agreed to recall the *Queen Elizabeth* and replace her by two old monitors. Fisher's and De Robeck's fears were strongly reinforced when, during the night of 12/13 May, HMS *Goliath* was torpedoed by a Turkish gunboat in Morto Bay with the loss of 667 of her crew of 750. The War Council, which had not met since 19 March, considered the whole matter on 14 May. Kitchener had tabled a paper which virtually favoured abandoning the campaign, but he admitted at the meeting that this was politically unacceptable. However he warned that the two extra divisions that Hamilton had asked for would not be enough. No firm decision was reached, Kitchener being asked to tell Hamilton to send a more detailed appreciation. The latter's answer was that, if he received help from, say, Greece or Bulgaria, his corps of two divisions would suffice, but if that was not forthcoming, a further two would be needed. A response to that was delayed by the political crisis sparked off by the 'shell scandal', orchestrated by the Northcliffe press, and Fisher's abrupt resignation on the grounds that he could no longer work with Churchill. This brought about the resignation of Asquith's Liberal administration and its replacement by an all-party coalition, Asquith remaining as Prime Minister, but Balfour, the former Conservative Prime Minister, replacing Churchill, who was kicked downstairs to be Chancellor of the Duchy of Lancaster. That put paid to any further idea of a purely naval operation. Any such thing was further discouraged when the U21 arrived off the peninsula on 25 May and promptly sank HMS *Triumph* off Anzac Cove, all but 75 of her crew being saved, followed to the bottom next day by the *Majestic* off W Beach, all but 43 of her crew being rescued. De Robeck's reaction was to withdraw all but the essential supporting ships to the safety of Kephelos Bay at Imbros.

During this period the ANZAC sector had been quiet, although very unpleasant for the soldiers. To avoid naval bombardment, the Turks had brought their front line as close as they could to the ANZAC defences. Any movement in or to and from the latter drew instant fire and had to be confined to the hours of darkness. Dead bodies lay everywhere: the stench was nauseating, food was meagre, and water had to be carefully rationed. Clothes and bodies were filthy and disease soon began to take a heavy toll. As a result of a visit by Enver and the arrival of another division, a fresh Turkish attack was launched at 03.00 on 19 May, principally against 400 Plateau. The ANZAC posts had been skilfully sited to give enfilading fire to each other, and the Turks were mown down, losing 10,000 men, most in the first two hours. All was over before midday and agreement was reached between the headquarters of Hamilton and Liman von Sanders for a nine-hour truce next day to bury the dead. Thereafter, with few exceptions, life for both sides in the sector settled down to the routine of trench warfare in disgusting conditions. Another Turkish attack at the end of June fared no better. At Helles conditions were significantly better: the terrain was more open and pleasant; the opposing lines were further apart, and there was space between the front line and the beaches.

On 24 May, by which time the whole of the 42nd Division had arrived, the three British divisions (29th, 42nd and Royal Naval) were formed into VIII Corps, command of which was given to Hunter-Weston (promoted to temporary Lieutenant General), Major General Beauvoir de Lisle taking over the 29th. General Albert d'Amade had already been succeeded in command of the French Corps by General Henri Gouraud. In spite of what he had said to Kitchener, Hamilton was not going to wait for the arrival of reinforcements before trying again, having been persuaded by Hunter-Weston and Gouraud that he should do so before the Turkish positions were further strengthened. The Third Battle of Krithia was planned for 4 June, this time with a preparatory artillery programme lasting four hours. On the left the depleted 29th Division was to attack on either side of Gully Ravine: on their right the 42nd would advance on a wide front to Krithia and to the east of it, while the Royal Naval Division attacked between them and the Kereves Dere, the French concentrating on the Haricot Redoubt near its mouth. The attack would be made in two waves, penetrating to a depth of 800 yards. There was no specific formation in reserve, only individual battalions of all five divisions. Hamilton himself, therefore, had nothing with which he could influence the battle.

The guns opened fire at 08.00, stopped for ten minutes at 11.20 to encourage the Turks to emerge from their dugouts, and then resumed until 12.00. 29th Indian Brigade led 29th Division's attack and suffered heavily. Two battalions of 88th Brigade, 1st King's Own Scottish Borderers and 4th Worcesters, reached the third Turkish line, but, no others having done so, were forced to withdraw. To their right 42nd Division's 127th Brigade penetrated to the last Turkish line and thought the way was clear to Achi Baba, while the Royal Naval Division also made significant progress, but at heavy cost. The French were met with intense fire, suffered very heavy casualties and could not reach their objective. When they began to withdraw, the Collingwood Battalion on the right flank of the Royal Naval Division came under intense fire from their right, and by 12.45 the division was back where it started, thus exposing the right flank of the 42nd. Hunter-Weston and Gouraud now faced the decision as to where such reserves as there were should be used. Influenced, no doubt, by the fact they were not under central command, they decided to use them to try and restore the situation in the Royal Naval and French sectors, starting at 16.00, instead of exploiting success in the centre; but at 15.00 Gouraud told Hunter-Weston that his divisions were not fit to launch another attack that day. It would clearly be folly for the Royal Naval Division to launch one on its own, so this was cancelled. 42nd Division was by then under increasing pressure, and at 18.30 was ordered to withdraw to the first Turkish line they had captured.

Lieutenant Reginald Savory (a future lieutenant general) was serving in the 14th Sikhs in 29th Indian Brigade and gave an account of their experience in that battle in a letter to his mother on 6 June:

There was some twaddle in the Daily Graphic about Sikhs crawling on their stomachs, with knives in their mouths, tracking snipers: all rot. Also, Krithia & Achi Baba are still in the hands of the Turks; in spite of fanciful stories about the occupation & sack of Maidos, which never took place. Our methods here seem to be based on a theory that all tactics are rot, & that the only way to do anything at all is to rush forward 'bald-headed', minus supports, minus reserves, &, in the end, minus a limb or two. Hence, the almost total wiping out of the 14th Sikhs on 4 June. We had, as our own special task, to advance up a nullah, a thing which one has always learned should *never* be done until all the ground commanding it is first seized, against the Turks who were in a wired trench at the end, & also on both sides, & at the top, & their machine-guns took us in front & rear, & from practically every side. Needless to say, we had no supports whatever! not a damned thing! Well at 12 noon we got up out of our trenches, got through their barbed wire (the only regiment that did) & bagged their first trench: total time taken, roughly twenty minutes: we hung on there all night, unable to go forward – because of having only two British officers left, the C.O. & a Capt Engledue of 89th P.I. [Punjab Infantry] who is attached to us, & also because of their machine-guns, their infantry being rotten: no one gives a damn for them. Not a single reinforcement did we get after repeated messages had been sent & so about 9 a.m. next day we had to come back having had 9 officers killed & three wounded out of fourteen & the regiment being 135 strong. The general who ordered the advance up the nullah is in everyone's opinion responsible for the whole thing. So bang goes one of the finest regiments of the Indian Army, & certainly the best on the Peninsula. We knew we were in for a hot time before we started, & it turned out to be right. I had a bayonet in my forehead, which luckily just went in under the skin & did little harm except for stunning me for a few hours, & giving me occasional headaches, but I am perfectly alright now.

These damned Turks mutilated some of our wounded, & fired on our stretcher-bearers & wounded, when they were trying to get back to cover. We have only got back the body of one of our British officers (Cremen) the rest are still lying out there; & so are all the rest of our dead. The smell in the firing-line now is awful. Every single officer who came out with the regiment has been either wounded or killed. Anyhow the regiment did damned well, & our men fought magnificently especially when they could get in with the bayonet. I myself had the extreme satisfaction of bayoneting three

Turks, only in the excitement of the moment I left it sticking in the third, & ran on with only a revolver: anyhow it must have hurt him, when he pulled it out, if he was still alive, & I hope it did. They are dirty, unwashen looking devils & nobody loves them: but from all accounts, they are getting fed up with the war in general & the Germans in particular: one prisoner I saw volunteered the information that he hated the Germans, by spitting & saying 'allemong' in quick succession. The German officers are mighty proud, & one of them refused to walk back to the base, but demanded a pony to ride, as he said he was too senior to walk with the others: so his escort just left him, sitting by the road, until presently a shrapnell burst unpleasantly near him, & he, thinking discretion the better part of valour, did not walk but ran! There are parties of marines & sailors from the Goeben & Breslau, fighting among the Turks, & running their machine-guns for them: but when they make an attack, they take jolly good care to stay behind.

By the way, before I forget, can you please send me a wrist-watch? as mine was bust on the 4th & I need one badly. Those 'screw-in' ones are best & stand lots of knocking about. Did I tell you that I am now doing the work of adjutant & quartermaster: the C.O. has been given temporary command of a brigade: so our mess is now reduced to three: Capt. Engledue, the doctor & myself: of course one gets used to it, in time, but at first it was awful; & I missed the cheery meals we used to have: everyone was always so full of buck, especially Fowle, who was one of the very best: I am awfully sorry for his wife, as they were such a very devoted couple, & she is an awfully good sort ... God knows what they are going to do with us, as we are no use as a fighting unit, & recruits are hard to get, especially in the numbers we shall need. Probably, they will order us to assault Achi Baba, single-handed & fling the survivors into the sea, so as to be rid of us: I assure you the powers that be (sitting in their comfortable dug-outs, drinking whisky & smoking cigars) are quite capable of it. Whisky, by the way, is an unknown quantity: rum is our staple drink.

On 3 July he had to write to his father to assure him that he was still alive, as the former had received official notification that he had been killed.

Captain Milward visited the area on 15 June and wrote in his diary:

Went all round the front trenches of the Indian Brigade high up along the sea coast – most wonderful arrangement of paths and trenches among the cliffs – then across the Gully Ravine, up among the trenches we captured the other day. I was taking round the photographer to shew him the best places to take photos of the enemy's trenches. One had to look carefully over the parapet with a periscope and we even had one of the periscopes broken by a bullet. Round the Gully Ravine the enemy and his snipers are very close. The trenches are very unpleasant in places, many dead still lying out. In front of the Indian Brigade, where the Lanc. Fusiliers failed to advance, the latter had 214 missing and all are lying out there still between the opposing trenches, with many Sikhs and officers. Many, too badly wounded to move, must have died from exposure, I'm afraid under the very rifles of our men. But the enemy kept up so hot a fire all night that burial or help was impossible.

16th June. Had 6 prisoners to examine, the result of a futile and costly attack the Turks made on the Essex and Dublins. They took twice our advanced sap, driving our men back with bombs, only to be driven out in the end, and forced to retire across the open under our machine-gun fire.

Sergeant Harry Hopwood of the 6th Manchesters in 127th Brigade of the 42nd Division was a veteran of the Boer War, in which he had served as a sergeant in their 2nd Volunteer Battalion. He wrote to 'Dear Mother and All' on 1 July:

There has been another advance on our part but it was on the flanks and we, the 6th, were in the middle of the line which is the most advanced so we had simply to stand fast all day and watch, being ready if necessary to support on the left. However, we were not called on and the 29th Division on the one side and the French on the other did very well. As it happened I was in the very trench that we got from the Turks on the 4th June when we, the 6th, made the charge. The stench of the dead was sickening, both our fellows and theirs being left about. We have buried several of ours but it is dangerous work and has to be done at night. There are hundreds of bodies to be seen, and it is no small relief to get back from the firing trenches to the reserve ones where we are now. We go up for anything from 3 days to 3 weeks, you never know, and then back to base for a few days only. However, personally, I am sticking it very

well and am feeling better than I have felt for months. Am sorry to
say that nothing has been heard of Tom Teare up to now. I hope to
goodness we do hear something before long, one way or another.
One has to be very careful here *in* the trenches, as any amount of
fellows get hit by bullets striking high on the parapet and coming
through. I have had some narrow squeaks, in fact everybody has. The
day before yesterday I was looking through a periscope with Capt.
Walker (one of our new officers) when one came through and
smashed the 'peri' throwing dirt and stones about and cutting the
Captain's face and head rather. It was a near thing for both of us.
How it missed me I dont know as I was holding it at the time . . . By
the way would you send me a bottle of Fruits Salts out, the water
here is very constipating and also a balaclava sleeping cap and some
Carters' Liver Pills. You done [don't] get too much exercise in the
trenches, there is no room . . . P.S. Since writing above have broken
a tooth off my top plate. Am posting it back. Will you have a go at it
Jimmy and return it. Have got a duplicate to go on with.

Hamilton and his staff thought that further effort to capture Achi
Baba would be futile – if pushed out of Krithia, the Turks would merely
create another line further back – but Hunter-Weston and Gouraud
wanted to continue to improve their positions on both flanks in order
to make a further advance possible. They would do so with concentrated
attacks to secure limited objectives, supported by concentrated artillery
fire, especially from howitzers firing high explosive. Hunter-Weston's
objective was Gully Spur, west of Gully Ravine, and Gouraud's Kereves
Spur, west of the dere. The French launched their attack on 21 June and
were successful, beating off several counter-attacks. 29th Division
launched its attack on Gully Spur a week later, reinforced by 156th
Brigade from the 52nd Division, which had landed a fortnight earlier.
87th Brigade was to attack west of the Ravine, the 156th to the east of it,
the former's artillery support being supplemented by French howitzers
and heavy mortars. 87th Brigade's attack was successful, capturing the
first two Turkish lines before the resuscitated 86th Brigade moved
through them, repulsing a Turkish counter-attack. 156th Brigade, with
less artillery support, had a tough time, making little progress and
suffering heavy casualties, especially in 1/7th Scottish Rifles. Turkish
counter-attacks over the next few days were successfully beaten off, after
they had suffered severe losses.

However Hunter-Weston and General Bailloud, who had replaced Gouraud, wounded when visiting a hospital, were not content. They wished to improve their positions in the centre also, Hunter-Weston employing the 52nd Division. Hamilton reluctantly agreed, having wished to deploy it in the ANZAC sector. The French, waiting until 12 July for more artillery to arrive, were to make another attack on the Kereves Dere, while 155th Brigade of 52nd Division attacked on their left. After a three-hour concentrated artillery programme, that attack was launched at 07.30, getting as far as the Turkish second line. Hunter-Weston then agreed that 157th Brigade, on the left of the 155th, could join in. They also reached the second line, but in some confusion. Consolidation of their positions in the former Turkish trenches in the dark proved difficult, and by dawn on the 13th the forward troops were still in a somewhat disorganized state and very tired. Hunter-Weston feared that 157th Brigade might not be able to hold its position against a Turkish counter-attack and ordered the Royal Marine Brigade of the Royal Naval Division to launch a further attack in cooperation with the French in the afternoon. There was a muddle about both their start line and their objective, and they lost 560 men in an almost useless operation. This brought these post-Krithia operations to a close, the three having cost 12,300 casualties, of which 7,700 were British.

While these indecisive operations were in progress, the new administration in London resumed its consideration of strategy, the War Council, having been renamed the Dardanelles Committee, meeting on 7 June for that purpose. Kitchener had tabled a paper rejecting either abandonment or major reinforcement and settling for Hamilton having to do the best he could with what he had. Churchill, in spite of his demotion, was still a member of the Committee. He tabled a rival paper, suggesting adoption of the defensive on the Western Front and application of the maximum possible effort to the Dardanelles. That would bring a rapid and decisive result, after which a greater effort could be devoted to the West. Kitchener, as before, changed his mind at the meeting and supported Churchill's line. As a result the Committee agreed that Hamilton should get his four divisions, including the 52nd already despatched. They would be the three new divisions of Kitchener's army not yet deployed to France, the 10th (Irish), the 11th and the 13th. Churchill, however, kept up the pressure for more to be sent, the Committee agreeing on 17 June that two Territorial Army divisions, the

53rd (Welsh) and 54th (East Anglian), should also be sent as soon as shipping could be made available. The first three were to be sent in fast passenger ships to arrive before the end of July. By then the Committee had become even stronger in its support for a major effort, influenced by disillusionment with the prospects of the Western Front and anxiety about Russia, which had suffered a severe defeat on the Carpathian front.

Hamilton had been dissatisfied with the arrangements for his logistic support, which was organized by Maxwell's headquarters in Egypt. The arrival of reinforcements from England would add to the problems. Accordingly a special staff was established under Lieutenant General E. A. Altham at Alexandria, known as Levant Base, charged with the task of ensuring that Hamilton's forces received adequate support from both Britain and Egypt. Major General G. F. Ellison, appointed as Deputy Quartermaster General at Hamilton's headquarters, was also directly responsible to Altham. He was an old friend of Hamilton's from the Boer War and the reorganization of the army after it, in which he had played a key role. He arrived towards the end of July and described his visits from Imbros to the Peninsula. On 24 July he visited the ANZAC area, which he described thus:

> The condition of affairs at this point of the Peninsula is perhaps the most amazing that has ever existed in the annals of warfare. As we approached ANZAC we could see the shore and the landing jetty being heavily shelled from both flanks and unfortunately some of the shells got home and caused rather serious casualties. Some 12 or 14 men being hit. Landing parties, bathers and those employed in the depots near the beach are never safe at any time during the day or night from incidents of this kind. The Turkish method seems to be to send down a considerable number of shells periodically, and then to give the beach a rest for a considerable period, very often for hours. For instance on the day I visited ANZAC the shelling I referred to took place before we arrived, and then there was no shelling until 4 o'clock in the afternoon, just at the time we were about to leave. Just before 4 o'clock they started a fresh fusilade from both flanks. They must have fired quite 30 shells in the space of about 20 minutes but hit no one. If no one is hit by the first shell, the chances of casualties are small, as every one near the spot, bathers included, at once bolt into certain shelters which have been made for the purpose of protection. The small jetty we landed on was well

riddled with holes made by shells. Of course the bulk of the landing of men and stores has to be done at night, but a certain amount of work goes on continuously pretty well all day. Close to the jetty are General Birdwood's Headquarters and there is quite a town of dug outs and sandbag shelters all huddled together on the face of the small ridge of cliff since our landing. The whole thing reminded me of the small villages in the hills in India with there [sic] little mud huts scooped out in the side of the mountains and giving on to some rough hill track.

He went on to the forward area, adding:

In such circumstances the difficulties of communication can well be imagined but no one with whom I spoke seemed in the least afraid of what any Turkish attack would do. The day I was there the Intelligence had a good deal of information to prove that a strong attack was pending. Enver, Von der Goltz and various notables from Constantinople were known to be in the Peninsula and everything pointed to an attack. No one asked for anything better. They have already beaten off two serious attacks with enormous loss and feel absolutely convinced that they can take on any number that come to attack them. I do not think I have ever met a more cheery lot of fellows than those I encountered in and around ANZAC. One great advantage of the curious conditions under which these men are living is that the dug outs on the face of the exterior cliff are practically immune from rifle or shell fire and the contingents at this point are accordingly spared the rather heavy daily losses that are experienced on the level open ground between KRITHIA and CAPE HELLES in the south Peninsula.

He visited the latter on the following day, landing at W Beach, about which he commented:

The wonder is how it is possible to remain on this beach at all during the hours of day light as from the Asiatic shore the enemy are able to fling shells right on to the beach. The beach itself is concealed from ACHI BABA, distant some 5 miles, but shells are constantly being aimed at the beach and any boats alongside the jetty, bathers etc are liable to be hit. As a matter of fact the beach presents an extraordinarily animated appearance. Stores are constantly being landed. Lighters filled by wounded were being sent off to the Hospital ship lying a mile or so out just as we arrived. A light railway to the front is actually in process of construction, and every form of activity such as baking, manufacture of bombs, digging out large water reservoirs and setting up pumping plant for them etc. is in progress in the quarter of a mile or so of sloping ground that separates the seashore from the plateau above which is in full view of ACHI BABA. Here too everyone is in the best of spirits and shells are regarded as being much less of a nuisance than the flies. The flies by the way are pretty bad every where, but not so bad, I think, as they used to be in South Africa or perhaps it is that the individual fly is not of such a persistent temperament as the South African species used to be. Thank goodness (by the way again) there are no mosquitos.

He went forward and described the scene in the following words:

When we got to the point where the troops in reserve are assembled, we found an enormous town of trenches and dug outs. Miles of the whole plain is nothing but deep trench after trench with the side towards the enemy undercut to give living and sleeping accomodation. Similarly there are deep pits in which horses, mules, etc. are picketted. Not that anyone thinks of living in these shelters permanently. It is only if a shell actually comes to any particular point that anyone feels justified in going to ground as it is quite probable that other shells will follow at the same point, otherwise everyone goes on with their work exactly as usual. The main industry which goes on all the time is digging. Cooking, washing, grooming of horses, and all the usual routine of camp life are constantly in evidence. Our men seem curiously indifferent to all that is going on about them. For instance when the French guns suddenly set up a furious fusilade no one seems to pay the smallest attention. On the other hand the French soldiers seem to take a much more active interest in all operations of war. Little groups of them were standing about with glasses or telescopes, watching the shelling of the Turkish trenches. They too have their system of shelters, but they appear to be much less substantial than those constructed by our own people.

4

Gallipoli: Suvla

For some time Hamilton had been favourably inclined towards sugges-
tions made by Birdwood that an attack on his northern flank offered
possibilities, leading, it was hoped, to the capture of the highest part of
the Sari Bair Ridge, Koja Chemen Tepe, north of Chunuk Bair. Its
seizure would threaten the whole Turkish position to the south of it.
Having sent patrols to reconnoitre routes up the ravines ('deres') leading
into the hills from the coast north of Anzac Cove, he proposed to
Hamilton an approach march by night up three of them, from south to
north, Sazli Beit, Chailak and Aghyl. From the heads of these ravines he
would attack and capture Chunuk Bair and Hill Q, between it and Koja
Chemen Tepe, and having secured these two, he would attack Battleship
Hill, Baby 700 and Plateau 400. He asked for reinforcement by the 29th
Indian Brigade for the night attack and by a complete division for
exploitation. It would be difficult to bring another division in through
the very restricted area of Anzac Cove, already overcrowded, and
Hamilton's staff turned their eyes to the area north of it, where there
were suitable beaches south of Suvla Bay. A landing in that area would
have the added advantage that it could deal with Turkish guns, sited on
the hills called Chocolate and W, which could threaten the rear of troops
taking part in the main attack.

When Hamilton received the news that he was to get three more
divisions, a Suvla landing seemed to offer the prospect of a more
ambitious exploitation of Birdwood's plan. The most suitable date, with
darkness for the approach to the shore and moonlight for movement
forward from the beaches, was the night of 6/7 August. Birdwood was
told to count on a reinforcement of two divisions in his area, while one
landed south of Suvla Bay. With this added strength he revised his plan
to include Koja Chemen Tepe also in the night attack. Hamilton's plan
was to land Major General Frederick Hammersley's 11th Division on
beaches C and B south of the bay. Having dealt with local defences, they

were to move inland to seize the hills, some four miles away, which overlooked the plain behind Suvla Bay, Tekke Tepe in front and Kiretsch Tepe on the left. Lieutenant General Sir Bryan Mahon's 10th (Irish) Division would follow up, and both would help Birdwood's force secure Koja Chemen Tepe. Major General F. C. Shaw's 13th Division, after gaining experience in the Helles sector, would join Birdwood's ANZAC Corps. The corps headquarters which was to arrive with the three new divisions and command the landings at Suvla was numbered IX. Kitchener had originally proposed that it should be commanded by the fifty-three-year-old Mahon, who had played a large part in raising his division; but Hamilton did not believe him to be up to it and asked for Lieutenant General Sir Julian Byng or Lieutenant General Sir Henry Rawlinson. Kitchener was not prepared to remove either from their commands in France. He insisted that the choice must be limited to lieutenant generals who were senior to Mahon, and the only ones thought remotely suitable were the fifty-four-year-old Sir John Ewart, then at Scottish Command, who was thought not to be physically fit enough, and Sir Frederick Stopford, aged sixty-one, who had been retired for five years and was Constable of the Tower of London. He had never held command in any significant operation, but was nevertheless appointed.

When he arrived and was briefed on Hamilton's plan, he expressed himself entirely satisfied; but almost immediately his staff began to raise difficulties. They argued that Chocolate and W Hills could not be taken without the fire support of howitzers, and, as the latter could not be landed until the morning of 7 August, the hills could not be captured before dawn as planned. That delay would mean that the infantry would not be able to reach the hills ringing the plain on that day. They also wanted to attack Chocolate and W Hills from the north and asked for the landings to be made in Suvla Bay, which the navy opposed as it was not properly charted. Hamilton's staff weakly gave way to the extent that Stopford's priority was no longer to give support to Birdwood's operation, but to establish a secure beachhead as a base for further operations.

The 13th Division was the first to arrive, landing early in July at Helles, where the troops gained valuable experience by taking their turn in the front line before being squeezed with difficulty into the crowded ANZAC sector. Major Claude Foster was commanding a company in the 6th Battalion of the King's Own Royal Regiment (Lancaster) in 38th Brigade and described their experience in a letter to his wife on 18 July:

We came out of the trenches yesterday morning after having spent four days doing our best to frustrate the enemy and make life a burden to him. We sniped him, we shelled him with a trench mortar, bombed him, and poured in 8 to 10 rounds rapid fire to draw him, which latter manoeuvre was successful, rather too much so, for not having asked anybody's leave I began to get apprehensive of what authority might say – However that blew over. But my attempt to draw fire produced a hurricane of lead from the Turks. They had some seven or eight machine guns opposite my company and all these were working furiously pouring lead into our parapets in addition to the ordinary rifle fire. The noise was so extraordinary I seemed for a time to lose the power of thinking. However not one of my people was hurt.

In observing the fire of the trench mortar through periscope I got hit in face and shoulder by splinters of stone. The bullet just failed to get through sandbag but drove some of its contents through with explosive energy. Result cut face – sore shoulder both forgotten now.

We came out of trenches for rest but have lost more heavily from shell fire here than in firing lines. Had lunch yesterday with shrapnel bursting all around. Too hungry to lose appetite. The flies, the dirt, the hardship are beyond description. Last night some of our wounded left for Alexandria. I could not help envying them.

The operations progress satisfactorily. Last Wednesdays battle turns out to be an unqualified success even though we did not succeed in holding all the ground gained.

There is generally an hour or two daily when conditions are pleasing. Last night the gloaming was exquisite. I felt more or less clean after a sea bath, there was a sweet breeze, our bivouac was on the cliff side and Imbros was fading out of view whilst the hospital ship was blazing with her belt of green lights and her bright red cross. It was so peaceful after the fatigue of the day and the merciless shelling . . . One quickly learns to take an extraordinary interest in one's grub here. Tell mother her periscope is most useful and not yet broken. The snipers break up periscopes at a great rate but mine has not yet been touched.

The 10th Division arrived next and were disembarked on the islands of Lemnos and Mitylene; the 11th last, disembarking on Imbros late in the month, their final destination kept a closely guarded secret. On the other side, Liman von Sanders detected an increase of activity in the ANZAC sector, but thought it presaged a further landing near Gaba Tepe, south of Anzac Cove, to which he directed the 9th Turkish Division, commanded by the German Colonel Hans Kannengieser. Defence of the Suvla Bay area was entrusted to another German, Major Willmer, with four Turkish battalions and a cavalry squadron, supported by nineteen guns, their forward positions being at Kiretsch Tepe, Hill 10, covering A Beach in Suvla Bay, and Lala Baba, covering B and C Beaches south of it.

The battle opened with a diversionary attack at Helles on 6 August by 29th Division between Gully Ravine and Krithia Nullah. The attack was roughly repulsed and cost the division 2,000 casualties. The 42nd Division, on their right, attacked on the following day with much the same result, after which Hamilton ordered the acting corps commander, Major General William Douglas, to stop. These attacks made no impression on Liman von Sanders, who ordered his reserve division in the area, the 9th, north to face the threat developing on Sari Bair Ridge. Birdwood also planned a diversion. The 1st Australian Division launched an attack at the southern end of 400 Plateau by its 1st Brigade against the Turkish position at Lone Pine at 16.30 on 6 August, followed by 2nd Brigade on 'German Officers Trench' to the north of it. The first succeeded after a fierce struggle lasting two days in which the brigade gained seven VCs. The second, which made use of tunnels dug towards their objective, failed at great cost.

Birdwood's plan was for Godley, commander of the New Zealand and Australian Division, to command the main attacking force consisting of his own division, reinforced by 29th Indian Brigade, 13th Division, the dismounted 3rd Australian Light Horse Brigade and 29th Infantry Brigade from the 10th Division. The assault force was divided into two groups, each formed into a number of columns and preceded by a covering force, guarding its flanks. These columns would move by night up the ravines from the heads of which they would launch their attacks on their final objectives. The right-hand group, commanded by Colonel Francis Johnston, consisted of the four battalions of his own New Zealand Brigade, the covering force being provided by the New Zealand Mounted Rifles Brigade. They would move up the Sazli Beit and Chailak Deres to capture Chunuk Bair. The left-hand group, commanded by Brigadier General Cox, consisted of his own 29th Indian and the 4th

Australian Brigades. They would together move up the Aghyl Dere: on arrival at its head, two Gurkha battalions would attack Hill Q, while the rest crossed over to the head of the next ravine, the Azma Dere, climb up Abdul Rahman Spur and attack Koja Chemen Tepe. The covering force, provided by the 40th Brigade of the 13th Division, would secure the left flank on the ridge of Damakjelik Bair, an extension westward of the Abdul Rahman Spur. All this was to be completed by dawn on 7 August. The leading troops started off at 21.45 on the 6th. On the right the covering force managed to deal with Turkish outposts on both of their 'deres', but fell two and a half hours behind schedule in doing so. This held up the columns, the Canterbury Battalion directed up the Sazli Dere, the other three battalions up the Chailak. Eventually the latter reached Table Top, short of Rhododendron Spur, where they were due to join with the Canterbury Battalion, of which there was no sign. It had got hopelessly lost and finished up where it had started. The columns of Cox's left-hand group had met virtually no opposition, but had become considerably disorganized, many of them lost, in struggling across the scrub-covered broken country, and by dawn were on the left of the New Zealanders, but no further forward.

Birdwood was now faced with a difficult decision. On the assumption that by this time Chunuk Bair and Hill Q at least would have been secured, the Australian Light Horse Brigade, in the original ANZAC positions near the Nek, was due to launch a direct frontal attack across it to take Baby 700; but both hills were still in enemy hands and the attacking troops more than a mile from them. He could cancel the Light Horse attack, postpone it or order Godley to go ahead. He decided on the last and the 8th and 10th Australian Light Horse Regiments made a series of gallant attacks which cost them dear and achieved nothing.

At 07.00 Johnston decided to wait no longer for the Canterbury Battalion, and with the Wellington and Otago Battalions started to advance towards Chunuk Bair, just as Colonel Kannengieser arrived there on a reconnaissance. The latter quickly and personally organized its defence to such effect that Johnston decided that he could make no further progress in daylight, reporting that to Godley at 08.00. The latter insisted that he must press on, Johnston allotting to it only the Auckland Battalion's three companies and two of the 2/10th Gurkhas, who had strayed into his area from Cox's disorganized columns. By then Kannengieser had organized a more effective defence, which easily held the attack.

Cox's group spent all day of the 7th, largely in vain, trying to sort itself out. Even the 39th Brigade of the 13th Division, sent up to reinforce him, managed to get lost in broad daylight. Cox therefore postponed any further attempt to make progress until 8 August. Lieutenant N. R. C. Cosby, with 1/5th Gurkhas in his brigade, gave this account of events:

Owing to several checks we were very late in arriving at the foothills near Chunuk Bair and then to make up for it someone in front started the column off (the Australian Major I believe), making people go so fast before we knew what had happened we had lost touch. We had now come out into the foothills below Chunuk Bair where we found lots of New Zealanders who had attacked across the back. We now had in front of us a hill called Q and beyond that was 971. Our D. Coy of the 1/5, one D. Coy of the 2/10 G.R. [Gurkha Rifles] and about a battalion of N. Zealanders were ordered to charge Q. We lay just under the crest of the slope before attacking and at the signal moved off, we being on the left. Directly we got over the crest we came under a very heavy fire and found that we had to go steeply down hill across some flat and then up hill to get at Q. They had M. Guns going and gave us a rotten time.

We moved off in the following dispositions ... [A sketch shows the New Zealanders on the right and, on the left in four successive lines; F Coy 1/5 G.R. with himself and Capt. Tomes; E Coy 1/5 G.R. with Mr Knowles; one Coy 2/10 G.R, with two British officers; one Coy 2/10 G.R. with one British officer.] The New Zealanders had to stop and then retired; it was a very long distance to go down hill and then right up to the M. Guns. Capt Tomes and I fetched up under the wall with a few men and Mr Knowles appeared with a few men afterwards. Gradually some more men came up singly and we finally mustered 38 i.e. 3 B.O.s 2 Gurkha Officers of 1/5 G.R.s 29 men of 1/5 G.R. 2 men of 2/10 G.R. and 2 N. Zealanders. We had a small stone wall for cover and a farmhouse about 15' × 10' just on our left. We could not advance as not one of us could hope to reach their trench alive so we held a parley. Capt. Tomes at first thought we had better retire but to do so we should have had to cross an open cornfield before we got into the bushes and I suggested that we had better stay where we were and dig in a bit and escape at dark as it was impossible to escape across the cornfield as they had now everything trained on it. This we did. The wall was very low being only 18″ high in front of us and a little more on the left. We put two men behind the farmhouse to watch the left flank and another man on the right to watch that flank and dug in where the wall was moderately high. We could not dig where we were as only by lying absolutely flat would the bullets skim over us. We made the left fairly deep so that if they got on our flank we could all crowd into it and give a good account of ourselves before they got us.

We arrived at the wall at 10 a.m. and lay there all day in the sun which was very hot. We decided to move off at dark about 8.15. At 8 p.m. dusk I was watching the right flank and saw a thin line of men creeping down the hill who were very difficult to see in the dusk. I told the others and we got ready and went across that cornfield in record time. The people on the hill thought the others were rounding us up and were taken by surprise but almost at once opened fire. Directly we got into the bushes we found a deep nullah into which we dropped and dashed straight down it to the bottom of the hill without losing any men. We did not know when we got to the bottom where our people were but eventually came across some British troops and spent the night in a nullah. At daybreak we found out where the rest of the Battn. were and rejoined them. They had rushed and taken some hills which they were then entrenching. Capt. Tomes stayed with us for 2 nights and was then sent to command the 6th G.R. where he met his death.

Godley's plan was that 4th Australian Brigade would go for Koja Chemen Tepe, while two battalions from the 13th Division, 7th North Staffordshires and 9th Worcesters, joined 1/6th Gurkhas at the head of Aghyl Dere to capture Hill Q. However, the two battalions got lost and by 08.00 the Gurkha commanding officer, Major Cecil Allanson, decided to set off without them. His men managed to get within a hundred feet of the summit of Hill Q; but, unfortunately, unaware of their achievement, Cox, at 14.00 with Godley's approval, called off any further attempt to make progress that day. 4th Australian Brigade tried to advance to Koja Chemen Tepe, but were stopped by Turkish defences on Abdul Rahman Spur. Lieutenant Savory was involved in these operations and wrote to his mother on 9 August:

Great doings going on now-a-days, of which you may possibly have heard by now, or even read in the papers. We are in a new place

now, and have got out of that infernal trench warfare, which has now
developed into mountain warfare: over very high country with dense
scrub, in places sometimes 6 ft. high, and as you can imagine perfect
for defence, but damned hard for attackers. Anyhow we go on slowly,
and I hope surely, and ought soon to have the Turks in a very nasty
position. If this show is a real success the problem of the Dardanelles
will have been solved ... We had a great bayonet charge yesterday,
with Australians alongside of us – all going for all we were worth –
and it really was great fun, up to a point where we got hung up
under a precipice with the Turks on top, and had a pretty stiff time
of it, so had to come back which was pretty annoying, but we ought
to get the place all right next time as we know the lie of the land
now. The Australians are great, when it is a case of going bald-headed
there is really no one like them, and a combined charge by them the
Gurkhas and ourselves was great fun. I haven't enjoyed myself so
much for some time, excepting of course when we got hung up by
that precipice which was pretty nasty ... This mountain warfare is
devilish tiring work and is accompanied by large casualties chiefly
from the infernal machine guns. None of us are very hard after three
months of enforced inactivity in the trenches, and consequently when
attacking up a very steep rough slope, which rises 900 ft. in a very
short distance, we all get so done that we have to stop for a bit of a
rest and, though partially hidden by the scrub, the bullets come
whistling through all right. When you read of all this new development in the papers you may realise what a perfectly marvellous show
it is, from a fighting point of view, as well as that of organisation.
The whole show was done with the utmost secrecy, and it was not
until we had actually started on our march, in the middle of the
night, that we realised what we were in for. The Turks just cleared
out and left their camps etc. standing just as they were, consequently
there was lots of loot going, of which the Australians and Gurkhas
took full advantage. I found one or two interesting things, but as it is
such an infernal sweat carting them about I left them alone or gave
them to some one else.

On the right Johnston's group resumed its attack on Chunuk Bair at
03.00 with the Wellington Battalion, followed by two from the 13th
Division, 7th Glosters and 8th Welch. They found the hill undefended,
but were subjected to enfilading fire from both Battleship Hill to the

south and Hill Q from the north, which inflicted heavy casualties on the Glosters and Welch as they climbed up to join the Wellingtons. The latter held the hill against Turkish counter-attacks until joined there after dark by the Otago Battalion and the Wellington Mounted Rifles.

Godley now realized that there was no hope of reaching Koja Chemen Tepe. He therefore planned to limit further attempts to taking Chunuk Bair, Hill Q and the ridge joining them. On the left, Cox was to renew his attempt to capture the summit of Hill Q with units from 29th Indian and 39th British Brigades. On the right, Johnston was to attack the southern shoulder of Chunuk Bair and, from there, Battleship Hill. Between them an ad hoc brigade of four battalions, commanded by Brigadier General A. H. Baldwin, commander of 13th Division's 38th Brigade, would attack the northern shoulder of Chunuk Bair. H-hour for all three would be 05.15 on 9 August, preceded by three-quarters of an hour of artillery preparation. On Johnston's advice, Baldwin decided against a move straight up the Chailak Dere and chose a complicated route which involved moving from that dere to Aghyl. The result was the chaotic muddle which these night moves across broken country inevitably produced, so that Baldwin's men had not reached their start line by H-hour. Johnston's New Zealanders, under heavy fire, never got started, and the gallant 1/6th Gurkhas, all on their own, gained the summit of Hill Q only to be driven off it by intense enemy fire. When Baldwin's men eventually reached their start line at the head of Aghyl Dere, they also were heavily fired on and dug in as best they could on the lip of the ridge.

Lieutenant Colonel H. F. N. Jourdain was commanding the 5th Connaught Rangers, from the 10th (Irish) Division, in Baldwin's brigade, but had not taken a very active part in the operation of 10 August, as he explained in his diary:

10th Aug. Tuesday. At 7 am I got the order to move to Anzac Cove, and I at once sent in to withdraw D. Company. These came in about 7.53 am, and I at once got all water bottles filled and ready for the march. D. Company had several casualties this morning alone. (five men wounded.) We marched down to Anzac Cove, and had to make a large detour to escape observation from Gaba Tepe, however guided by Major Nicholson we reached Anzac Cove at 9 am.

We hardly stopped there only to take 3000 sandbags, and then we passed on through a tunnel where we met large numbers of wounded walking or being carried towards the Cove. I met Lieut. Craske and Lt Col Bewsher of our Brigade and Capt McCleverty Brigade Major all wounded. On we went as fast as we could as we heard that the services of the Battalion were urgently needed. I reached No.2 post sometime about 10.15 am and here met Lieut Gen Sir W. R. Birdwood, and Major Generals Shaw and Sir A. Godley. They told me that the Turks had massed and driven in part of the line, and asked me to push on as fast as possible & report to Gen Cox. I did my best to get the men along but I found it hard to push them so hot was the weather, and such hard work they had had lately. We reached General Cox's headquarters and he showed me the Turk position and the point where General Cooper and his staff had been demolished. It was heartrending to see the long lines of bloodstained men being carried down, and the dry river bed was simply chock a block with wounded and dying men. I stayed with General Cox, and then had Battalion concentrated at 11.40 am. We passed up the Argyl Dere until we reached the Headquarters of 39th Brigade under Brig. General Cayley. I reported myself to him and he got orders from Gen Cox to take 2 of my companies for action at once. These two A & B began to advance at 2.10 pm on the farm, which was only weakly held by a few men of various corps – I did not like the idea of sending these 2 Coys to almost certain destruction but I did so at once. I kept C & D Coys with me at H.Q. and sent on A & B under Major Money & Capt. Cooper. I went up to watch the progress of these 2 Coys – these companies progressed slowly and had a terrible hill to climb. On they went and it was not until some hours afterwards that the leading platoons suffering heavily from snipers reached the edge of the ridge. They held on gallantly, and at a quarter to 4 I went up to see General Cayley and learnt the position I was to take up at night. I did not consider it a good one, and I told Gen C. so, but he asked me to try and get it. I sent out C & D Coys to try and do so, and at 6.10 pm I began the new advance. These companies soon found the task beyond their power and after several losses they were driven back, and I at once went up and ordered a sap to be dug right across the donga, between Green Hills and 14th Sikh's Hill – C. Coy did this excellently but D. did little and I went out to put them right. I came back to H.Q. and saw Gen. Cayley about 8 pm and told him what I had done. He agreed that as I was on the spot it was all right. I then went to get some wounded in and get them sent on. After giving various orders about rations water etc, I went back to H.Q., and at about 11.40 pm I went out again to where the Sap across the trench was being made. I found most of the men quite awake and doing good work. I came back with the Adjutant of the N. Staffords who wanted to see me. I went to Brigade H.Q. to see Gen. Cayley and advised him to let me hold present line and to withdraw Major Walker. I went down and sat with my men and assisted the wounded to water. At 4 am on the *11th August Wednesday*, I went out and got the men to stand to arms. Afterwards we had tea and biscuits and awaited orders. The G.O.C. sent for me about 8 am and told me he had made up his mind to try and hold the ridge a little in front of my position and asked me if I would go on and reconnoitre the position and try to occupy same this evening. I said I would try to do so, but I did not think scheme good. I went out at 9 am on my journey and got to the Barricade, and there erected the Batt. H.Q. I put B. Coy into the trenches and took out C & D to have a rest. I left A Coy in bivouac for the present, and because they had a very hard time. I settled down for the day, as several machine guns and snipers barred my passage to the new position. I waited till nightfall as the enemy shelled the North Staffords on my right and part of one my Companies (B.). I spent a quiet day but regardless of the shells that fell near. The sight of our camp at 4 am this morning was terrible, wounded and dying men lying all over the place. Men groaning and dying without a murmur. I assisted as many as possible but it was too horrible to contemplate.

Major Claude Foster and the King's Own were also involved. He wrote a long account of his part in the battle to his wife on 12 August, having on the previous day told her of his unpleasant experience while his company was waiting in reserve, being shelled by a heavy gun, fired from the Asiatic shore. His batman was killed and many of his company wounded there. They were then moved forward to join the main battle, as he related:

On the evening of the 8th I was detached with ½ Bn to assist the 4th South Wales Borderers who had lost heavily on the extreme left of our line. I was marching most of the night, spent two or three hours in trenches being shelled and was then ordered back to the main battle on the morning of the 9th. The Turkish counter attack reached its culmination about 8 A.M. that morning. Many of our positions were captured and the slaughter of our men was enormous. When I arrived in the main gulley on my way to the battle field the sights were tremendous and suddenly a torrent of fugitives bore down the deep and narrow waterway panic stricken, horrible to see, lashed by the hostile machine gun fire (for from some part of the enemy's position every part of the gulley was visible). I drew my revolver and did what I could to arrest the flight. To stop the fugitives was easy enough, to get them to return much more difficult. However I managed to struggle forward with my own men and about 10 o'clock reached the H.Q. of 39th Brigade. General Cayley pointed out to me a line of trench ¾ of the way up Chunuk Bair which was full of khaki clad figures and he said to me 'Take your men up to that trench. Our people are holding on to it splendidly. If we can hold it till reinforcements come from Anzac the situation will be saved.'

To get from where the General was to the point on the hillside where I was to commence my advance (this avoiding the gully which was a regular trap, a filthy shambles) I had to cross the gully. My company was immediately cut in two by the tide of fugitives and thinking it was best to get on with those I had rather than wait to try and collect the remainder, I started my advance through the prickly scrub, up hill down dale towards my objective, the sandbag trench.

Many a time I had to halt to try and close up and collect the half company which started dwindling at once and was obviously reluctant, thoroughly upset by the panic in the gulley and weakened by lack of food and water. The men having had no water since 4 P.M. the day before and possessing no rations for the day. It is a foolish thing to send men out to fight famished.

When we had got half way up the hillside of Chunuk Bair, I found myself feeling pretty exhausted, dragging my weary limbs up the precipitous slopes and somewhat discouraged to find my half company was already reduced to 18 men. I thought well 18 men at the critical point will be better than nothing and so went on. The last stage led up to a steep narrow water course quite over hung by scrub. A wounded man was dragging himself downwards pluckily enough. One more struggle and we emerged on the shelf on which was situated the sandbag trench.

I felt bewildered by the number of wounded, wailing for water and saying they had been abandoned for two days. But what about the trench? Surely it has seldom fallen to the lot of any man to witness such a sight before. It was crowded indeed, but there was not a single live man in it. Perhaps 800 yards of trench garrisoned by the dead alone, lying about in every posture of death. And I was soon to see the reason for it. I left the men at the head of the watercourse under cover and went with a young officer to the North Staffords to reconnoitre. As far as I went nothing but corpses and some wounded raving with the agonies of thirst. The Turks had worked round the flanks of this trench in their successful attacks and had annihilated the occupants with utter completeness by shrapnel and machine gun fire. It was clear that my party could speedily incur the same fate and also that General Cayley distraught by the trying situation had made an astounding error. There was fighting going on both to the right and left of me. I decided to join the conflict on my left. The most frightful part of the situation was abandoning those miserable naked and wounded. I parted with all the water I could spare and started down the journey downhill across the gully and up to the spur to the east. It was slow work. Crossing the gully I had some men hit and a panic arose that the Turks were on them, for climbing the steep bank one man was hit through the foot and fell back into the gulley carrying those following him with him in his fall. Nothing I could say would persuade the survivors to advance. So I found myself reduced to the command of three soldiers, the acting Co. Sgt Major a corporal and a private soldier, all of them quite exhausted from lack of food, water and sleep and demoralized by the scenes of the day.

By coaxing and abuse they were got to the summit of the ridge, a long knife-board feature, running at right angles to Chunuk Bair. Some 200 yards south of me was a British redoubt. The ground between my party and the redoubt was very exposed and the fire hot, so I put the men into some abandoned machine gun emplacements and they promptly threw themselves down and went to sleep.

I watched the Turks and tried to get the C.S.M to do some sniping at the Turks, three of whose machine guns were visible within 600 yards of us. In the end it turned out to be more like a front seat in a theatre than anything else for I could see everything going on on the side of Chunuk Bair. Soon the roar of battle died down. The air was still full of bullets which whizzed and banged in every direction. The heat was terrific, one felt an immense thirst. I still had some

water in my bottle but dared not do more than wet my mouth for it
was impossible to say when, if ever, we should come down from the
mountain. I sat wondering what had become of Lloyd Williams and
the rest of my company and of No 1 Company which was to have
followed me. The Colonel of the South Lancashires had told me as I
crossed the gully for the last time that a big attack was being planned
by us, I concluded for the recapture of the lost sandbag parapet with
its hecatombs of dead. It seemed to me my duty was to await the
coming up of the attack and join in it. For we were obviously far
ahead of the British firing line and with the exception of the little
redoubt quite isolated.

I dozed now and again and every time woke dreaming of water
fresh and cold, sometimes in a trench, sometimes in a bucket. At 5
o'clock there was a complete lull, the Turks seemed to have withdrawn from the redoubts immediately to my front so I made a dash
for the British post and arrived with my 3 men without having a shot
fired at me. There I found 4 guns of the South Lancashire regiment
½ a company of the Worcesters and some odds and ends of men. I
was the senior officer and so took command.

In a shorter letter of the same date he had written:

I don't know what is wrong with me – I simply cant write. I have
only myself and 80 men left of the 6 officers and 226 we left
Blackdown with. And I am mortal tired. Longing for a rest, a change
of clothes, cleanliness. Water is more precious than gold. O for taps
and baths! But that hill has to be won yet! On 9th August we suffered
a heavy local defeat and lost our hold on Chunuk Bair. The slaughter
was appalling – the scenes indescribable. The 38th Brigade staff was
annihilated and its battalions destroyed with the exception of our
own which still numbers about 400 men ... Thompson is alive and
well. He has been transferred to the command of No 2. Company.
All my other young officers have gone.

He himself was promoted lieutenant colonel to command the 9th
Worcesters in 39th Brigade.

These setbacks were due to the arrival of Turkish reinforcements. The
7th and 12th Turkish Divisions of XVI Corps had reached the area after
an exhausting march from Bulair late on the 8th, the 7th to the northern
end of Sari Bair Ridge, the 12th to face Suvla. Their commanders

protested to the corps commander, Feizi Bey, that they were too tired to attack that day and he agreed to postpone one until dawn on the 9th. When Liman von Sanders heard of this, he promptly sacked him and replaced him with Mustafa Kemal, who ordered a counter-attack by the 7th Division for 04.30 on the 9th. It was this that hit Cox's men, driving the 1/6th Gurkhas off Hill Q and stopping the rest of his troops in their tracks. Further south another attack was launched on Chunuk Bair, where the New Zealanders had been replaced by the 6th Loyal North Lancashires, who were in the process of being reinforced by the 5th Wiltshires. They and the New Zealanders with them were driven back to Rhododendron Spur. Baldwin's men, after making a valiant attempt to advance, were also driven back to the edge of the ridge. There was now no doubt that Birdwood's plan to secure the whole Sari Bair Ridge had failed, and no help had been forthcoming from the direction of Suvla.

The landings there must rank as one of the worst fiascos in the history of the British army. A fatal step in the planning stemmed from Hamilton's weak acceptance of Stopford's change to GHQ's plan, which resulted in the change of priority from helping the ANZAC attack to establishing a firm beachhead. Although Stopford's chief of staff, Brigadier General Hamilton Reed, was the holder of a VC, he appears to have been averse to taking risks. He did not like the idea of a direct advance from Beach B to attack Chocolate and W Hills. In the GHQ plan, this would have taken place in moonlight. As a result of waiting for the howitzers to land before attempting it, it would be in daylight over open ground. Stopford decided that the attack on these hills should be made from the north and therefore pressed for the use of A Beach within Suvla Bay and for those landing on B to move round the northern side of the Salt Lake, which nobody seems to have realized was dry at that time of year, no obstacle to movement. In spite of naval objections to landing in the bay itself, De Robeck and his staff gave way. The assault was to be carried out by the 11th Division. The troops were to be embarked on ten destroyers and ten special motor landing craft with bow doors, relics of Fisher's madcap Baltic project, 500 on each. Each destroyer would tow one of these craft, which it would release as close to the shore as possible at 21.25 on 6 August. The craft, having discharged its troops, would return to the destroyer to pick up the other 500. Brigadier General William Sitwell's 34th Brigade would be landed at A Beach, north of the mouth of the Salt Lake, called the Cut. Its task was to take Hill 10, overlooking the beach, and advance to the ridge of Kiretch Tepe on the left flank of the plain. Once those objectives had been secured, the battalions landing in its second wave, hopefully at 01.30, would move round the Salt Lake to attack Chocolate and Green Hills. The main landing would be on B Beach, south of the bay and the Salt Lake. The first two battalions of Brigadier General Henry Haggard's 32nd Brigade would land at the northern end of the beach, attack and capture the Turkish defences at Lala Baba, at the south-west corner of the Salt Lake, and then move north between the sea and the Salt Lake to Hill 10, where they would await the arrival of the brigade's other two battalions before joining 34th Brigade's attack on the Chocolate and Green Hills, under the latter's overall command. Brigadier General Robert Maxwell's 33rd Brigade would land at the southern end of B Beach, its first two battalions forming a defensive line facing south between the beach and the Salt Lake, the next two following 32nd Brigade to Hill 10 and remaining there as a divisional reserve. It was a complicated, laborious and needlessly cautious plan. It was appreciated that the supply of water would be a problem: four water lighters were to be towed to the beaches by a special water tank ship. Hamilton wanted Stopford to remain with him at Imbros until he could land at Suvla, but Stopford chose to embark in the sloop HMS *Jonquil*, which had very inadequate signal facilities.

No opposition was met at B Beach and all four battalions were ashore unharmed by 22.00. By midnight the 6th East Yorkshires had taken the Turkish post at Lala Baba, having suffered significant casualties, and the first battalions of 33rd Brigade had landed. Unfortunately, further north, the navy's reservations about landing in Suvla Bay had proved well founded. The three destroyers ran into shoals and anchored too far out and in the wrong places, with the result that the leading battalions, 11th Manchesters and 9th Lancashire Fusiliers, were landed south of the Cut, the latter in deep water. The Manchesters managed to make their way north to their objective, Kiretch Tepe, clearing away Turkish posts on the way, and by 03.00 they had reached a point two miles along the ridge. The Lancashire Fusiliers could not find Hill 10 and were troubled by snipers. The two battalions of the brigade in the second wave had not yet landed, owing to craft grounding. Meanwhile Brigadier General Haggard, with the whole of the 32nd and two battalions of the 33rd Brigade at Lala Baba, waited for the situation north of him to be clarified.

GALLIPOLI

1. Vice Admiral John De Robeck and General
Sir Ian Hamilton

2. HMS *Implacable*, in support of the 2nd Royal Fusiliers off X Beach, Cape Helles,
25 April 1915

3. V Beach from the *River Clyde*. Casualties litter the barge below;
the survivors shelter behind the earth bank ashore

4. Captain David French,
1st Royal Dublin Fusiliers

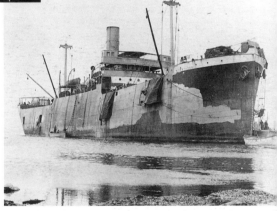

5. The *River Clyde*, in
use as a storeship later in
the campaign

6. X Beach

7. 2nd Hampshire Regiment, Battalion water cart, X Beach

8. Generals Baillaud and Gouraud at Sedd-el-Bahr

9. Stores accumulate at Anzac Cove

10. Gully leading to the hospital at Anzac

11. Lieutenant General Sir William Birdwood

12. Clearing the dead, Anzac, 24 May

13. Bomb-throwing
catapult

14. Soldiers take
a bath

15. Suvla Bay:
a scene of inactivity
reminiscent of the 6–7
August landings

16. Trench at the foot
of Chocolate Hill,
Suvla Bay

17. British warship bombarding Chocolate Hill

18. Dead Man's Ditch, Suvla Bay

19. 5th Gurkhas

20. 14th Sikhs in the trenches. In the background, a beturbaned Lieutenant Reginald Savory peers round the traverse

21. Lieutenant Colonel F. W. Jarvis, Suffolk Yeomanry

22. Finsbury Vale leading to Bedford Gully, Anzac

23. Lord Kitchener, second from right, with General Maxwell (foreground) at Gallipoli, November 1915

24. Symington Bridge, Cape Helles, December 1915

25. Christmas Day, Cape Helles

Eventually, at 03.00, he despatched four companies only, who found themselves absorbed into the confused situation of the Lancashire Fusiliers. Lieutenant C. A. Elliott was commanding a platoon in the 9th West Yorkshires in 32nd Brigade. He described his experiences in a long letter to his mother after he had been wounded later on:

> It was about 10.30 when we landed. The beach was pretty dark and there was no firing. We got off the boat and lined up on the beach just as the firing started. I being No. 4 platoon was right on the left of the company and had to send out a section to the left as a flank guard. I never saw that section again. By now the firing had started but only a few stray bullets were passing over us. We advanced in column up the hill. Lupton disappeared at once which was as well as Fraser took charge. We were the rear company. We all had orders that there was to be no firing before dawn.
>
> A sudden burst of rapid fire and loud gutteral cries of Allah! Allah! and we knew our first line had got into someone. Silence again, and then heavier fire than before. We now approached the top of the hill. Bullets were sweeping over the crest and each line had to double over the top and to a safe distance on the other side. The Brigade formed up in the hollow and we took stock of our losses . . . The [6th] Yorkshires however we knew had been badly hit. I suddenly noticed a group of men groaning like a Salvation Army meeting. My temper was a bit frayed so I hove up to them and asked what the thunder they thought they were doing. 'Oh, Sir' one moaned, 'we're all that's left of the Yorkshires.' My boys began to look interested. I cursed them roundly and swore there were three full companies in front whereat they ambled off shamefacedly. I, of course, had no idea where the Yorkshires were.
>
> Suddenly the whole valley seemed to start chanting 'West Yorkshires' 'West Yorkshires'. A most weird uncanny sound. I looked round for a reason and then saw a battalion in column charging down on us from the hill we had just come down. We officers rushed up and managed to stop their front rank just as they came up to our rear ranks. It was of course the Y & L.* They had been in reserve and seemed to want to fight somebody.
>
> We now moved on again. The moon had come up throwing a

---

* 6th York & Lancasters.

most ghastly and romantic light on the glittering lines of bayonets. The firing was getting heavier and as the light improved men began to fall fairly fast. B Company in front of us were going too slowly and we had orders to go through them. We pushed on as fast as possible. The country was open and sandy with big gorse bushes studded thickly across it. These swarmed with Turks who retreated from bush to bush as we advanced. We had to poke bayonets into each bush as a few of the more pronounced fatalists stayed to snipe succeeding lines.

He then made contact with the 8th Duke of Wellington's (West Riding) on his left and came under shrapnel fire. After a discussion with other subalterns, he decided to escape from it by going forward and found himself with only three men. He continued:

Things looked rosy [?]. I got my 3 men up and we wired [?] off as hard as we could. If the fire had been warm when we advanced, it was really sultry now. Every rifle in Gallipoli seemed on us and there was that awful 'Whoree' of shrapnel. I never knew before I had so many pulses in the roof of my mouth. Many times I passed wounded men lying, some still rolling about in their agony. A hero would have stopped and pulled each one to cover and adjusted his field dressing. I did not. I ran on to the crest of a little hill some 1,000 yards behind my bank. Here I dropped behind a convenient rock and remained for 10 minutes dead to the world. When I recovered my wind I found Major Wood and the Adjutant. We each enquired for the battalion, for Brigade headquarters, for any orders or news and found each as ignorant as the other. We seemed to have about 200 men, Yorkshires, West Yorkshires, West Ridings, Y & L, Northumberland and Lancashire Fusiliers and a few Dorsets. A lovely jumble.

Major Wood was for an advance. He gave the word and ran forward 20 yards. Barely a man followed. I went down the line cursing, persuading and even kicking, but it was no use. The men were tired out, hungry, thirsty and a little cowed. They had been forward and had been driven back, they had lost pretty heavily, they had seen nothing to fire at and had been under pretty heavy fire for 12 hours. They wanted a rest. Once we tried to get them forward. Davenport had rolled up and the three of us went forward. A few men came but very half heartedly. Two were hit and Davenport was knocked down by a bullet that only grazed his shoulder.

There was nothing for it but to get back to cover. I stopped to ask Davenport if he wanted help but he called out that he was alright and told me to clear and not draw fire. To lend point to his remarks a bullet drilled a hole through his helmet.

With only an hour to go to daylight, Brigadier General Sitwell managed to get ashore and sent a message for help to Haggard, at the same time ordering the Lancashire Fusiliers to attack Hill 10 at dawn. They set off to attack a small hill, but it was not Hill 10, which was 400 yards to the north and from which the Turks enfiladed them effectively. Captain G. W. Atkins, of the 25th Punjabis, was serving with the 8th Northumberland Fusiliers in 34th Brigade. In a letter after he had returned, wounded, to England, to Colonel Moberly of his regiment, he described his experience:

> By the time we had got ashore the 32 Bde, with slight opposition, had crossed our front & gone on to help the Lancs Fus at hill 10. All of us just got our companies together & hurried off into action – everything was disorder. The G.O.C's of Brigades had no orders to give, or didn't know what to do! ours, Sitwell, certainly didn't – He was sent back over it, with several others. How we made as much ground as we did the first day, I can't think, except that the C.O's caught coys of various units & used them. Shortly before daybreak their guns started off . . . we had no guns, not even naval ones, till 6 pm that day, when the navy started on hill 53!!!* . . . Orders went round that hill 53, which up till midday had been left alone, owing to hill 10 being so strongly held, would be stormed at 6 pm! so you can imagine our losses taking it, as the line had to extend into the Salt Lake, which is just white sand (its dried up or was).

By this time Hammersley, who had landed and set up his head-quarters near Lala Baba, began to realize what had happened and ordered Haggard to move his brigade north to join the 34th. On their arrival, Hill 10 was attacked, the hundred Turks defending it withdrawing, after which, instead of reorganizing for the advance round the Salt Lake to attack Chocolate and Green Hills, the battalions involved, apparently ignorant of the plan, moved north-east to join the Manchesters on Kiretch Tepe. Brigadier General Felix Hill, whose 31st Brigade of the

* Chocolate Hill.

10th Irish Division, with two battalions of the 30th Brigade, had arrived offshore, boarded *Jonquil* to get orders from Stopford. The latter had intended to land them on A Beach and use them to complete the capture of Kiretch Tepe; but the confusion in the bay caused him to order them to land on C Beach, south of the Cut. Hardly had Hill left the *Jonquil* than Roger Keyes boarded it to report that he had found a suitable landing place on the north side of the bay; but Stopford refused to change Hill's orders. When Sir Bryan Mahon arrived with another three battalions from his division at 07.30, he was directed to this new beach, separating the two brigades of his division: the third, the 29th, had already joined Birdwood's ANZACs.

A long period of confusion, delay and dithering ensued while the various commanders got at cross purposes with each other. Stopford had hurt his knee and stayed on board *Jonquil*, almost completely out of touch. Eventually Hill set off with his 31st Brigade to follow all the others round the completely dry Salt Lake to launch an attack on Chocolate and Green Hills. While on this circuitous route, he was stopped: a major attack by the 11th Division was to be launched at 17.30. Hill's brigade reached the lower slopes by 19.00, after dark, and, having been reinforced by the reserve battalions of the 33rd, 6th Lincolns and 6th Borders, the hills were taken; but, instead of pressing on to the important W Hill, a mile to the east of Green, the 31st dug themselves in while the two battalions of the 33rd were recalled into reserve near Lala Baba. Meanwhile Mahon and his three battalions faced one delay after another, eventually joining up with the Manchesters on Kiretch Tepe, but making no effort to get further forward towards its junction with Tekke Tepe or to make contact with Stilwell's 34th Brigade on their right.

Lieutenant N. E. Drury was with the battalion headquarters of the 6th Royal Dublin Fusiliers, one of the two battalions from 30th Brigade which landed with the 31st. His diary records his frustration:

> The 6th R Dub. Fus landed about 06.00 at a spot about 250 yards south of NIBRUNESI point and we rushed the men up the little beach to a low bank about 6 feet high and piled arms and took off equipment. We then started bringing ashore the tools, machine guns ammunition, water and food. We had some gunfire but not anything like what I expected, and there were very few casualties in the 6

R.D.F but the 7th Dublins had more. One shell dropped in the water between the 2 lighters (6 ft apart) without hitting anyone, but soaking us to the skin. The 6th R. Inniskilling Fus. landed 100 yards south of us and also a field ambulance. There was also an aeroplane over dropping bombs but I saw no one hit, although I heard someone say that a steamer had been struck. While this was going on, the Colonel was looking around for someone to give us our orders but no staff were to be seen. I could see no sign of Turks anywhere nor any trenches. After a long delay we came across General Hill 31st Brigade who told us we would not join our own 30th Brigade but would remain with his Brigade. I didn't hear the orders he gave but gathered that we were to move north and attack the high ridge we could see across the plain. We were told to follow the 7th R. Dub Fus across the sea side of the hill LALA BABA where we dumped the mens packs and left them in charge of the C.Q.M.S's. Then about 13.00 we started off in artillery formation to cross the spit of sand between the Salt Lake and the sea. This isnt really a lake but a sort of marsh in which the salt water has dried up leaving a coating of glistening salt shining in the sun.

By the end of the day, therefore, little progress had been made towards Tekke Tepe. Both divisions and their brigades were in a confused state, uncertain of the plan and what their orders were, the men equally confused, weary, hungry and many desperately thirsty as the water supply arrangements had broken down. Morale at all levels was low. The initial direction of effort had all been to the left, away from the ANZACs, to help whom no effort was made: indeed many of the commanders did not seem to realize that that was an aim of the operation. Hamilton meanwhile was bursting with frustration and impatience. While getting bad news from Helles and Anzac, he was receiving almost none from Suvla. What he did get appeared to indicate that both divisions had landed successfully.

When 8 August dawned, Mahon on Kiretch Tepe reported that he would need more artillery before he could advance. Hammersley gave way to the pleas of all his brigade commanders for time to rest and reorganize, and merely ordered Sitwell to move some of his battalions forward from the area of the Cut to form a line joining Chocolate Hill to Kiretch Tepe. Stopford acquiesced, ordering that no attempt to advance should be made until late that day at the earliest. Hamilton suspected that all might not be going according to plan and despatched a staff officer, Lieutenant Colonel Cecil Aspinall, to find out. The only destroyer available had boiler trouble and he was forced to use a trawler, not reaching Suvla, accompanied by Hankey on a visit from London, until 11.30. Meanwhile 32nd Brigade made their way forward against no opposition to Sulajik, but, becoming disorganized, withdrew to the area of Hill 10, except for the 6th Yorkshires, who had reached Scimitar Hill, a mile east of Chocolate Hill, where they remained, although under fire from W Hills to the south of them. Before Aspinall arrived, Stopford had been reminded by GHQ of the need to secure Tekke Tepe, in response to which he issued the feeble order: 'If you find the ground lightly held by the enemy push on. But in view of want of artillery support I do not want you to attack an entrenched position held in strength.' When Hamilton learned of it, he realized that he must go himself to stir things up. At the same time Aspinall had seen Hammersley and was appalled at the inaction. He went to see Stopford, still in *Jonquil*, who was smugly complacent. The horrified Aspinall then boarded Rear Admiral Christian's flagship, HMS *Triad*, and signalled his concern to Hamilton. At last Stopford went ashore to see Hammersley, but missed him, leaving a message to say that he left it to him to decide when to launch a further assault. Returning to *Jonquil*, he found a message from GHQ saying that air reconnaissance showed no sign of Turkish troops on Tekke Tepe and that he would be reinforced by Major General John Lindley's 53rd (Welsh) Division. Stopford then ordered an advance to the hills beyond the plain, 11th Division on the right, 10th on the left, still leaving timing to Hammersley, who had already decided not to start until the morning of the 9th, 33rd Brigade directed on W Hills, 32nd to the Anafarta Spur at the southern end of Tekke Tepe. Mahon was to complete the clearance of Kiretch Tepe and then clear Tekke Tepe from the north.

5

Gallipoli: Last Fling

Hamilton, who already knew that the Turkish XVI Corps had started to move south from Bulair, reached the *Jonquil* at 18.30, furious to find that no attack was intended until the following day. He set off by picket-boat to go ashore and see Hammersley and try to bring it forward. He insisted that Tekke Tepe must be occupied that night, but was met with every sort of excuse. Hammersley eventually admitted that 32nd Brigade, which he wrongly believed to be concentrated round Sulajik, might be able to advance from there that night. Hamilton demanded that they should do so and extend it to the Anafarta Spur on the right and the centre of Tekke Tepe on the left. The Brigade was not in fact concentrated. 6th Yorkshires were still on Scimitar Hill, 9th West Yorkshires were beyond Sulajik, and the other two battalions were scattered about the plain. The two Yorkshire battalions could in fact have advanced directly from where they were to Tekke Tepe, which patrols had earlier reported as only lightly held; but the acting brigade commander, Lieutenant Colonel J. O'B. Minogue, decided that he had to concentrate his brigade before launching the attack. This took all night and it was not until just before dawn, at 04.00, that the attack got going, by which time the soldiers were tired and browned off, and two important positions had been evacuated. Lieutenant Elliott described what happened:

A beastly night. I suppose I dozed occasionally but most of the time I spent staring up at the beautifully brilliant stars, wondering if I should see another night. Dawn was breaking very grey and dim when there was a burst of rapid fire from the right that grew rapidly. Suddenly from the front bullets began to come in. Two men went over at once and one more was yelping with a wound in his stomach. Then from the left came that awful cry Allah! Allah! and more spluttering rifle fire. Fraser rushed past me from the left. 'The devils have got right into D. Coy' he yelled as he passed. Almost directly a sheet of bullets came down on us from that flank. I got my men to face round to the left and started firing back. Cries of 'Don't fire, they're your own men, they're Gurkhas – they are coming in to surrender, they've got their hands up and are unarmed' were passed from mouth to mouth. Even then I wondered who started these cries. Had some German in our uniform got into our lines? We were blazing promiscuously and blindly into the scrub on our left. I looked to the front and saw some shadowy figures not 100 yards away. One big man was waving his hands urging them on. I got him balanced nicely in my foresight and let go. He came down alright and I got one more a minute later. The din was terrible. The cries of the wounded and the stench of blood were sickening me. The Adjutant came up revolver in hand. 'What's this about our own men?' he yelled. I told him we were enfiladed from D Coy's position. He rushed back to send me more men. Spencer ran up with a few men and yelled to me where I wanted them. I showed him and just as he got down he got it through the body. I think it killed him outright but I had no time to see. We could not stay where we were. There were more hit than sound where I was.

I nipped up the line to get orders. I found Davenport with a sergeant tying up a wound in his leg. He told me he had been hit twice – I asked him where Fraser was. 'There' he said and I saw I was kneeling by him. One glance at his face already blue showing the gleam of his teeth under his moustache was enough. Curtis and Ghat were down. Our left was turned and already bullets were coming from the hill the East Yorks had held on our right while a few snipers in the rear hit their mark every time. We could not see to fire. I passed the order up to retire to the bank of gorse the other side of the clear strip. We could not be in a worse position and should at any rate have some field of fire. No one seemed to want to leave the shelter of the tiny bank. The men seemed dazed. They fired wildly and looked apathetically at their neighbours who were hit. I staggered to my feet and rushed back. Halfway across I felt an electric tingle in my leg. My first feeling was one of elation – I'm wounded, I can clear out, and the second of thankfulness, I was not knocked down and I can still walk. I dropped behind the first gorse bush and found Evers there. I told him what had happened and that he was in charge. I got my puttee undone. There was a hole on each side of my leg. I put the field dressing on the largest. Took the bolt out of my rifle and chucked it away. I was too tired and weak to carry my equipment so I slipped it off and put my revolver in my pocket. I scrambled to my feet and with my arm round a man's neck, hopped off to the rear.

While the day of the 8th had thus been frittered away, the 12th Turkish Division was arriving from Bulair, reaching Tekke Tepe at almost the same time as 32nd Brigade launched its attack. The latter was met by a fierce counter-attack and driven back, exposing the flank of 34th Brigade to the north, which had been joined by 159th Brigade from 53rd Division. On Hammersley's right, 33rd Brigade, advancing towards W Hills, came under fire from Scimitar Hill, leading to a struggle for the hill in which the brigade was reinforced from both 10th and 53rd Divisions. The latter's 158th Brigade advanced on the right flank to try and make contact with the extreme left flank of the ANZACs, but could not do so, meeting intense Turkish fire and finally being withdrawn to Lala Baba. Meanwhile, on the left, Mahon, supported by naval gunfire, made progress along Kiretch Tepe, but failed to reach Kidney Hill, a mile short of its junction with Tekke Tepe. There the momentum of the attack petered out, more from exhaustion of the hot, tired, hungry and thirsty soldiers than from the strength of the opposition, which came from only 350 Turkish gendarmes.

Lieutenant Drury's account of the day reads:

By 06.00 the firing line was taken over by us with C. Company (Capt. J. LUKE) on the left and B. Coy. (Capt. W. H. WHYTE) on the right. Casualties began comming [sic] down at once, among the first that I saw was Lt. Charlie Martin of C. Company who had his arm smashed by a bullet near the elbow, he was without coat, helmet or equipment. Captain John Luke of C Coy came down soon afterwards with all the fingers of his left hand cut off by a piece of shell which smashed his rifle in pieces. He said there were several snipers up in the trees we had passed, and several of his men had been shot from behind. He was in fearful pain and was damming [sic] the Turks and their snipers in awful language. He turned up again in half an hour without having gone to the dressing station at all, and carrying a lot of water bottles of wounded men, to get them some water from the well. I could see the white bones of his hand sticking up out of the flesh. Paddy Cox cursed him and ordered him off. The well became a death trap as the bullets were banging into it like hailstones and Couper's dressing station in a slight hollow near it had to be moved as several bearers were hit and wounded men hit again.

The firing was worse than I imagined it would be and I felt very scared but I saw our good old Regimental Sergeant Major, Jock Campbell, going about his job of looking after ammunition supplies with the greatest coolness, and I profited by his good example. We had no messages from the front line and could not hear what was happening, nor could we get any messages from 33rd Brigade, so I went over myself to Chocolate Hill. I could not find anybody at the place they showed me, and I found they had moved round to the sea side of the hill facing LALA BABA where they got down into a Turkish trench, and from which they could not see us or Hill 70 at all. General Maxwell in the devil of a funk and incapable of giving proper orders.

About 09.00 we had to send the reserve (D) Company under Capt. P. T. L. Thompson to help the 6th Border Regt on the right in response to their urgent messages. These orders to reinforce the front line should of course have come from the Brigadier General but he seems useless and doesnt know what is going on and doesnt try to find out. By this time the Irish Fusiliers seemed to have gone up into the line as I didnt see any of them about. 09.30 Colonel Cox decided that as his whole battalion was now involved he would move up nearer the front line, leaving the R.S.M. and a couple of orderlies at the Well Headquarters in case of messages being sent there. We moved up to a point about 500* [500 yards] near the line . . . 10.00. We met Bill Whyte comming to explain the position personally as all the messengers had been knocked out, and he had had no acknowledgement of his messages. He was as cool and collected as on a Field Day at home, and said that instead of our supporting the Lincolns, that we were doing the attacking and trying to keep the Lincolns from running away. Major Jennings reported killed also several junior officers. I went barging about in the scrub trying to find where people were and I found parties of Lincolns and Borderers all over the place lying up in funk holes. Finally when I got to D Company, who were on the right in touch with A Coy, a whole lot of these 2 regiments started running away like mad, shouting out that they were 'cut to ribbons' etc. Thompson, Billy Richards & I had a job to prevent them clearing out altogether, and even had to threaten to use

our revolvers, even to the officers. I found that there were no troops
on D Coys left to the south of Hill 70 for several hundred yards so I
managed to persuade a party of Borders about 20 strong with 2
officers and a C.S.M. to follow me up the track leading towards
ABRIKJA and I got them lining a bank ... with a good field of fire
in front (East) and also towards HILL 70. I couldnt succeed however
in making any of them put their heads up and fire although I showed
them good targets. The worst of them was a fat Co. Sergt. Major who
would only lie down in the ditch and announce 'We are all cut to
bits'. Then an extraordinary thing happened. A big hare got up
behind us and raced out past us through a gap in the bank and on
towards the Turk. The brave C.S.M. and one or two others lifted
their rifles and started blazing away after the hare although they were
too much afraid to shoot at the Turks.

Hamilton had spent the night on board *Triad*, and came ashore to
find Stopford busy supervising the establishment of his headquarters
there. Thoroughly disillusioned, he went off to see Birdwood, while his
chief of staff, Major General Walter Braithwaite, urged Stopford to renew
the attack next day. Stopford, assuming it to be an order from Hamilton,
allotted the task to Lindley, who was not certain where all his troops,
haphazardly committed to battle, were. He planned to use what he could
collect of his 159th Brigade to recapture Scimitar Hill, 158th Brigade
following through to Anafarta Spur. He launched the attack at 06.00 on
the 10th. It was a total failure at heavy cost.

Drury's diary records:

No information about what positions are to be attacked, nor at what
time, nor even what part we are to take in the advance. Apparently
only attached units to move, the 33rd Brigade to sit still like yesterday
and leave us to do the work. Many of them did not even sit still but
cleared off to the beach and some got into the lines of the 31st Field
Ambulance near A Beach and were found by Colonel Shanahan who
drove them out with his fists. Father Murphy tells us it was the only
time he was ever in a rage – 'God forgive me, I hit some of them.'
    We had a very clear view of a Brigade of the 53rd DIV comming
up to the line. They marched out from behind LALA BABA about
06.00 in column of route (!) and then deployed in the plain and
advanced in lines of Battalions about 100 yards apart. They came
along in the bright sun across the plain on a frontage of about 1000

yards, without a particle of cover, with bayonets and brass work glinting in the sun. They were simply plastered with shrapnel and long-range rifle and machine gun fire all the way and suffered heavy casualties. It was a wonderful sight and would have looked well on a Field Day at Aldershot, but whoever ordered it should be shot. They landed yesterday and I know of nothing to prevent their leaving before dawn and get under cover before daylight. (I notice the Turks have more guns firing today than yesterday.) The attack was a fiasco. Most of them stopped when they were about level with us, but some charged right up to within 200 yards of point 70, only to retire immediately at the double. A lot of Turks followed them over the crest, but we opened fire and drove them back at once. It was a rotten show with no method and devoid of any show of determination. A lot of sniping all day, with a good many casualties. It is impossible to find where the snipers are firing from, but sometimes it seems as if they are somewhere in the trees behind us. The ALI BEY CHESME is almost unapproachable as they have the range of it to a yard. The Turk gunners often spray it with shrapnell if men are seen at the well. I had a bit of interesting shooting during this afternoon at a sniper I spotted with my glasses away on our left front. I had Sergeant Fuller spotting for me and I got him after 4 or 5 rounds. Range 850☆

Captain Atkins takes up the tale:

The line ran through hill 53 & we had joined up with the ANZAC CORPS (6th Gurkhas) – Our division [11th] had lost about 60% of its men and nearly all its officers. The 53 & 54 Divisions (Terriers) landed two days after us & I hope they are better than when I saw them. The Welsh Bde ran away, throwing their rifles & equipment down. They were held up by two of our Coys (Passy's & Tyrrell's)* they were both hit that morning – the 10th – We were flank guard to the 53rd Div that morning – I went along the line to see them when things quieted down & found them both in a trench together. Poor Passy, plucky old man, had been hit through his leg but refusing to give in, stuck with his coy hobbling on two sticks – having no food in him at the time, the doctor held out great hopes of his

* Major De L. W. Passy and Captain C. H. Tyrrell, both also officers of the 25th Punjabis.

getting over it. Tyrrell got a compound fracture of his thigh &·was in great pain but Mrs T says he is getting on well & soon coming home.

I was wounded when we were very badly cut up – the last effort of Genl Sitwell – We were told to attack trenches that we had never seen & knew nothing about – not even the direction in which they ran! Everyone expostulated, even myself! but that was because being second in command I had to lead it! We started off and I swear if those trenches could have been taken we should have done it – The men were splendid, no noise, no firing everything was perfect, I finally got to within 20 yards on my left & about 40 on my right before giving the order to charge – Hell let loose was nothing to it, we ran our noses into a most fearful snag – they were not trenches but field works & they had two dense tiers of fire belching from them. I was hit twice in the head just under their parapet – I had dropped on my knee to draw my revolver, as I saw a fat brat on the parapet in front of me & suddenly remembered I had nothing in my hand. I thought I'd been poleaxed – my servant took me out of it, how, without being hit, I can't think. We lost all our officers.

While the attack was in train, Major General S. F. Inglefield's 54th (East Anglian) Division landed. GHQ intended it to mount a concentrated attack on Tekke Tepe, but Stopford used it to plug holes in his line. GHQ sent a further order that it be used for the purpose Hamilton intended on 12 August, while all the other divisions held the line and supported it; but Stopford took no notice, prompting Hamilton to return and insist that it must be used as he had ordered, starting at dawn on 13 August. As a preliminary, its 163rd Brigade should advance towards Tekke Tepe on the 12th to secure a start line nearer to the objective: if they met strong opposition, the main attack would be cancelled. No reconnaissance had been carried out and orders to the lower level were vague, if they were received at all. Not surprisingly the brigade's attempt to advance met strong resistance, particularly from artillery fire, incurred severe casualties, and failed. Hamilton agreed to the cancellation of the attack next day.

Lindley had reported that his 53rd Division was no longer fit to fight. Stopford agreed and also expressed doubts about the 54th. This brought Hamilton back to see him, telling him, after discussion, to consolidate his positions as far forward as possible and continue reorganizing his corps so that it would be ready for another operation. The meeting however finally persuaded him that Stopford and several of his subordinates must go. On his return to Imbros, he reported to Kitchener: 'There is nothing for it but to allow time to rest and reorganize unless I order Stopford and his divisional generals to undertake a general action for which, in their present frame of mind, they have no heart. In fact, they are not fit for it.' However, perversely, Stopford had decided to order Mahon to complete the clearance of Kiretch Tepe with his own two brigades and the 162nd from the 54th Division. Typically, he issued his orders at 08.40 on 15 August for an attack that afternoon. After some gallant fighting, the Irishmen reached the summit near the eastern edge of the ridge, but a series of fierce counter-attacks at dawn on the 16th drove them off it. 162nd Brigade, on the right flank, secured Kidney Hill on the southern side of the ridge, but they also were driven off by counter-attacks and forced back to their start line.

Meanwhile Kitchener's reaction to Hamilton's report was to offer him Byng, Horne or Kavanagh from the Western Front, to replace Stopford. Hamilton chose Byng, whom he had originally requested. If that request had been met, the story of Suvla might have been different. As a temporary measure until Byng arrived, de Lisle from the 29th Division was to take Stopford's place, to the anger of Mahon who outranked him and threatened to resign. Instead he spent a short spell of rest at Mudros, Hill taking over temporary command of the 10th Division. Hammersley, Lindley and Sitwell were also dismissed. De Lisle's orders from GHQ were to capture W Hills and Anafarta Spur as soon as possible. He would have the help of a brigade from the ANZACs on his right. The 2nd so-called Mounted Division, actually dismounted Yeomanry regiments acting as infantry, was on its way from Egypt. Even with them, de Lisle assessed that he would not be able to muster enough men for a successful attack. Hamilton added 87th Brigade from 29th Division at Helles and, after further discussion, the rest of the division. All these had arrived by the time that de Lisle issued his orders on the afternoon of 20 August for the attack to start at 15.00 on the 21st, preceded by half an hour's artillery programme. 29th Division, on the left, starting from Chocolate Hill, was to attack Scimitar Hill with 87th Brigade, and, with 86th Brigade, 112 Metre Hill, south of Scimitar and between it and Anafarta Spur. 11th Division, from the Azmak Dere, was to attack W Hills, while a composite brigade from the ANZACs, commanded by Cox, was to secure Hill 60, a mile south of the Azmak

Dere. The 2nd Mounted Division and 30th Brigade of the 10th Division were in reserve, hidden from view near Lala Baba. Lieutenant Drury's battalion was back with 30th Brigade. His diary records:

Theres to be a big attack made, so far as I can learn, on a front from CIMITAR HILL (Hill 70) to the left of ANZAC with 3 Divisions, 11th, 29th & 2nd Mtd Div, including the 29th from Helles. The 10th DIV is in reserve to the other three and the 30th Bde is reserve to the 10th DIV. I dont know where the 31st Bde is but I think they must be over to our left. We met our 1st Battalion during the morning. They have only one of the original officers left and they have got through over 3,000 men since they landed at Helles. I suppose as we are so far behind the fight that we will get all the overshies. The Navy commenced a tremendous bombardment about 13.00. There were big monitors with 14.2″ guns also the Swiftsure, Chatham, Canopus and Triumph (fitted with big derricks for some purpose). All were firing hard with 6″ and 9″ guns and occasionally 12″ guns. The noise was perfectly ear-splitting as the ships were close to the shore, and were firing just over our heads. There was a queer mist or fog over the ground and I dont know how they can see where they are shooting. I suppose they had observation posts ashore and some way of signalling hits or misses. Some of the guns make magnificent smoke rings when they are fired, which circle up in the still air for hundreds of feet. We did not move off till about 17.00 and then we went with Battalions in artillery formation and moving in Echelon. It was very hard to keep direction with the fog and dust of shells falling. We got a heavy shelling most of the way up, but we did not get it as badly as the Munsters who were more in the open away from the trees. Major Aplin was wounded in the foot but is carrying on. Gen Nichol was walking along at the head of the 7th R. Dub. Fus when a big shell exploded beside them and hid the General in a cloud of smoke and dust. Some hard case in the 7th sang out 'Thank god there's the ould divil gone at last' 'Not yet my boy' said the General emerging from the stour without a scratch, and quite amused at the incident.

We lost touch with A Coy under Lt. Arnold who had the R.S.M. with him, and the whole battalion got a good deal scattered. There seems to be heavy fighting in front, but we have no news of what is going on or how far they have got. A lot of casualties are passing down. Heavy fighting all night with a lot of bombing.

The artillery bombardment was weak and ineffective, in contrast to the Turkish counter-bombardment. 87th Brigade gained Scimitar at considerable cost, but lost it to counter-attack. This almost guaranteed the failure of 86th Brigade's attack, which took place through burning scrub. De Lisle's reaction was to order forward the 2nd Mounted Division to regain both objectives. Their 2nd (South West) Brigade, sent to regain Scimitar Hill, made a gallant attempt to do so and held on to the near slope until withdrawn before dawn on the 22nd. The two brigades sent to reinforce 86th Brigade lost their way, came under heavy fire and achieved nothing. On the right, 11th Division's 32nd Brigade met strong resistance on the way to W Hills, suffered heavy casualties and withdrew to their start line. 34th Brigade on their right succeeded in reaching their objective north of the Azmak Dere at considerable cost, but were there subjected to heavy fire from the south. The four battalions of 33rd Brigade were then moved up, two to each of the forward brigades, but no further progress was found possible. Further to the right, the composite ANZAC brigade reached Hill 60, but could not dislodge the Turks from the summit. They held on there, reinforced by the 9th and 10th Australian Light Horse Regiments, and fought doggedly up the southern slope, but had not reached the summit by 27 August, by which time it was clear that the combined ANZAC and Suvla offensive had totally failed. Captain R. S. Hawker was in the Devonshire Yeomanry, manning machine guns in the 2nd South West Mounted Brigade on Manchester Ridge at Suvla. His diary records:

I attended a Court Martial at Brigade HQrs on two N. Devons who were found asleep at their post. Channer W.S.Y.* was president & I must say gave them a most awfully fair trial. We gave them awfully heavy sentences as we could do no other being tied down by regulations though I must say I was very sorry for them. Miers was on the Court-Martial & it seemed very funny to be senior to him & he almost old enough to be my Father. I heard afterwards the evidence entered up against them was not considered sufficient & they were let off. When we left the Trenches we handed over to the 6th Border Regiment they did take a time getting in too with their guns & I only just managed to get out before the whole of their Regiment came in. I had been up about 9.30 am with my returns & had stopped to pass

* West Somerset Yeomanry.

the time of day with Teddy & we were talking about a Bath on the Prince George & how nice it would be to get back to our dug-out. I moved on & the next thing I heard was Douglas at it again dropping in 3 shells into Jefferson's post in quick succession then a man came rushing down the Trench saying poor Teddy was blown to pieces, also several men of the R.N.A.S [Royal Naval Air Service] two officers and a man, Teddy's dug-out & the R.N.A.S Armoury being blown to atoms. Langmaid had his leg broken by a shell falling on him luckily it did not explode & Cobley Teddy's servant was also hit & hustled along to the Dressing Station being told there was nothing much the matter with him. As a matter of fact the shrapnel bullet went so close to his heart they could not operate. I did not go up to see poor Teddy as I would rather remember him laughing and joking as he was with me about ½ an hour before the shells came along. He was buried that afternoon at Karakol Gap Cemetery, I could not go as I was waiting for the Borderers to take over. We were jolly glad to get back to our dug-outs & have a good rest. I tried to get permission next day to send Teddy's private things direct to Mrs Teddy but was not allowed to, anyhow I got them all done up & posted them. I locked his bag & Hockey & I checked the things in his valise practically nothing & had them taken down to the Beach. The Colonel put a very nice 'order of the day' in Regtl orders saying how we had all sustained a great loss. I took up the Cross made by men in Teddy's Squadron & placed it in position, Sergt Lock showing me the place. I shall never forget that place it reminded me so much of a picture a camera study at Anzac entitled 'Goodbye & Good Luck' showing a man looking at a new grave on the skyline just a silhouette it was getting dark when we came away the picture came back very vividly to me. There were 4 other poor fellows on stretchers there awaiting burial all from that horrible Green Knoll below the Pimple.

At about this time, on 22 August, a soldier called David wrote to his mother, who lived in London. His unit may therefore have been in the 54th Division. It is typical of many letters sent regularly by soldiers to their mothers:

Just a line to say how I am getting on. I have been down here at the base since Friday, sick with diarhea, but I am better now only a bit weak, and I expect to go back to my pals in the trenches in a day or so as I am getting better. I feel a bit weak though. I shan't be sorry to go back, as the Turks shell the Red Cross sometimes and its safer as far as shell fire is concerned in the trenches. There are plenty of wounded here, and it makes my heart bleed to see them. There are very few killed, the majority are wounded, and they get attendance at once. I don't know where we are, except that it's some part of Gallipoli, and even if I did, I would not be allowed to tell you. Only one thing worries me, and that is you all at home. You must not worry too much about me. I will do my best to look after myself. I don't think this war will last very long now, and I hope to be home with you again before very long. It's very hot out here in the day time, lovely and cool in the evening, and a bit cold at night. We don't get such good food as they do in France, but we don't feed so bad considering everything. I have had one lot of cigarettes since I've been here, but they are all gone, and I have to cadge now. I expect we will get some more before long. Well, mother dear, I must close now, don't worry if you don't hear from me for a bit, as paper is like gold. P.S. Please let them know in London how I am getting on. I've had no letters yet.

Before then, on 17 August, Hamilton had asked Kitchener for 95,000 men, 45,000 to bring his British divisions up to strength, and 50,000 as reinforcements. He said that this would give him 'the necessary superiority, unless the absence of other enemies allows the Turks to bring up large additional reinforcements'. On the previous day Kitchener and Sir John French, the Commander-in-Chief of the British Expeditionary Force in France, had agreed to cooperate with an autumn offensive there planned by General Joffre. They announced this to the meeting of the Dardanelles Committee which considered Hamilton's request on 20 August. The Committee decided on a weak compromise: 13,000 replacements and 12,000 reinforcements. As Hamilton relapsed into a mixture of anger and gloom at the news, the French Government decided to send four divisions to effect a new landing on the Asiatic side of the Straits, removing the two at Helles to take part also. When Kitchener told Hamilton this, he promised to replace them by two regular British divisions from the BEF, the 27th and 28th. Hamilton's spirits rose, but it was not long before they were dampened again. Joffre refused to send the four divisions from France until his autumn offensive had finished. He also expressed his fear that the landing might grow into a greater commitment and he had no faith in the general chosen to command,

Maurice Sarrail. After a meeting with Joffre and Sarrail on 11 September, Kitchener told Hamilton that Joffre's reservations might be less if all the French divisions were committed to a specific task on the peninsula. These discussions, however, were rendered irrelevant by Bulgaria's adherence to the Central Powers and threat to Serbia at the end of September. The latter appealed to Greece for the help of the 150,000 men which she was bound by treaty to provide; but Greece pleaded the need to defend her own borders and asked Britain and France to provide them instead. The obvious response was to divert Sarrail's force there, with a British contribution from the Dardanelles. On 25 September Kitchener told Hamilton to send one of his French and two British divisions to join Sarrail at Salonika, suggesting that he might need to withdraw from Suvla, adding: 'but it must be clearly understood that there is no intention of withdrawing from the peninsula or of giving up the Dardanelles operations until the Turks are defeated.'

In the event only one British division was sent, Mahon's 10th, but the 2nd Mounted Division was sent back to Egypt owing to its high rate of sickness. That was high in every formation, Hamilton protesting that he had '100,000 men on the peninsula, 50,000 of whom are unfit'. Claude Foster's letter to his wife on 4 October bears out Hamilton's complaint:

> The ravages of sickness are terrible here and most distressing: with all our drafts we can barely keep our strength up. During the last fortnight we have lost five officers and 120 men.The resources of the nation in men can hardly keep pace with such a drain on its manhood.
>
> People come one day and are gone the next. I appoint an officer to a particular duty knowing too well that it may be a day or two or week or two that I will have his services but hardly longer. Dysentry and diarrhoea account for nearly all. Today I lost two good officers, my adjutant and a gallant young regular officer, who has fought with the greatest pluck both against the enemy and disease. This loss of officers operates so adversely on discipline of course. Officers continually being changed so that the men do not know their offficers or officers their men. The result as you can imagine most destructive of confidence and efficiency. (Great big shells are whizzing over and my natural anxiety as to whether one intends to land in my dugout makes my writing and spelling worse than usual).

Harry Hopwood, now Company Quartermaster Sergeant, was one of those affected. He wrote home from hospital in Malta on 3 October:

I have been suffering from diarrhoea for about six or seven weeks, but never went sick with it, as nearly everybody has the same complaint, and a lot had dysentery so as long as I kept clear of the latter complaint I didn't bother the doctor. However I found myself going weaker every day so that I finally found it hard work to walk about. One morning I got up at 'stand to' (4 a.m.) and when I got on my feet I reeled about like a drunken man and nearly fell down. I felt very bad that morning and took my temperature it was 102 so I went to see the doctor. He told me to lie up all day in my dugout and have a rest. Next morning I went again, and my temperature was 103.4 so he told me to go down to the hospital at the base. I told him I couldn't walk (it was about four miles away) and he sent me down to what is known as the 1st Receiving or Dressing Station on a stretcher. There I had to wait about three hours for an ambulance van, but it turned up at last and with three more we got down to the beach some time in the evening. Here we changed into another one a motor which poisoned me with the petrol fumes, and this ran us another two or three miles to Cape Helles. We were put into a marquee here for the night, and next morning taken on a mine destroyer to one of the hospital ships (the Gascon). I was just about done it is a long time in fact I never remember feeling worse. However in two or three days I began to feel better, and on the fourth day she ran over to Lemnos, and we were told to get ready to transfer to another boat. I had to be carried again, and the Ausonia was just about as bad as the other one was good. Anyhow to make a long story short, she ran us to Malta in three days, and the people were very nice ladies in the streets offering you milk, tea, cigarettes, etc. They put us on motor ambulances and ran us to the different hospital, of which there seem to be a lot here. I am very comfortable here and am just getting rid of the fever.

Lieutenant Colonel F. W. Jarvis, commanding officer of the 1/1st Suffolk Yeomanry, kept a diary, noting the strength of his regiment daily. On 24 October it was 23 officers and 322 men, on which he commented:

There are now 94 cases in hospital mostly suffering from dysentry. It is difficult to account for so large a number of cases. This gully seems to be exposed to the cold wind more than other gullies in which troops are bivouaced, which may have something to do with it. It is certainly much colder than other gullies I have visited today. It is also of interest that there are fewer cases in D Sqdn. than the other Sqdns. & this I attribute to the fact that 'D' Sqdn. are almost entirely country dwellers from a cold heavy clay district in E. Suffolk, whereas the men of A & B Sqdns come mostly from towns like Cambridge, Newmarket, Bury St. Edmunds.

At about this time Ellison appears to have been in correspondence with Colonel Maurice Hankey, with whom he had worked closely in Whitehall when Ellison had been on the staff of Richard Haldane, at the time that he was Secretary of State for War. In his papers is a letter from Hankey, dated 16 October:

I have two interesting letters to thank you for. More especially do I thank you for your remarks on my Memorandum on the prepara-tions for a winter campaign. They arrived just as I was revising the Memorandum and bringing it up to date, so are very opportune. You seem to have made a wonderful deal of progress since I was out, and the new piers at Walker's Beach must be a God-send. We received the other day a telegram from Sir Ian describing the effects of the first fierce southerly gale, which must have caused you a good deal of perturbation. I do hope, though, that you have surmounted the difficulties.

At this end our preoccupations have been mainly with regard to the Balkans. It is very much feared here that if once the Germans establish communication with Constantinople your position may become untenable, or very nearly so, owing to the great increase in shelling to which your beaches would be subjected. Personally, I do not think it is possible for the Allies to do anything in time to save the situation in Serbia, except by giving moral support, and such things as ammunition and heavy guns to the Serbians, which may enable them to prolong their resistance until the weather comes to their assistance. It is, however, rather a gloomy outlook.

Nevertheless, I am not a bit gloomy about the general result of the war. There is a lot of evidence now that the Germans are heartily sick of it. There is reported to be great depression in Germany, owing to the heavy casualties and the comparative lack of success. Prices also are almost intolerably high there, and wages have remained almost stationary. Our own Government is at the present moment very distracted by this compulsory service agitation. In my opinion, it is most unfortunate, as it takes people's attention away from fighting the war. The difference between the numbers that can be obtained by compulsory and voluntary service, in my opinion, is not worth all the pother.

On 11 October Kitchener startled and angered Hamilton by asking him to estimate what his losses would be in an evacuation. Hamilton replied that, as it would depend on circumstances, he could not give a straight answer but that 'it would not be wise to reckon on getting out of Gallipoli with less loss than that of half the total force'. Criticism of Hamilton in London had been growing, Stopford and an Australian journalist, Keith Murdoch, leading the pack. His reply to Kitchener sealed his fate at a meeting of the Dardanelles Committee on 14 October, Kitchener telling him next day that General Sir Charles Monro had been appointed to replace him.* Hamilton left on 17 October in HMS *Chatham*, Braithwaite leaving with him. He wrote this letter to Ellison from Marseilles on the 21st.

Have had a perfectly charming voyage and with my singular, water-on-a-duck's-back sort of disposition I have quite enjoyed it. On arriving here I have a message indicating that the reason that they have sent for me has been that the general conditions in the Balkans now made it absolutely necessary for the Government to consult me about the whole question; Whatever this may mean; whether it is wholly blarney or half blarney; it is a nice way of putting it.

Have just had a call from the Governor, who is putting chariots and horses at my disposal wherewith I shall go out to a restaurant and make merry. Please give my little bit of news to Altham, to whom I wrote a hurried farewell when I had no idea even of the ostensible reason of my recall.

Best of luck to you and to the new Chief. Please give the latter my salaams and good wishes.

Birdwood assumed temporary command until Monro arrived on 28 October with his own chief of staff, Major General Arthur Lynden-Bell, with instructions from Kitchener to report as soon as possible on the

* Lieutenant General Monro was made a temporary general to command at Gallipoli.

situation at Gallipoli and in the Near East generally. After visiting Helles, Anzac and Suvla and talking to all the corps and divisional commanders, Monro signalled to Kitchener, reporting his view that another offensive would not offer any hope of success: the Turks could always reinforce their defences to counter the effect of any additional troops sent: he therefore recommended evacuation. Birdwood, however, was opposed to it.

Since the end of August, Roger Keyes had resuscitated his project for a new naval attempt to force a way through the Straits. De Robeck was still opposed, but allowed Keyes to go with Hamilton to London, where he did his best to persuade everyone in authority to back his proposal. The Dardanelles Committee, renamed the War Committee, met on 3 November to consider Monro's report. As usual they could not reach a firm decision and asked Kitchener to go to the Dardanelles himself and assess the situation. Kitchener then appeared to be even more unpredictable than usual. He had been persuaded to support Keyes's project, combined with a new landing at Bulair, and signalled Birdwood, telling him to replace Monro, who would be switched to command British forces at Salonika. Birdwood, who had a high regard for Monro, kept the signal to himself, while the First Sea Lord, Admiral Sir Henry Jackson, vetoed Keyes's plot.

Life in the front line at this time was described by two very different people. One was Second Lieutenant Howard Hicklenton of the 2/4th City of London Regiment (Royal Fusiliers) in 29th Division. In a letter to his mother dated 21 October he wrote:

Well today I have been sent up to the firing line for instruction, so that I have had a chance to see what things are really like – well I am up here for 48 hours & up to the present I have seen quite enough. Now, please don't think this is gruesome but I must tell you as I know you are anxious to know what I have to put up with now, for the thing just outside our trench or the one I am in now, lay about 600 bodies, they are the Worcester Regt, they went out to attack on Aug. 5 and were absolutely wiped out & they are still where they have fallen just skeletons now, but still wearing their equipment and helmets there is one I saw quite near the trench absolutely no flesh on the body at all, and it would be madness to try to get at them, some of them have been buried but I am told as soon as you pick them up they fall to pieces, so now you can imagine I am well hardened for anything. At one place the trenches are 15 yds apart & bombing goes on there. There is a machine gun just behind the dugout I am in at the present moment. These dugouts I must say are not underground, but kind of trench houses exposed to the sky. This machine gun keeps on opening fire & it sounds rotten, an awful rattle all of a sudden & then quiet.

The other was David Maxwell, who had served as a sergeant in the Imperial Light Horse in the Boer War and was now a major in the Scottish Horse. He paid a visit to the ANZAC sector on 10 November and described it in a letter home:

How the landing was ever effected & the very high perpendicular cliffs ever scaled is beyond imagination & speaks wonders for the N.Z. & Australians. The works are wonderful – miles of deep trenches 8–10 ft deep – miles of tunnels (deep level to counteract mines & high levels for saps, through the roofs of which they make little holes & use them for sniping). Some of these wonderful places are within 20–30 yds of Turk & men lie all day picking Turks off . . . I had a lovely view of a Turk about 15 yds from me, but it was too cold-blooded a business even for me to shoot him so I let him go. We & the Turks are always blowing each other up by mines & it is most exciting work – they get so close to each other that only talk in whispers is possible & bayonets have to be used instead of picks to loosen the ground & hands instead of spades. The Turks trenches are covered with wire netting to catch our bombs & are also covered with timber & earth – most difficult to capture they told us.

All the officers (British) are full of praise of these N.Z. & Australians & say they are wonderful workers as well as the staunchest & most enterprizing fighters. Their dress consists usually of a very short pair of shorts – shoes, & an identity disc. They are burnt as brown & black as black men. They all seem such a good class of man – so different to the kind that were in S.Africa. Trenches were beautifully clean & few flies . . . possibly due to the height (tops of high cliffs) & dryness of the trenches . . . The Australians & N. Zealanders take no account of their officers, & use their own good horse sense . . . the whole place was such a maze of trenches zig-zagging in & out of the deep gullies that one never knew if a trench a few yards ahead of one was ours or the Turks. In lots of places even our own people get mistaken so they shove up little flags in very doubtful places, but of course they get constantly shot away.

A week after his visit, on 17 November, there was activity in the sector held by the Suffolk Yeomanry, as Lieutenant Colonel Jarvis recorded in his diary:

Effective strength Officers 19 Men 275, 178 in hospital, 9 excused. 12 evacuated from Peninsula, including Capt. Greene, Lieut. Musker, 2nd Lt. Leslie, 2nd Lt. McKelvie.

The centre posts of the trench were rather severely shelled between 9 and 10 a.m., & a few shells fell again on the same posts between 4 and 5 p.m. A strong patrol under Lieut. Eversden went out at 6 p.m. to try & rush a supposed observation post of enemy in front of the centre of the trench, but nothing was accomplished the weather being extremely bad, a gale of wind, torrents of rain and thunder. The patrol was heavily fired upon by the Turks, being lighted up suddenly by a vivid flash of lightning, but returned safely. During the height of the storm at 7.45 p.m. the Australians sent up rockets & started firing, this led to heavy firing all along the line by the enemy, to which we replied. Two companies of the 1/11 London in reserve to this Regt. were telephoned for to come to our assistance, as the situation appeared to warrant the assumption that an attack by the Turks was about to be made, & on account of the weather it was very difficult to see whether an attack was being made or not. The reserve arrived at 8.30, but by that time the firing had died down & all was quiet for the rest of the night.

Kitchener reached Mudros on 9 November and held discussions with Monro, Birdwood and Maxwell from Egypt, who had persuaded Monro to support a landing near Alexandretta to counterbalance the political effect in Egypt and India of an evacuation from Gallipoli. Kitchener then toured the peninsula, accompanied by Birdwood, and on 15 November signalled London supporting Monro's report, but recommending that the Suvla and ANZAC sectors should be evacuated, but that Helles should be held for political reasons. At the same time he appointed Monro to command British forces both at Gallipoli and Salonika, with Birdwood as his subordinate at the former and Mahon at the latter. He set off back on 24 November, on which day the Cabinet discussed his message. The majority were in favour of total evacuation, but were persuaded against it by Lord Curzon, the Foreign Secretary, who painted a lurid picture of 'half crazy men, the swamping of craft, the nocturnal panic, the agony of the wounded, the hecatombs of the slain'. In De Robeck's absence on leave, Wemyss, acting in his place, revived Keyes's scheme, but the Admiralty again vetoed it. The French had objected to the removal of British forces from Salonika to take part in a renewed offensive. Monro remained adamant in favour of total evacuation. On 7 December the Cabinet finally approved the partial evacuation that Kitchener had recommended. Preparations for this had been quietly going on, and, when he heard of the decision, Birdwood ordered its immediate implementation. Godley, now commanding the ANZAC Corps, proposed to thin out gradually, holding his forward positions until the last moment, so that the Turks would not realize that an evacuation was planned. Byng at Suvla had proposed successive withdrawals, but Birdwood ordered him to emulate Godley. The final evacuation of ANZAC and Suvla was planned for the two nights of 18/19 and 19/20 December. Everything went according to plan, 83,048 men, 186 guns, 4,695 horses and mules, none of them being left behind, and 2,000 vehicles being shipped away without a casualty. This posed a problem of morale for VIII Corps left at Helles. Its commander, Lieutenant General Sir Francis Davies, tried to uphold it with his Special Order of the Day on 20 December:

> The position at Cape Helles will not be abandoned, and the Commander-in-Chief has entrusted to the Eighth Corps the duty of maintaining the honour of the British Empire against the Turks on the Peninsula and of continuing such action as shall prevent them, as far as possible, from massing their forces to meet our operations elsewhere ... We must by strenuous labour make our positions impregnable, and while driving back every attack we must ever seek to make steady progress forward and maintain, both in spirit and action that offensive which, as every soldier knows, alone leads to success in war.

Three days later, however, the forceful Lieutenant General Sir William Robertson succeeded the ineffective Sir Archibald Murray as Chief of the Imperial General Staff. On his appointment Robertson had insisted that it was he, not Kitchener as Secretary of State for War, who should be the channel for orders to Commanders-in-Chief in the field. On 24 December he told Monro to initiate planning for the evacuation of Helles. Having persuaded the Cabinet to support him, Robertson confirmed to Monro on 28 December that evacuation should go ahead. It was successfully implemented on the night of 8/9 January, 35,268 men, 3,689 horses and mules, 214 guns, 328 vehicles and 1,600 tons of stores being shipped away without loss. 508 mules were shot and 1,590 vehicles left behind. The British Empire casualties of the campaign totalled 37,000 dead and 83,000 wounded and sick. Of the dead, 25,200 came from Great Britain or Ireland, 7,300 from Australia, 2,400 from New Zealand, 1,700 from India and 22 from Newfoundland. The French lost 47,000 killed and wounded. The Turks are believed to have lost 350,000 killed and wounded.

6

Up and Down the Tigris

Barrett's force had, to all appearances, fulfilled its tasks: Basra and the oilfield at Ahwaz had been secured; but rumours soon started circulating that the Turks were planning a counteroffensive and concentrating troops at Ruta, eight miles up the Tigris from Qurna, and at Nasiriyeh, the ancient Ur of the Chaldees, 110 miles up the Euphrates from Qurna and rather more, round the southern shore of Lake Hammar, from Basra. A combined river and land reconnaissance towards Ruta on 1 January 1915 found the river blocked and defences firmly held just south of Ruta. Early in February information was obtained from Arab sources that a Turkish force had left Amara, a further sixty miles up river, heading for the oilfield at Ahwaz, near which the pipeline had been cut. To counter this, at least to see that the local Arabs did not switch to the Turkish side, Barrett, in the middle of the month, sent his Commander Royal Artillery (CRA), Brigadier General C. T. Robinson, up the Karun to Ahwaz with the 4th and 7th Rajputs, thirty men of 2nd Dorsets, thirty of the 33rd Cavalry and two mountain guns. Robinson found a force of Turks and Arabs north-west of the town, went out to discover more, was ambushed and was lucky to get away, losing his two guns. Barrett was forced to send more cavalry to restore the situation. Lieutenant E. C. Staples of the 11th Rajputs was with the force and described the action in a letter to his parents:

> Well at 2 am on 3rd March we were marched out, a force of less than 1,000 men All told to make 'reconnaissance in force' (Father knows all the meanings of that mysterious phrase). We had two field guns & two mountain guns. About 6 am we got to a place about 3 miles from the Arab Camps & it got light, so we wished them good morning by plumping shells into the Camps. We watched the Arabs with our glasses come buzzing out like a disturbed wasps nest & thought they were going to run away. We all felt sorry for them when

we saw the shells bursting on them – However they didn't run away but produced green, red & white banners exactly the same shape as those used in May processions at Greenwich (I remember that thought occurring to me). They also had a very large number of mounted men, who, keeping a distance of about 2 or 3 miles, galloped round both our flanks & some got on to hills between us & our Camp. The footmen for the most part remaining in front of us. Then they proceeded to advance upon us from three sides simultaneously & very rapidly & rifle fire soon started. We were all ordered to retire, which we proceeded to do. The enemy closed in upon us in rear with wonderful rapidity & stuck to our rearguard (with which I was most of the time) the whole way back to camp keeping an average distance of 150x [150 yards] from us. In this manner we drifted back the eight miles or so to camp. We had to make the rear guard retire at a walk, to steady the sepoys, as we dared not let them double. Personally I never expected to get back to camp as we were being pelted with bullets from never less than three sides all the time & were cruelly outnumbered – Two things to my mind saved us – One (& the most important) was the surprising inaccuracy of the Arabs' fire. The second was that they never had the pluck to push us & cut us all down, which I am sure they could have done. They used to make spasmodic efforts to do so, but only about 50 men would start & gallop in on us, shouting – & as soon as a dozen or so were shot, they used to wheel off. They exposed themselves very recklessly to get hold of any loot, such as a loose horse or a dead mule & many of them got bowled over trying to secure these prizes. I got hit very early in the show, as we were retiring a bullet flopped between my feet, ricocheted up and through the inside of the ankle of my left boot, my sock and part of my puttie & made a small channel about an inch long on the skin over the ankle bone little more than a graze really thus [sketch of his foot and ankle]. It felt as if some one had thrown a stone & hit one & I remember a hop skip & a jump with a shout of 'damn'. I took a rifle then and had one shot with which I got an Arab, who never moved after he fell. My ankle didn't hurt much at first but it soon began to get very stiff & swollen & I had to draw my sword and use it as a walking stick & a very good one it proved. We continued like this through low hills till about 2 or 3 miles from camp, where the hills ended & there was an absolutely level plain. Just before the rearguard left the hills the Turks brought up their guns & started shelling the main body the shells passing over us before they exploded. I saw one burst apparently into the main body. The last bit across the plain I did with the detachment of the Dorset regiment (about 20 men under a corporal). There were at least five other British officers of the 7th and 4th with them. Tell Father to ponder that over. The shells continued to fly over us, but the Turks fortunately mistook a building with a mud wall round it for our Camp & proceeded to vigorously shell it. I must say shells *do* make a damnable sound just after they burst. There is a sort of 'swish' as all the bullets strike the ground. They were not using shrapnel but what is called 'Segment shell' which is much the same. Well we continued across the couple of miles of plain with the Dorsets whom we extended widely & fixed bayonets because we were followed at about 300 yards by swarms of their mounted men, who fired at us from the saddle with no effect. We were also being enfiladed by a collection of their ragamuffins from a hill at long range, but they did no harm – About four times anything between 50 & 100 of the mounted scallywags plucked up their courage, shouted vigorously & galloped in to cut us down. We used to halt & face about & start firing when they got to about 200 yards & by the time they had got to 100 yards from us, they always had about 12 empty saddles & the rest would invariably wheel round & gallop off. If the whole lot of them had really made a determined charge upon us, they *must* have got in & finished us. As it was, little lots of 50 or more had no chance. By the way, the shells were flying over us all this time. The horsemen gave up chasing us about a mile from camp but all these halts to repel their charges and pick up wounded had made my ankle so stiff that I could barely hobble, even with the help of my sword, so that I had to put my arm round the neck of a Dorset Tommy, he passed me on later to a sepoy, because he had to help a man who couldn't walk at all & Major O'Keeffe, our doctor, took me on for a bit & finally about ¼ mile from camp, Sheepshanks of the 12th Cavalry who was out there attached to the 33rd rode up & he & O'Keeffe heaved me on to Sheepshanks horse which I rode in, but I am glad to say I didn't have to be helped till the enemy's attacks ceased. I never saw anything so absolutely steady as those few men of the Dorsets. It really was a joy to see them. The RFA too were grand. I never saw a European anything but absolutely cool & collected although I don't think any of them expected to live to see camp. The private soldiers were as steady as the officers & one felt glad one's skin was a white one. The three doctors were magnificent – Major O'Keeffe Captain Arthur both IMS [Indian Medical Service] one very Irish & the other very Scotch & Capt McCreery RAMC – his father I believe in AMS. They were all three of them dressing wounds all the time under fire & helping wounded & I know little O'Keeffe was one of the last into camp. McCreery took his boots off for the first time 36 hours after we got into Camp, having been treating wounded most of the time. When I got into Camp I had to be lifted off the horse – The boot being an ordinary Tommy's boot, they took off easily enough. 'Saves a lot of trouble that' said the hospital orderly Tommy, when he saw that the bootlace was cut through by the bullet.

Attention then switched to Nasiriyeh, where the Turks under Sulaiman Askari had concentrated some 6,000 soldiers and 10–20,000 armed Arabs, supported by twenty-one guns. At that time of year the whole area round Basra was extensively flooded and Barrett had established a camp on the nearest dry land to the west at Shaiba, nine miles away, to meet any Turkish force which moved south by land towards Basra, stationing five battalions from Delamain's 16th and Fry's 18th Brigades there, with the 10th Brigade Royal Field Artillery, under Fry's command. At this time Barrett was reinforced by the forty-seven-year-old Major General Sir Frederick Gorringe's 12th Division from India, which had only two brigades (30th and 33rd), each of three battalions, and very little artillery. The fifty-eight-year old Lieutenant General Sir John Nixon, who had been Commander-in-Chief of India's Southern Command, arrived on 9 April to assume command of the corps formed by these two divisions. Barrett being evacuated sick, his place in command of the 6th Division was taken by the fifty-four-year-old Major General Charles Townshend, who came with a high reputation. Nixon arrived just as Sulaiman Askari opened his offensive, bombarding Qurna as a diversion, but moving his main body south from Nasiriyeh west of the flooded area.

His forward troops were contacted by cavalry patrols west of Shaiba on 10 April, and early next morning the camp was attacked as the fifty-two-year-old Major General Charles Melliss's 30th Brigade was sent over in the local flat-bottomed rowing boats known as *bellums* to reinforce the garrison. On the morning of 13 April the Turks could be seen passing round to the south, heading for Old Basra and Zubair. A charge by a squadron of the 7th Hariana Lancers met with a rude rebuff, as did two attacks by the 104th Wellesley's Rifles, but a subsequent attack by 2nd Dorsets and 24th Punjabis drove them away. Next day, 14 April, Melliss, in overall command as the senior brigade commander, sent out a reconnaissance in force towards Old Basra. Leaving his own brigade at Shaiba, he set off with Delamain's 16th on the right and Fry's 18th on the left, Brigadier General B. G. H. Kennedy's 6th Cavalry Brigade covering the right flank. The Turks were found to be occupying positions in the Barjisiyeh woods, five miles to the south-west. Changing front to attack them, both brigades became involved in a close-quarter battle which, just as it seemed to be grinding to a halt after significant casualties, was saved by a charge led by 2nd Dorsets that put the Turks and their Arab hangers-on to flight. Blaming his defeat on them, Sulaiman Askari shot himself. Hemmed in with their backs to the flooded area on the right flank, the cavalry made little contribution to the victory. Melliss, who had won a VC in operations in Ashanti in 1900, gave a full description of the operation in a letter to his wife on 22 April:

> Nixon decided to send me out with one battalion in canoes. A large number were collected & by 4 pm I started, you should have seen my fleet! the men poling & of course awkwardly being new to it. It was a very scattered fleet, as we drew near Shaiba camp the enemy tried to shell us but it was getting dark & they could not get the range. About 8 pm I arrived & some of my divisional staff in the leading canoes. It was quite dark incessant firing going on all around for the enemy were attacking. We were afraid of being shot by our own side or by the Turk, however we got inside the defences alright, my canoe man being shot in the arm. Bullets were flying all over the camp, maxims going, star shell rising in the air & falling in blue green lights to show up the enemy. It was picturesque but unpleasant as I had over a mile to part of the defences where General Fry who was commanding was. There was nothing to be done that night so having got something to eat lay down in my clothes & tried to sleep but the incessant firing close at hand would not let me do much sleeping ... I felt much at sea trying to get the hang of things in this huge camp & try to grasp the situation. Fortunately for me I made my way to where the 119th were holding part of the defences to enquire what they had been firing at so

heavily & there I met old Chitty* who was commanding them. He took me on top of what must have been an old Babylonish tower which stood near his part of the defences. That tower proved my good friend & was the cause of my good fortune. The whole situation lay before me, there were thousands of Turks & Arab riflemen on all 3 sides of us at a distance of ¾ mile & nearer in some places, behind trenches in houses & holding sandy ridges they simply swarmed, & there was the cavalry brigade just moving out! It was too late I could not stop them one cavalry regiment made a gallant charge against a body of the enemy on a sand hill with their standards stuck on the crest. They drove some of the Arabs before them & got into them with the lance but the fire was too hot on all sides & they had to fall back leaving a Major Wheeler & an Indian officer dead on the mound where the standards were, they had ridden most gallantly at it to seize the standards. The rest of the cavalry brigade were fired into from the flank and had to retire too. I then sent for General Delamain & ordered him out with 3 battalions (I gave him the 24th Punjabis) to attack the mound & the house etc in its vicinity & I got up my C.R.A. (an old friend Colonel Cleeve) on to the mound where we overlooked everything & told him to support the infantry with all the guns. From there we switched them on to whatever point we wished. It was as we just pounded them with shells & under cover of it the infantry advanced & captured the enemy's position & houses with little loss. The houses were blown up & over 90 dead were found on one mound called the north mound. The enemy had now begun to clear from the direction viz our north face, so I sent orders to continue the operation towards the west, pushing out the 119th, Norfolks & 48th Pioneers. We continued to shell the enemy hard & by 2 pm had driven him from the vicinity of the camp westwards & southwards, those advancing to their help from west & south were infiladed by the latter regiments & many dreading to leave their trenches on account of the hot artillery fire directed on them stood up in their trenches & surrendered . . . The enemy who I had driven off were chiefly Arabs, & there still remained the regular Turkish troops in the background.

* Lieutenant Colonel W. W. Chitty.

During the quiet night that followed, Nixon suggested sending up the other two battalions of 30th Brigade, and Melliss decided to await their arrival before resuming the attack. His account continues:

But when I went out early next morning to look out from my tower I thought I could see through my glasses some movement in the direction of Barjisiyeh woods as if a retirement was commencing back to Nakheilah. These woods were a long belt of trees edging a sandy plain very difficult to define owing to the mirage. I thought I might miss an opportunity of hitting him again if I waited so ordered all troops (except 2 battalions & 2 guns to guard the fort) & started out at 9 am to advance on the Barjisiyeh woods. I first came on the out posts & drove them back easily but as I advanced against the woods I found the enemy entrenched along a front of nearly 4 miles & the rifle fire began to get very hot & then shells to fall amongst us. It would take too long to tell you all the incidents of the fight, very early in the action my C.R.A. (Cleeve) was shot in the leg near me as I talked to his successor the next moment he was also mortally wounded poor fellow, my signalling officer was shot & we had a warmish time from shell & bullets. The fight lasted from 10.30 to 5 pm. I never want to go through the anxiety of some of that time, reports came into me of heavy losses on all sides & doubt if further advance was possible. I had thrown in my last man into the fight – still it hung very doubtful, I could see through the mirage with difficulty movements of masses beyond the woods, probably the Kurds and Arabs but whether retreating or coming on it was impossible to say. At last came a time when word came that our gun ammunition was running out! There was nothing for it but to prepare plans for retiring (can you imagine my feelings!) one of the two regiments left to guard the camp was ordered out & all transport carts also to collect wounded & I sent word to the brigadiers to come to me to receive [orders] about falling back. When to my joy a report came to me that the Dorsets & others had carried the enemy's first line of trenches some 900 [yards] in front of the wood & that they were on the run. Can you imagine how thankful I felt, but still decided not to make any further advance against the wood where I expected the enemy would probably have prepared a 2nd position & would hold it, the day was going, my men exhausted, we had suffered great thirst & heavy casualties (which amounted as I learnt later to

1076 more than a 5th of my force) gun ammunition running out &
so at 5–30pm when all the wounded had been collected in carts, (we
had to leave our dead) I gave the order to retire & we slowly
withdrew without a shot being fired at us. It was dark some time
before we got back, you may imagine my feelings, the heavy losses 14
British officers killed & nearly 40 wounded & the result uncertain
though I felt I had hit them hard I did not sleep much that night
wondering if I had been rash & foolish & had thrown away good
brave fellows lives in vain. Well early next morning I sent out the
cavalry with carts with some bodies of infantry, the former to
reconnoitre the wood & the latter to bring in the dead & soon the
joyful news came in that the enemy had fled leaving camp standing,
arms, ammunition, gun & rifle 700000 rounds of the latter, clothing,
even their cooked food untouched. It was a complete victory.

He told her that Nixon had warmly congratulated him on the action,
but complained that if it had only taken place earlier, and the news of it
reached GHQ in India before Nixon's arrival, he, and not Gorringe,
would have got command of the 12th Division.

Basra was now firmly secure, but conditions for the soldiers there
and at Qurna, most of whom were Indian, were extremely trying. It was
intensely hot and humid, and there were few facilities of any kind to
alleviate it. The administrative and logistic back-up, inadequate for the
6th Division alone, was still deficient in almost every respect, notably in
the medical field. Sickness of every kind was rife. There was every reason
to restrict operations to the essential, and initially the governments in
London and Delhi were united in demanding that they be limited to
what was necessary to secure Basra, the oilfield at Ahwaz and the pipeline
to Abadan. However, divergence between them soon began to develop.
As early as November 1914 Sir Percy Cox had suggested to Lord
Hardinge that British occupation of the Basra *vilayet* (province) should
be declared permanent, Lord Crewe, the Secretary of State for India,
rejecting the suggestion on the grounds that the allies in the Entente had
agreed that there should be no acquisition of territory until the war was
over. It was the Indian Government, off its own bat, that decided to
send a second division and gave Sir John Nixon a directive which told
him to consider a plan to advance to Baghdad; but, when, on arrival, he
asked for another cavalry brigade, he was refused. Having heard of his
request, Crewe cabled to Hardinge:

No advance beyond the present theatre of operations will be sanctioned, although an advance to Amara with the object of controlling the tribes between there and the Karun River might be supported because it adds to the safety of the pipeline. Our present position is strategically a sound one and we cannot afford to take risks by extending it unduly. In Mesopotamia a safe game must be played.

Nixon's first reaction to this was fully in accord with it: to send Gorringe with most of his division on 22 April up the Karun to Ahwaz, where it was even hotter and more uncomfortable than at Basra. Nixon's eyes then turned to Amara, an advance to which Crewe reluctantly agreed, warning that Nixon would get no more troops. Four days later Asquith's coalition administration replaced his Liberal one, Austen Chamberlain becoming Secretary of State for India. He asked what was intended and was assured by Hardinge that Nixon would not go beyond Amara. While Gorringe gave the impression that he was planning to advance there from Ahwaz, Townshend launched a methodical attack upriver from Qurna on 31 May, mounting every gun he could on some form of floating platform, the whole collection, with the navy's sloops *Espiegle* and *Clio* and launches *Shaitan* and *Sumana*, earning the nickname 'Townshend's Regatta'. It was a remarkable success, the Turks fleeing upstream, hotly pursued by Captain Nunn* and Townshend, both transferring to a launch when the sloop could get no further. Accompanied by only about a hundred sailors and soldiers, they reached Amara and received the surrender of its garrison on 2 June, anxiously awaiting the 2nd Norfolks, who arrived next morning. Not content with this remarkable victory, Nixon wanted to secure Nasiriyeh, arguing that to do so was essential if Basra were to remain secure, and asked permission of Simla (the hill station to which the Indian Government removed itself in the hot weather). On 14 June the Viceroy cabled Chamberlain recommending it, and, when no reply had been received by the 22nd, told Nixon to go ahead when he was ready.

At that time of the year most of the land on either side of the seventy miles of both the Old and the New Euphrates channels to Nasiriyeh was flooded: fifteen miles of it was the Hammar lake. Once again it would be an amphibious assault led by Captain Nunn's dauntless little fleet.

---

* He had replaced Captain Hayes-Sadler, who had returned to his ship HMS *Ocean* and taken her to the Dardanelles.

Gorringe was in command, his division providing the force. They set off on 27 June, 30th Brigade* in the lead, attempting to force their way out of Lake Hammar into the Hakila channel. The first problem was the obstruction which the Turks had placed in the channel and were defending, as Captain A. R. Ubsdell, of the 2/66th Punjabis, Gorringe's ADC, described in his diary:

> *Sunday June 27th.* We arrived at the other side of the lake at about 1 o'clock & were just going into the Channel when the two gun boats sent back word that they had been fired on, & as we drew up to where they were, the enemy opened fire on us. They were pom-poms & came from the two Thorneycroft boats the Turks have. They have built a big obstruction across the river just above where we are anchored, & just above that again there is a bend in the river hidden by a clump of date palms – Their two boats (each had two pom-poms) kept rushing round the corner & blazing off a few rounds & then returning behind the trees again – We blazed a few rounds at them with our two 4.7, which are being towed by the second of the two gun boats, but I don't think we did any damage – At 2 o'clock the G.O.C. & two or three officers went up to have a look at the obstruction to ascertain the best way of blowing it up. On their way up the pom-pom let off a regular fusilade & on their way back at about 4.30 they did it again. We were out of range really, although a few of the 1lb shells fell about 20 yards ahead of us – At 6.30 a party went off to blow the obstruction up. Some of the 48th & some 4th Hants went as pickets, while the S & M [Sappers and Miners] got things ready. They met with no resistance, but did not get the thing blown up at 12 o'clock as expected owing to the fuses not working properly.

There were two more attempts to blow up the obstruction before the river was cleared by a 60lb charge electrically detonated on the 29th.

Further progress up the river involved fighting in difficult conditions. Once that was over, there was little opposition until they were six miles short of Nasiriyeh, where the Turks manned a strong defensive position. Gorringe brought up Brigadier General K. E. Lean's 12th Brigade,† who were not ready to attack until 13 July. When they did so, they became

---

* 24th and 76th Punjabis and 2/7th Gurkhas.
† 2nd Queen's Own Royal West Kents, 67th and 90th Punjabis and 44th Merwana Infantry.

entangled with hostile Marsh Arabs and progress came to a halt. Gorringe decided that he needed more troops. Meanwhile those already in the marshes were going down with fever like ninepins. Difficulties of movement were great, and it was not until 24 July that a further properly organized attack was made. With stalwart help from Nunn's launches, it was successful: the Turks withdrew and the town surrendered next day, the operations having cost 500 casualties.

Major General Melliss wrote several letters to his wife during the course of these operations. On 11 July he wrote:

I am very glad Gorringe has seen the wisdom of asking for reinforcements & another brigade arrives tomorrow, rather 3½ battalions & 2 five inch howitzers, with this we ought to do the job without serious losses although I don't think it is by any means an easy one. They have a dreadful open field of fire in front of both their positions on the right & left banks & across their front on the right is a water channel 5 to 6 feet deep at a distance of 200 yards from their rifles, the plan of attack is for my brigade to make a turning movement in boats through the marshes round his right which will cut off his retreat from Nasiriyeh & the other brigade make a feint attack to attack his left. I dont like my job the men crowded up in boats offer a beastly easy target & if their guns get on to us we shant like it & we shall like it still less if our guns dont succeed in knocking the Turks out of some dry ground (islands) in the middle of the marshes which guard their right flank. However let us hope it will all pan out well & that we shall get to Nasiriyeh & have some rest for we are all feeling tired out with this climate. My brigade is only the skeleton of one now 1500 men & lots of British officers sick & wounded Smithett 76th Punjabis wounded his 2nd in command sick Colonel Taylor & Colonel Haldane both invalided to India, the Hampshires are merely a scratch lot of 240 Officers & men, not a regiment. The 24th Punjabis is the only regiment of any strength Viz 577, the 76th only 350 7th Gurkhas 340. What do you think of that for a brigade? Yesterday & today I got into a hot fire, drawing quite unintentionally the whole fire of the enemy's position guns, rifles & maxims. They are evidently jumpy & thought we were attacking them the reason yesterday was that I pushed out a couple of Gurkha companies through a strip of palm grove to make closer reconnaissance of the enemy, as I was lying down with the scout line taking in their trenches through my field glasses they spotted me & opened a devil of a fire of course I had to order a withdrawal at once & luckily thanks to the many trees & their high fire we got back with only 1 man killed & the Gurkhas say they accounted for 5 Turks of a picquet in the palm groves which first opened fire on us.

On 19 July he described how things had worked out:

On the 14th my Brigade was detailed to make turning movement through the marshes against the enemy's right in order to seize a sort of island from which we could take the Turkish position in rear by gun & rifle fire, of course the movement had to be carried out with the men in native canoes (called Bellums) which hold about 10 men & are poled or paddled through the marshes which vary in depth from 2 to 4½ feet & sometimes of water with clay & mud at bottom. I had made my arrangements to carry this out when the G.O.C. (Gorringe) changed the plan & said he would prefer the movement to be carried out by one battalion only & detached the 24th Punjabis for it supported by 4 guns of the Mountain battery. Alas with disasterous results the 24th by canoeing through the night arrived by dawn some 1000 yards from the island in the marshes & proceeded to advance against it on foot through the mud & water of the marshes, all went pretty well (although men were exhausted with the heavy wading) until they got within 200 yards of the island when their attack was blasted by hot fire from trenches held by the Turks, our poor fellows were shot down right & left trying to charge the position Majors Cook Norton, Capt Leslie Smith were shot dead, Lieut Haverfield mortally wounded Lt [blank] killed missing or captured. Then old Climo* made a gallant attempt to save the situation & got together a few officers & men & advanced again, his adjutant poor young Birbeck was shot dead & a number of his party killed & wounded & he had to retire. The casualties were over 123 out of some 400 men, only Climo 1 subaltern & 1 Dr left. Many missing, no doubt wounded men who fell into the water & were drowned. You may imagine how we of the 30th Brigade felt this & felt for Climo & his regiment. All those good fellows we have known in Suez all gone. Climo is left with 2 subalterns, young Pim, whose chubby face has grown quite old looking & Rind the Qtr Master. Pim

---

* Lieutenant-Colonel S. H. Climo.

was both at Shaiba & this last affair. How I wish now Gorringe had not altered his plans.

A letter of 1 August, written from Nasiriyeh, described the final stages and a row which erupted between him and Gorringe, apparently originating in Melliss entering Nasiriyeh and hoisting the Union Jack there before Gorringe himself arrived. Melliss insisted on referring the matter to Nixon, and the matter was resolved by allowing Melliss to go on a month's leave to India, which he admitted to his wife he needed:

> I require a change I felt very ill throughout the fighting of the 24th the effects of the constant sun exposure. Little Hickley kept me going through it all with tinned milk & water & occasionally egg & Worcester sauce. I was at the end of my tether you know how I feel the sun & had been constantly exposed to it all day for 2 weeks at least with only a matting overhead for shade. I dont know how I should have got through without Hickleys constant doses of milk & water. He is ill now, poor little chap bad with fever. I am going to take him down & get him invalided to India. Curiously enough the only one who didn't break down of myself & my staff was Dickenson, the great hefty McKenna went down after the fighting was over.

By now sickness was widespread, one of those succumbing to fever being Townshend, who was temporarily replaced by Fry.

Ever since Nixon, on his departure from India, had been told by the Commander-in-Chief, General Sir Beauchamp Duff, to 'Consider a plan for an advance on Baghdad', he had seen this as his ultimate goal; but, aware of London's desire to keep the campaign limited, he did not openly espouse it. However, as soon as Nasiriyeh was in his hands, he proposed to Lord Hardinge that his forces should occupy Kut, 120 miles up the Tigris from Amara. His argument was that Kut was where an ancient canal, the Shatt-al-Hai, left the Tigris to join the Euphrates at Nasiriyeh: a force stationed at Kut would be more effective in countering any renewed Turkish threat against Basra and the oilfield than two widely separated forces, one at Nasiriyeh and the other at Amara. He had no difficulty in persuading the Viceroy, who cabled London: 'As Nasiriyeh has now been occupied, we consider it a matter of strategic necessity that Kut should be occupied', adding that he proposed to remove the 28th Indian Brigade from Aden for that purpose. Chamberlain gave a confused reply, countermanding removal of the brigade from

Aden, emphasizing that no other reinforcement would be made available, and asking for Nixon's views. The latter suggested that the brigade at Ahwaz might be withdrawn if the Anglo-Persian Oil Company would pay the local Arabs to protect, or at least not to interfere with, the pumping and oil line. He argued that a force at Kut would have a significant effect on the attitude of the inhabitants of Persian Arabistan. When Chamberlain expressed doubts, Nixon replied that he could not guard Ahwaz and advance to Kut at the same time. The authorities in India gave their full backing to Nixon and Chamberlain weakly gave way, on 20 August authorizing an advance to Kut.

A week later Townshend returned to the 6th Division at Amara, as anxious for action as were his soldiers who had had little to do since arriving there, other than try to endure the boredom, the stifling heat, poor food, flies and general sickness.

Captain Ubsdell was equally bored and frustrated stuck with Gorringe at Nasiriyeh, as his diary reveals:

Friday Sept. 3rd. Up at 5 for a long ride in the Desert. Got back to breakfast at 9.15. The GOC still peevish & did a lot of cursing about the breakfast which every one else thought excellent. Poor old Wilson was put on the mat after breakfast. Really I can't stand being with this man much longer & I'm sure Wilson won't either. He is the most unspeakable cad. At eleven the Bishop* arrived with two Chaplins [sic]. It is amusing to see Gorringe with him, trying to be pleasant for once. He even graciously smiles & makes remarks to us in the Bishop's presence, but its a sore trial to him, for as soon as the B. has retired to his tent G bursts in full flood again & bites everyone with rage.

    Saturday Sept 4th. Up at 5 & got the Bishop & party off on the T.4 down to Asari where he is going to consecrate the graves of the men killed in the show. He expects to be back by mid-day. The G.O.C. stayed in writing letters this morning. The Bishop got back at about 1.30. Wilson tells me that the sights down there were absolutely horrible. Almost all the bodies had been dug up by jackals & had to be reburied.

---

* The Bishop of Lahore.

From Amara, the nearest Turks were thirty miles away upstream, more trouble being caused by the local Arabs than by them. Largely to impress the Arabs, a mobile column was sent sixty miles up river to Ali Gharbi, no Turkish defences being found on the way. Delamain's 16th Brigade was sent up there at the beginning of August, the nearest Turkish forces then being established astride the river at Es Sinn about twenty-five miles east of Kut, where Yusef Nur-ud-Din, a former police chief of Basra, had some 5–6,000 men with twelve guns. Townshend's plan was to move his whole division forward, part in boats but most on foot, until they were concentrated near Sheikh Sa'ad, eight miles east of Es Sinn. He hoped to surprise the enemy by making it appear that his main effort would be made on the southern (right) bank of the river, where the ground was more favourable, whereas he would attempt to outflank the Turkish positions on the other bank, which was intersected by marshes. He began his move forward from Amara on 11 September in a temperature of 110–120 degrees. One of his problems was that at that time of year the river was low, and he was very short of land transport – 300 mules below establishment. After a pause of ten days near Sheikh Sa'ad for the artillery to catch up, he launched his attack on 26 September, 18th Brigade on the north and 30th, with the bulk of the cavalry, on the south bank closing up to the Turkish defences. Under cover of darkness a pontoon bridge was laid across the river by which 16th and 17th Brigades crossed to the north bank. On the 27th, while Fry's 18th Brigade attacked the defences immediately north of the river, Delamain, with two battalions, attacked a Turkish position about four miles to the north. Brigadier General F. A. Hoghton's 17th Brigade was then intended to wheel round the northern flank of that position, but found itself embarked on a wide detour between two marshes. When he realized what was happening, he sent two of his battalions back to join Delamain, whose attack then succeeded, relieving the pressure on Fry. Just before sunset, it looked as if the attack was petering out, but a final charge won the day. The soldiers, almost mad with thirst, rushed to the river while the Turks made off upstream, abandoning Kut.

Nixon's immediate reaction was to press on the 120 miles to Baghdad. He told Delhi on 3 October that he was 'strong enough to open the road to Baghdad' and asked for another division to enable him to stay there. Townshend took a different view, writing in his diary that day:

The Army Commander does not seem to realize the weakness and danger of his line of communications. We are now some 380 miles from the sea and have only two weak divisions, including my own, in the country. There is my division to do the fighting and Gorringe's to hold the line of communication from Kut to the sea. There is no possible support to give me if I receive a check, and the consequences of a retreat are not to be imagined. Thus, I feel it is my duty to give my opinion plainly to the Army Commander whether he likes it or not!

On the same day Chamberlain cabled: 'If on account of navigational difficulties there is no probability of the enemy being caught up and smashed, there is no object in the pursuit being continued,' followed next day by a definite order for Nixon to stop; but the latter pooh-poohed the difficulties which, he argued, could be overcome by lightening the loads of vessels and marching overland. The subsequent exchanges between Basra, Delhi and London centred more on whether Nixon would have enough troops to reach and secure Baghdad than on whether even his existing force could be moved and supplied, the War Office being under the impression that he had received the additional river transport he had asked for, which he had not. It was finally agreed on 24 October that he should go ahead and that two Indian divisions from France would be sent to him as reinforcements. Nixon thought that the Turks had no more than 9,000 troops in Mesopotamia, whereas the Viceroy was told in a secret telegram from London on 21 October that Khalil Pasha, with 30,000 men, was on his way there from Turkey, as was the German General von der Goltz to take command of them.

While these arguments were being bandied to and fro, Townshend had moved Fry's 18th Brigade sixty miles upstream to Aziziyeh, halfway to Baghdad from Kut. From there he discovered that Nur-ud-Din, with an estimated 11,000 men and forty guns, was occupying a strong position at Sulaiman Pak (the ancient Ctesiphon) some twenty miles south of Baghdad. He considered that his division was not 'strong enough to open the road to Baghdad' and that, in any case, the low level of water in the river hampered the move forward of his troops. On 3 October he signalled Nixon's chief of staff, Major General G. V. Kimball, recommending that his division be halted at Kut, and that, if the government decided that it wished to occupy Baghdad, this should not be attempted until it could be done by a corps of two divisions advancing by land. He received an abrupt reply telling him that it was Nixon's intention to open the way to Baghdad, and adding that a reinforcing division was expected from France. That was irrelevant because, of course, it could not arrive for some time. Even before Nixon had received the authority he was seeking, he had ordered Townshend to concentrate forward, 16th Brigade leaving Kut to join the 18th at Aziziyeh, followed next day by the 17th, leaving the 30th, with only two battalions, at Kut. The weather had now hotted up again and the marching troops, cutting across bends in the river, suffered heavily from heat and thirst.

A combination of delays kept Townshend's force at Aziziyeh until 18 November. By then, largely from aerial reconnaissance by the eight aircraft supporting him, he had a fairly clear idea of Nur-ud-Din's defences. The latter's 11–12,000 men were almost all manning two lines of defence on the east (left) bank of the Tigris, the first immediately south of the ruins of Ctesiphon, overlooking a bend in the river at Bustan and extending six miles inland on firm ground to a redoubt named VP. The second, parallel to it and about two miles in rear, on the far side of the village of Sulaiman Pak, followed a slight rise in the ground. Behind it was a pontoon bridge leading to the division manning defences in difficult broken ground on the other bank. It was the nature of that ground that dissuaded Townshend from making his main effort on that side of the river. His plan was for Hoghton's 17th Brigade (Column C) to advance conspicuously close to the east bank and attack the centre of the first line. Deploying to their assembly areas overnight, Brigadier General W. G. Hamilton's 18th Brigade (Column B)* would attack beyond the end of the first line at VP, heading for the centre of the second line. An hour later Delamain's 16th (Column A), between the two, would attack and capture VP and then turn left behind the first line to weaken the resistance to Hoghton. About three miles beyond Hamilton, a 'Flying Column', consisting of Roberts's 6th Indian Cavalry Brigade and the 76th Punjabis, the whole commanded by Melliss, would attempt to outflank the second line. Captain H. S. Cardew of the 1/39th Garhwalis commanded No. 34 Signal Company, providing communications between Townshend's headquarters and those of his brigades. He

---

* He had succeeded Fry.

was pleased to have been able to obtain some wireless sets to back up the telephone cable network, as he related in his account:

> Now regarding 'wireless'. I had learnt my lesson at Essein & demanded a pack set both for the Flying Column & Column B, & also if possible with Column A. However there was no wireless set available for this column & it was with the greatest difficulty I got the other sets, & even then each set was terribly under-manned. Horses could only be found for the pack set proceeding with the Flying Column. This set was complete before leaving with regard to horses & equipment but mounted men of the Signal Company with the Flying Column, & any others who could be found, were requisitioned when erection was necessary. The set with Column B was sent out packed on two mule carts – the jolting over the desert in carts was hardly good for such delicate instruments & the dust played havoc with it. Again the signallers with this column were detailed to assist in erection, when necessary. With Divisional Headquarters was one pack set, taken off the Mejidieh. At Lejj was one wagon set. Divisional Headquarters could thus be kept in touch by wireless with the Flying Column, Column B & Lejj.

The whole force concentrated at Lejj, twenty-one miles beyond Aziziyeh and seven from the Turkish defences, on 20 and 21 November, such launches as could negotiate the shallow water moving up also. At 16.00 on the 21st Hoghton's brigade marched forward for five miles and then halted for the night, before resuming their march in the early hours, during which they had difficulty in maintaining direction. At dawn on the 22nd they were not certain where they were, except that they faced formidable defences, covered by barbed wire, which Hoghton hesitated to attack. Expecting to hear the sound of battle from him as his signal to start, and hearing nothing, Hamilton asked Townshend for permission to launch his attack, which he did at 08.00, Delamain joining in an hour later and driving the Turks from the VP redoubt. Interpreting this wrongly as their abandonment of the first line, he made straight ahead for their second, instead of trying to roll up the first, which Hoghton was struggling against on his own. Meanwhile Melliss had not gone far enough east to outflank the second line and found himself up against it. The result was a confused situation on open ground exposed to the fire of defences which, for the most part, were still intact. Casualties were very high: the Turks showed no sign of quitting and Townshend, to whose headquarters Nixon had attached himself, had committed all his troops. Together they decided to try and hold on to what they had gained and see what the morrow would bring: hopefully the Turks might withdraw, as they too had suffered heavily. They were to be disappointed. As day dawned on 23 November, it was clear that the second line was intact and strongly held. However counter-attacks from it during the day failed. They were renewed during the night of 23rd/24th with greater vigour, but did not dislodge Townshend's men from the area they were occupying. By now, however, they had been seriously weakened. Of the 8,500 men of his division who had taken an active part in the battle, half (not surprisingly, almost all infantry) had been killed or wounded. Townshend realized, and Nixon agreed, that he had no alternative but to withdraw the hundred miles to Kut.

Lieutenant H. C. Gallup, serving with the 1/5th Hampshire Howitzer Battery of the Territorial Force, was there and described his experience:

Tuesday, November 23rd. We marched out of camp at 7.p.m. and got to our appointed places at 2 a.m. There were only the 82nd battery R.F.A. and ourselves with our Column A but we were very strong in infantry. The rest of the night was spent by what few men we could spare and some sappers digging our emplacements, while Flux and I were left behind a bank with twenty gunners and the guns so as to cover the working party in case of an attack, but none took place. The last mile or so of our march we passed large sand mounds which are probably the ruins of the old town of Ctesiphon.

About 7.30 a.m. our flank columns attacked, but we did not come into action until 9 o'clock. It was so cold waiting there all that time. When we got to the gun emplacements they were found to be useless and we had to advance much closer to the enemy's position. After several hours' fighting the enemy's chief position was carried and occupied by our troops, and we then turned our attention to their left flank, where our people were not getting on well at all, and were in fact retiring. It was about 3 o'clock in the afternoon that the Turks counter-attacked so strongly. We found afterwards that they had been re-inforced at that time with about 5000 fresh troops. The 82nd and ourselves were sent forward to try and stop it. I think we managed to do so, for a time anyhow, but it was a very *warm* time. They then attacked from another quarter and drove our infantry in and we had to limber up and get out as quickly as we could under a most beastly hot fire. We retired to another position and started again and kept them off for some time, some of the heavy guns also got on to them. It was now getting dusk and I was very thankful when we got orders to limber up and retire for the night to the captured Turkish position. I was frightfully weary and utterly sick of the sound of rifle bullets fizzing by. We spent the night in one of the barbed wire enclosures surrounded by a deep trench full of Turkish prisoners. We wanted a snooze badly . . . We were very surprised that we were left to sleep in peace and quiet, as we fully expected a noisy time. I do not know yet what is the number of casualties but they are heavy on both sides. We captured eight guns yesterday morning, but I think we lost them again in the counter-attack in the afternoon. The Dorsets and Oxfords have lost heavily. We lost two men and two horses killed and several more wounded, but why it was not more serious I cannot say . . .

Wednesday, November 24th. I left off writing to you at eleven o'clock yesterday morning and we have had a *very* lively time since. I went out at eleven o'clock to water my section from a dirty ditch about a quarter of a mile away and just as we were finishing shrapnel started coming over again. On my return into the wired enclosure, I found great commotion going on, horses being sent away for safety and the guns in our battery were then being protected with sand-bags. The other battery moved a little way off. Nothing much happened except that they kept on putting a few shells over us and it was supposed that they were doing this to cover their retirement, but at 5 o'clock we were rudely awakened by seeing very large bodies of Turks approaching all deployed for the attack. They had apparently been re-inforcing. From then onwards until this morning we have been attacked. A very noisy night, heavy rifle firing and things humming over us and most beastly close. At one time we lay flat on our faces for a time and then during a lull, made for the low shelter of our sandbags and lay there all night during the intervals of firing an occasional round in the hopes of hitting something. A cheerful night!

During the night it was decided that our force was too weak to hold the position and a retirement was ordered to take place at dawn. At dawn there was another burst of rifle fire and we again carried out a retirement under fire losing two drivers only. It was rather fine to see the teams come galloping up to fetch us. My horse could not be found so I retired on a gun limber, seated on the knees of the smallest gunner in the battery. We only retired for about an hour and a half and took up another position and were then joined by two other batteries and waited for the enemy to come on. A gun boat was amusing itself by putting shells round about us for about an hour, while we eat a little bully beef and awful dry biscuit and after a bit we were told that the Turks were retiring again.

Captain Cardew described the withdrawal of Townshend's headquarters from Aziziyeh:

November 30th was rather an awful day. Ever since dawn was a scene of motion, the bridge being hastily dismantled, the barbed wire defences being torn down & thrown into the river to prevent if possible the Turks getting the wire which they were in great need of. By 9 a.m. most of the ships had departed downstream, the Naval ships still remaining. About 9 a.m. from the direction of El Ketmin [?] could be seen bodies of something moving in the mirage. It may have been columns of men or it may have been cattle. The General Staff were on the top of the Telegraph Office, much perturbed by these sights, & very impatient for the ships & land transport to get away. Waggons had to be destroyed hastily. One waggon wireless set was on a mahela under tow, for the other we raised some 'bhiles' of the cow gun teams to drag it along with us. We had only got it off by about 10 a.m. when the order for the troops to commence retiring was issued. It was lucky this set was got away & saved, as it proved invaluable in Kut. At one time it looked as though, for the want of horses, mules or any animals to draw the waggons we should have to destroy it, till the idea of using the cow gun waggon 'bhiles' was thought of. The wireless was of course far more valuable than these waggons, which were at once destroyed. Finally, smashing up the Telegraph office, we left Azizieh about 10 am on our march to Umm-al-Tubbul.

The withdrawal was a gruelling experience for all who took part, but for none more so than for the wounded. Those who could not walk were carried to Lejj, thirty miles back, in unsprung carts jolting over rough ground. Having been transferred to boats, many no more than lighters which had brought up supplies, they made their way, held up by one accident after another, usually caused by grounding, all the way to Basra, a horrifying thirteen-day journey. If they survived that and were lucky, they were then taken by hospital ship to India. The medical arrangements, both for evacuation and treatment, were scandalously inadequate. Even for those who were not wounded, the retreat was a grim ordeal. Pressed by the Turks from the rear and harassed by armed Arabs, who clustered round to rob the defeated, they marched and stumbled on, their pace sometimes deliberately retarded in order to protect the launches and boats, which were having difficulty navigating the shallow channels of the river. Fortunately the Turks, following only a few miles behind most of the way, were also delayed by difficulties of their own. Had they not been, Townshend's exhausted men might not have reached Kut, as they did on 3 December. Captain W. C. Spackman of the Indian Medical Service was with the 48th Pioneers and kept a diary which he intended should eventually be sent to his parents. In the entry for 7 December, he described the final stage of the withdrawal:

A furious rifle fire began as our brigade went into the rear-guard action & only by dragging the mules could we prevent the carts from swerving off to the right into the ditches. Once on the road we got along well, but several men & mules & camels were hit. The brigades & the guns & the ships & cavalry held them off, in fact gave them a very severe handling, tho' they were 3 divisions. We trekked 30 miles to Monkey Village & the brigades followed, some of them doing 44 miles that day & fighting too. (The troops were arriving all thro' that night and the confusion in camp was appalling; it was a bitter cold night). The ships fared badly, the FIREFLY (monitor) was riddled & had one thro' her boiler; her commander chucked his breach-blocks overboard and she was abandoned. The COMET, the famous little gun-boat of the British Resident at Baghdad, went aground. A tug dropped her two barges in order to try and pull her off but failed. She was set ablaze and her commander dived from the stern as the Turks swarmed up her bows. The tug got away but lost her barges, one full of wounded. The A.D.* Supplies, a well-nourished full colonel of sedentary habits, leapt off the barge and did a record 2 miles across a difficult country to reach the retreating column, where he got a lift on a mule cart. The SHAITAN (a small gunboat) sank;

* Assistant Director.

but they had plugged Hell into that Turkish camp before being scuppered.

We cleared sick & wounded on to the BLOSSE LYNCH at 'Monkey Village' and marched off at 4am. doing the 50 miles between Aziziyah and Kut in 30 Hours, and getting into Kut midday on 2nd. Dec. We started digging at once, as we knew a siege was certain and I hurried round the bazaar after Mess stores with fair results. The Turks did not worry us till the 5th. But since then the frequent bouts of shell fire and almost incessant streaming of bullets have put a great strain on us all.

His next entry was on 12 December.

Our camp is by a palm-grove where some guns are & so we get a terrible lot of shells and have already had some very close shaves from direct hits, and shrapnel clatters on the dug-out roof. Yesterday, during a typical 10 minutes I counted 50 shells in and around our camp: the whole place is very large, but this & one or two other spots come in for most of the shells.

The BLOSSE LYNCH went down river with sick & wounded on the 4th. & the cavalry got away on the 6th. The 5th. is, I believe, counted as the first day of the siege. The Turks have made some spirited attacks but are held off fairly easily as our wire defences are strong and the river is on 3 sides semicircularly. A post holding the further end of the boat-bridge was scuppered unfortunately & led to a most gallant deed. The bridge had to be blown up that night & Matthews, a sapper friend of mine, with a band of sappers and 3 of ours (48th Pioneers) did it. M. had to dash across the bridge carrying 50 lbs of guncotton, lay it across the bridge 30 yds. from the far side & light the fuse. As the enemy were strongly holding the other side, it sounded impossible. There was no moon & it was timed for 9 pm. We listened anxiously for a blaze of musketry, but amazing to relate he was not fired on and the two explosions announced success before their fire broke out. The bridge was some 300 yds.long.

Townshend's first reaction was that he would defend Kut as stoutly as he had Chitral on India's unruly North-West Frontier in 1895, for which he had been created a CB. Nixon, back at Basra, signalled that he was glad to hear this and that reinforcements would be 'pushed up to you with all possible speed'. Townshend had explained that his men needed rest and that his prospects did not look too bad 'with one month's rations for British troops and two for Indian, as well as plenty of ammunition' provided that the reinforcements Nixon promised reached him within two months. However his optimism faded when he received Nixon's reply which reiterated that every effort would be made to relieve his force 'and it was hoped that this would be achieved within two months', adding that, as the Turks would probably invest him, it would both reduce the numbers he had to feed and help a relieving force to send out the cavalry brigade and any transport that could be spared, as well as return as many ships as possible, before they did so. Townshend's reaction was to suggest that as, after two months, his food would have been exhausted and the Turks would probably have built up their force to possibly six divisions, he had better get out while he could. In any case he sent out the cavalry brigade over a specially constructed bridge to the south bank. Nixon forbade any such attempt and tried to reassure him by saying that two months was 'the outside limit' and that he had asked for yet another division and more heavy artillery. On 7 December, the day on which the Cabinet in London accepted Kitchener's recommendation for evacuation of Gallipoli, the Turks closed the ring, leaving Townshend's force of about 10,000 men, some 3,500 Indian non-combatants and 6,000 Arab inhabitants shut into the loop of the river 3,000 yards long and 2,000 wide, the smelly little town of Kut itself taking up 2,500 square yards in the south-west corner and the mud fort standing on the river bank at the extreme north-east corner. The British Empire's war against the Ottoman was not going well.

Three successive defence lines across the loop were hastily dug, Hoghton's 17th Brigade being allotted the north-east sector, Delamain's 16th the north-west, Hamilton's 18th the southern, where most of the artillery was sited. Melliss's two-battalion 30th Brigade was in reserve.

The first attack came in the north-west on 9 December and was repulsed. Attacks, all of which were held, continued at intervals up to and including Christmas Eve, which saw one of the fiercest, in which the garrison lost 315 men, having killed 907 of the enemy. This was described by Major A. J. Anderson, Commanding Officer of the Volunteer Artillery Battery, which was supporting 17th Indian Brigade, holding the fort in the north-east corner of the defences. The battery was formed from European and Eurasian volunteers in India and Burma, mostly employed

in transportation. Anderson had been serving in the Rangoon Port
Defence Volunteers.

Dec. 24. This was the great day of the siege. It was the only occasion
on which the Turks made a serious and sustained effort to do
anything by assault. Immediately it was light enough, soon after 7
a.m., a very heavy bombardment began and was kept up more or less
throughout the morning. The town and front line got a share but
there were 22 guns concentrated on shelling the Fort alone and it
was soon evident that they had special intentions towards the latter.
The position of the enemy's batteries formed almost a semi-circle to
the northward of the Fort from about N.W. round to a little S. of E.
where a battery was posted on the left bank of the river. Both our 15
prs. were early put out of action for the day, various shells having
smashed the wheels, besides doing other damage. It was also at a very
early staqe that the telephone communication from the observation
post to the C.R.A. and the Field and Heavy Batteries was cut. In spite
of continued attempts to restore it this communication remained
broken for the rest of the day. For a time also both the lines between
the O.C. [Officer Commanding] Fort and Brigade H.Q. were broken.
The observation post was a most unpleasant spot, but shells coming
from so many directions, no cover anywhere was safe. According to
one account, shells were several times timed falling at the rate of 80
per minute in and around the Fort and one felt a continual buffetting
from the concussion of the bursts. Personally I found the ear
protectors which I had, a real blessing. Capt. Freeland and I were
both knocked down by one shell but the burst was just beyond us
and we were only warmed and covered with earth and atta. Another
burst in the entrance of our mess dug-out (which was luckily empty)
filling it with shrapnel bullets and breaking treasured whiskey bottles
etc. About 10 a.m. a segment shell penetrated and burst in the centre
gun dug out, wounding 4 gunners. 3 more shells entered the same
dug-out afterwards. All this time the walls on the N., N.E., and S.E.
including the N.E. bastion were gradually crumbling and along big
stretches were practically demolished, as also the barbed wire outside.
It was about midday when I saw from the O.P. [Observation Post]
the enemy issuing from their trenches near the river, and immediately
blew the alarm on the whistle. It had been arranged during the morning that in the event of attack our gunners should join the infantry

with rifles at the barricade in the N.E. bastion, on which was also posted a detachment of the Oxford L.I. under Lt. Mellor. By the time I got down from my post into the communication trench, they had already doubled off to their position. I paused in following them to order the removal of the 4 wounded gunners to safety behind the Fort.

I may here mention that my Madras servant Chakharia carried one of them Gr. Gilbert, the greater part of the way into Kut on his back and then came back again at once in spite of everything which might have discouraged him. All the other native servants whom I sent off to look after the wounded remained in the safety of Kut, but my servant showed himself all through to be quite exceptional and was beyond praise.

Finding on trying to proceed along the trench that the way was completely blocked by the men of the Indian Regiment from the N.E. wall and river or E. corner, I realised that something was wrong. I could find none of their officers (I subsequently learnt that Capt. Brickman and Lt. Keeling were the only B.O.'s remaining) so on looking over the parapet and finding that the Turks were already appearing on the debris of the wall and learning that the intervening trenches were denuded of any of our troops I did all I could to organise a firing line out of the men who were blocking the trench and got the trenches lined both N. and S. of the Observation Post. On retracing my steps for the second time going towards the N.E. bastion. I eventually found Capt. Brickman, the acting C.O. who informed me that he was on his way to the O.C. Fort to explain the situation to him. I explained to Capt. Brickman what I had done and then proceeded to join our own men in the N.E. bastion.

That attack was beaten off, and the Turks withdrew. His account continues:

During the afternoon more shelling took place and before dark the enemy were seen to be receiving considerable reinforcements, so that the subsequent night attack was expected. The C.O. of the Oxfords, Lt. Col. Lethbridge was now in command of the N.E. wall and bastion and the Vol. Artillery Battery were again posted on the barricade in the bastion. It was as the moon was rising behind clouds about 8.15 p.m. that the attack started.

The outer walls of the bastion were lightly held by men of the 103rd M.L.I. [Mahratta Light Infantry] and it was arranged that they were to retire to the side galleries as the attack developed, the idea being that a treble cross fire should thus be maintained from them and the barricade to prevent the enemy penetrating inside the bastion. The signal I arranged with Capt. Goldfrap 103rd M.L.I. was three short blasts on the whistle as soon as his men were clear of the front and on this signal, which soon came, fire was opened from the barricade. Smoke and dust in the very difficult light soon made it impossible to distinguish details but the enemy got to work with bombs, and first I was warned by Capt. Goldfrap that casualties had reduced his tenure of the left or W. gallery to only a few men near the barricade, and later the whole of the right or E. gallery was open to the enemy from the same cause. We had also had many casualties at the barricade, so it was impossible to do more than station men at each end ready to deal with any attempted rush round the flanks. The din all this time was appalling, as in addition to the enormous volume of rifle and machine gun fire at such close quarters, and constant bursting of bombs, we heard afterwards that our own batteries, 104 Heavy and the Howitzers, were keeping up a strong fire of lyddite on the enemy trenches outside the fort, besides which one of the Field Batteries was also helping us with shrapnel and star shell. The only way of making one's self heard, and that was indistinctly, was to shout close to the other person's ear. For a while a steady exchange of fire was kept up, the only particular incident being the putting out of action of our machine gun in the centre of the barricade, which belonged to the 103rd M.L.I. First the native gunners working it were one by one knocked out and then Capt. Dorling R.F.A., who was with us, attempted to get it going again only to find that the gun itself was out of action. In doing this he himself was hit through the shoulder and we continued to have other additions to our casualty list. Then probably about 9.30 p.m., though it is difficult to fix the exact hour, one of the enemy's rushes brought them within more effective bombing distance, and one bomb which fell right among our men cleared the whole of the right half of the barricade, its area also extending to the left half. Incidentally it knocked me over with a slight wound in the shoulder and splinters in the face. I shook myself together to find that there was only a handful left on the barricade (including Capt. Freeland and Lt. Davern, who also had a gash in the hand) and the position seemed very difficult to hold as, besides the gaps on the flanks, there was also a trench running under the middle of the barricade and the other end of this was held by the enemy. However I found enough men and we remanned the barricade in sufficient strength to hold on. Luckily the enemy failed to follow up their advantage at the moment, and simply settled down to rifle fire again where they were. I made another effort to get the machine gun going again with the help of 2 specialists from the Oxfords for whom I had sent but it was useless, so I got them to remove it.

Captain Cardew described what it was like at Townshend's head-quarters:

During the morning we in Kut were having a pretty thin time of it from shells which were bursting in the town in every direction. Many shells came over the Gen Staff houses. I remember going up to see the Staff in Gen Staff No 1 house where the CRA and his staff were carrying out observation work – bullets were fairly phitting over the roof though we were protected by the parapet. I was quite pleased to get below again and on entering my office met Captain Beg our ordnance officer. We had a little chat together as I knew him well, & he then said 'I must be off to see the staff.' Barely had he reached the roof when a 40 pounder shell hit the parapet fair and square carrying it away. Poor Beg was killed instantaneously, Col Courtenay the CRA had his leg shattered and Capt Garnett, his staff officer was badly wounded and burnt. Garnett died two days later delirious. Col Courtenay on arrival in hospital showed much pluck telling the Doctors to amputate his leg if they considered it necessary – he wouldn't mind. A few days later his leg had to be amputated but he died from shock & blood poisoning poor man. That shell did its work pretty effectively, three important gunner staff officers in one fell swoop.

Not long after this, in the middle of the night, his office received a near miss, as he related:

The shell just passed through a bit of the roof or ceiling above my head & exploded on the far side, bang into the Signal Company Courtyard. Men were sleeping in the courtyard at the time. One fragment of shell shattered the leg of Pte Lutener, another tearing through a window shattered the knee of Sergeant Murray sleeping in the room. This sergeant had been badly wounded by a shell on May 31st in the action at Kurna on board H.M.S. Espiegle. We were standing together at the time, when the one & only shell of the, I might say, hundreds fired at the Espiegle hit her & laid us both out. He had gone back to India, recovered & had rejoined us just before Ctesiphon. It was very hard lines on him getting badly smashed up a second time. Col Browne-Mason* & I were down below with them in a second, improvising splints, bandaging etc. We got them off to hospital at once, both in pretty bad pain. One wondered if another shell would come along whilst we were at this work, but we were spared. One huge piece had entered the signal office burying itself in the stone floor within an inch or so of the head of one of the operators, who was sleeping in there till it was his time for duty that night. This was Pte Howrie, a Scotchman. He just turned over & went to sleep again. He also had recently returned from India having been invalided from rheumatic fever. The operators on duty showed much pluck, continuing work as though nothing had happened though from dust, smoke & filth caused by the explosion it was almost impossible to see in the courtyard for some considerable time.

Sergeant Murray died in hospital some 5 weeks later from blood poisoning & exhaustion. I think he worried himself too much & hastened his end. However we managed to cheer Lutener up in our visits & he survived. His leg had to be amputated eventually & he himself was an absolute skeleton but he lived & was taken down stream on the capitulation of Kut. We had little nourishing food for men in hospital, the tinned milk soon ran out & men had to exist on the ordinary ration of meat & bread. We used to make up soups & send them to Murray & Lutener. Both of them, like all the others had a terrible time in hospital apart from their wounds & what one has to suffer when they are being dressed. Both had draining tubes in their wounds to allow the 'puss' to flow out by. Great pieces of shirt & trousers had been dug out from inside of their wounds. I think Lutener underwent at least 6 operations. Murray seemed to be in terrible pain till his death, never getting a wink of sleep. Once he rallied & seemed to improve but his heart failed at the end. The hospital was for ever getting its share of shells – I refer to the British General Hospital. This was situated in the covered bazaar of Kut, the roadway & stalls or bunks on each side of it being crammed with beds, or mattresses. The worst cases had beds, the others lay on

* The Assistant Director of Medical Services.

MESOPOTAMIA

26. HMS *Miner*, a river gunboat,
on the River Tigris at Qurna

27. View up the River Tigris from
Outlook Tower, Qurna

28. 120th Rajputana Infantry
covering the retirement from
the Arab village of Alloa,
30 January 1915

29. Lieutenant General
Sir John Nixon

30. Moving by *bellum*, May 1915

31. Major General Melliss
VC and staff, July 1915

32. Indian troops passing
through a communications
trench

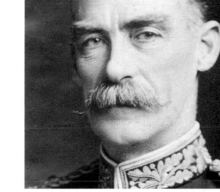

33. Lieutenant General
Sir Percy Lake

34. Arab prisoners from the
Turkish 35th Division captured at
Sheik Sa'ad, 10 January 1916

35. 60pdr gun at
Hannah, February 1916

36. Wireless station receiving the last message from Kut

37. The surrender at Kut: Major General Charles Townshend (seated, middle) with, to his left, his captor, Khalil Pasha

38. British artillery limbers captured at Kut

39. 'The Lane' at Yozgat, taken with an illicit camera

40. Building a pontoon bridge across the River Diyala

41. British troops at breakfast

42. Rolls-Royce
armoured car,
December 1916

43. Sergeant John Farnol, 1/5th Buffs,
convalescing in India

44. Indian Army donkey
transport entering Baghdad,
March 1917

45. British troops crossing
the North Bridge, Baghdad

46. Ford Motor convoy on
the Jerizeh Reconnaissance,
March 1917

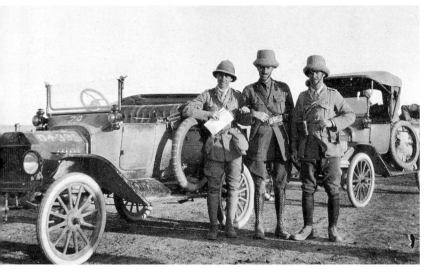

47. Russian visit to British
General Headquarters,
Baghdad, April 1917.
Lieutenant General Sir
Stanley Maude is seated
second from the right,
front row, with Major
General Money on
the far left

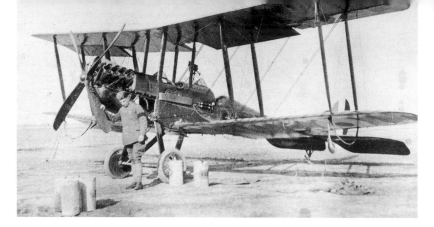

48. Captain G. Merton RFC and his BE2c reconnaissance aircraft

49. Indian cavalry

50. Observation balloon going aloft

mattresses on the ground, in the bunks. There were also the Indian General Hospital & four smaller hospitals or Field Ambulances where the wounded were treated & if serious enough sent on to the General Hospital for operations. All operations were done in the General Hospital but cases of dysentry & other sicknesses were retained in the Field Ambulances. Each Field Ambulance was situated in as good houses as could be found but overcrowded owing to the amount of sickness. I suppose as many men died in the Field Ambulances as in the General Hospital. It was a marvel that with the amount of filth & squalor about, anybody ever survived an operation however great precautions might be taken. Operations often had to be carried out on the patient's bed, quite exposed to the eyes of all other patients. Every day found one if not more beds vacant, the occupant having died & having been removed at once so that his bed could be available for another. The British dead were taken to an improvised mortuary, a room in a house, where at first they were sewn up in their blankets but later, as blankets were so urgently required owing to the cold, were sewn up in white cloth. Each afternoon about 5 p.m. the procession to the cemetry [sic] would start; a few men belonging to the unit of the deceased attending as pall-bearers. The body covered with a blanket was carried on a stretcher to the cemetry where a party was always on duty grave-digging, so that the graves were always ready. Some days it might be one only, though generally about 5 or even more. Then each was laid to rest, & the padre would read the burial service once, for all, & the parties would march away. Even whilst the funerals were in progress shells often hurtled over the cemetry, & one was never free from bullets. At one time till the floods came we buried at night only. The Rev Spooner was the Church of England Chaplain, & the Rev. Father Mullen the Catholic priest. No words can express the admiration that these two men were held in by all ranks. They worked unceasingly and unflinchingly – always with the wounded, cheering them up, helping them. Father Mullen was on one occasion wounded in the hand by a splinter of shell. The day we buried Sergeant Murray was one that I shall not forget. It had poured all night – the roads were inches deep in mud, slush & water, & very slippery. It was with the utmost difficulty that we got him to the cemetry & during the service many bullets whizzed past us & a few shells were fired into the town. We were a bedraggled, dirty, wet lot by the time we returned.

Major General Melliss wrote to his wife in the form of a daily diary. She seems to have received the entries somehow and he mentions that he was able to send her telegrams. She had managed to get a plum pudding to him before the siege started. Having on the two previous days described the attack on the Fort and the anxiety it caused him, although his brigade was not directly involved, and to Townshend, he wrote on 25 December:

> Townshend is a hopeless incapable dreamer & ass – vain as a peacock & full of military history comparisons, but as a practical soldier one's grandmother. would be as good. Sometimes one doesn't know whether to laugh or cry at his incapacity – He never goes near his men or rarely – never goes near the front line of trenches & sees things for himself. But he is not the only rotter – there are several in high places. I tell you honestly although it sounds conceited for me to say it, but I can say it to you. I am the best man in this force of the senior Generals & what I suggest is accepted at once. It is not saying much though, but there are amongst the seniors an awful set of incompetents. Later. I have [had] a dinner of a tough goose & your plum pudding the latter very good. I am [illegible] in a very peaceful night the Turks very quiet – no horrid jarring sound of maxims & rifle shots the night through. I hope it'll keep quiet all night. Am relieved tomorrow by Delamain. I have been up here 10 days.

Most of the garrison's casualties in these attacks were caused by artillery fire. After Christmas the Turks moved away, having fired shells carrying pamphlets calling on Indian soldiers to rebel against their Imperialist oppressors. At first Townshend thought they were withdrawing, but Nur-ud-Din, under the overall command of von der Goltz, had decided to concentrate on preventing any relief and was moving his troops to hold a position beyond Sheikh Sa'ad, thirty miles downstream.

7

No Relief for Kut

With the impending arrival of the 3rd and 7th Indian Divisions from France, Lieutenant General Sir Fenton Aylmer, the Adjutant General in India, was sent to form and command Tigris Corps,* the troops which would be 'pushed up' to relieve Kut. By an ironic coincidence, he had, as a major in the Royal Engineers, played a prominent part in the relief of Chitral, which Townshend had been defending, in 1895. He reached Basra in the first week of December. The first of his reinforcements, the 28th Brigade† of the 7th Division, commanded by Major General Sir George Younghusband, had already arrived and been sent straight upriver as soon as it disembarked. A major limitation on the speed with which Aylmer could assemble an adequate force to carry out the relief was the scarcity of all means of movement, of which rivercraft was the mainstay. At that time its total strength was thirteen paddle steamers, three stern-wheelers, nine tugs, three screw-boats and fifty-seven barges. There were many other logistic bottlenecks and deficiencies, not least the totally inadequate unloading facilities at Basra. Nixon had asked Delhi to build a railway from Basra to Nahiriyeh, but that had been turned down as too expensive if the *vilayet* was not to be retained after the war. The 7th Division's engineers, as soon as they arrived, began to build a rough road from the Shatt-el-Arab to Amara, up which most of the division had to march, taking ten days to get there and four more on from there to Ali Gharbi, where Aylmer was assembling his corps. There Younghusband took over command of the division.

The intelligence available to Aylmer told him that Nur-ud-Din had five divisions (roughly the equivalent of British brigades) totalling some 22,500 men, supported by seventy-two guns, most of whom were

---

* It had originally been intended that he should command the 7th Division on its arrival at Basra.

† 2nd Leicesters, 51st and 53rd Sikhs, 56th Punjabi Frontier Force Rifles.

thought to be round Kut, but an unknown number believed to be manning their old defences at Es Sinn. It was estimated that only an advance guard of 900 cavalry, 1,100 camelry and one infantry battalion, with two light guns, was nearer to him than that. On 4 January the 7th Division (19th, 21st and 35th Brigades), preceded by the 6th Cavalry Brigade and supported by three gunboats, set off to advance on both sides of the river to make contact with the enemy, its first stage being to secure Sheikh Sa'ad. Aylmer followed two days behind with the rest of the force, 9th and 28th Brigades, most of the artillery and a number of unbrigaded infantry battalions. After Sheikh Sa'ad, Younghusband would continue his advance cautiously the fifteen miles to Sannaiyat, his troops on the north (left) bank of the river having to follow a narrow strip of land between the river and the Suwaikiyeh Marsh. From there it was only seven miles to Es Sinn. As they were setting off, Aylmer received a message from Townshend that two Turkish divisions had been seen moving past Kut in his direction; but bad weather prevented Aylmer's aircraft from confirming this. By nightfall of the 4th Younghusband was five miles short of Sheikh Sa'ad, where an aerial reconnaissance at midday had reported about 10,000 men in defences astride the river. Younghusband was confident of being able to defeat them, but Aylmer told him to 'hold' them while he brought up the rest of the force. At the same time he suggested to Nixon that Gorringe's 12th Division should advance from Nasiriyeh up the Shatt-al-Hai to give the impression that he also was moving to relieve Kut. Younghusband's concept of 'holding' the enemy at Sheikh Sa'ad was to launch an attack on both banks of the river, Brigadier General G. H. B. Rice's 35th Brigade* on the north (left) bank, Major General G. V. Kimball's 28th on the southern (right), the rest of the division following Rice, except for the cavalry brigade which would operate on Kimball's left flank. Younghusband himself was on board the gunboat *Gadfly*, leading the supply flotilla, at the rear of which was the ancient paddle steamer *Julnar* acting as a hospital ship.

Dawn on 6 January found the area blanketed in mist, in which 28th Brigade started forward at 09.00, covering four miles before it lifted to reveal the Turkish trenches two miles ahead and cavalry behind them.

---

* 1/5th Buffs, 37th Dogras, 97th Deccan Infantry, 102nd King Edward's Own Grenadiers, 128th Pioneers.

The leading troops soon came under fire and, trying to find the flank, moved further away from the river, only to find that the defences extended further south than they expected. By 15.30 they were still 500 yards from the Turkish line and had not assaulted it. Rice on the other bank had done no better and the flotilla had not been fired on, but had had to dodge mines floated down with the stream. Younghusband decided that he could get no further that day and told his brigade commanders to stop and dig in. Communications between him and Aylmer had broken down and it was not until 21.00 that the latter knew of the situation. He told Younghusband not to get involved in any further serious action before they met at first light at the pontoon bridge which had been laid across the river behind Younghusband's leading brigades. This, combined with another early morning mist, meant that nothing happened until the middle of the day. Action was further delayed by having to switch artillery to deal with a Turkish threat to Rice's right flank. The plan was that Rice should 'hold' the enemy while Dennys's 19th Brigade* would move round his right and, with the 16th Cavalry, outflank and roll up the Turkish left. They would be followed by Brigadier General C. E. de M. Norie's 21st Brigade† in divisional reserve. On the other bank 28th Brigade, reinforced by the 92nd Punjabis from 19th Brigade, was to advance 'vigorously', helped by the cavalry brigade and followed by Major General R. G. Egerton's 9th Brigade‡ from 3rd Indian Division in corps reserve. Nobody was certain exactly where the Turkish defences on the north bank were, and in any case the weight of artillery fire with which to engage them was seriously inadequate. 19th Brigade began their advance at noon and after two hours had veered too far north, leaving a wide gap between them and 35th Brigade. 21st Brigade was then diverted into it, while 19th Brigade was ordered to turn left to the north of them. This, however, did not bring them round the Turkish left, but directly against it. Both brigades then found themselves making a frontal attack on formidable defences with little artillery support. While they were being mown down, another threat to the right flank developed, to deal with which two of Norie's battalions and most of the artillery were diverted. On the other bank

---

* 1st Seaforth Highlanders, one company 92nd Punjabis, 125th Napier's Rifles.
† 2nd Black Watch, 6th Jats, 9th Bhopals, 41st Dogras.
‡ 1st Connaught Rangers, 1/4th Hampshires, 62nd Punjabis, 107th Pioneers.

28th Brigade had been more successful. They launched their attack at
14.30, and by 16.00 had taken the Turkish first line, but at considerable
cost – 1,000 casualties, 2nd Leicesters alone losing 16 officers and 298
soldiers. Fire from the second line was intense, and Kimball decided not
to try to get any further that day.

Aylmer agreed and told him and Younghusband to plan for a
renewed attack during the night of 8/9 January. Once again the medical
arrangements had been scandalously inadequate, made worse by rain
and the mud it caused. Provision had been made to handle 250
casualties: by the end of 9 January there were 4,000. Younghusband
planned an extensive reshuffle of his brigades for the planned night
attack, which involved much marching and countermarching in the mud
and pouring rain, exhausting the soldiers. It was therefore fortunate that
it proved unnecessary to launch it, as the Turks had begun to withdraw,
abandoning Sheikh Sa'ad which 28th Brigade occupied the following
afternoon. Nur-ud-Din's reason for withdrawal was not clear and von
der Goltz sacked him for it, Khalil Pasha taking over command. Their
withdrawal brought no surge of euphoria to Aylmer, who took a cautious
view. In a signal to Nixon on 13 January he said that, although he was
determined to continue the advance to Kut, he needed more men. He
expected to meet a strong position at Es Sinn. He pointed out the
weakness in his medical services, saying 'the wounded cannot receive
proper attention', and that he had only one aircraft for reconnaissance.
Nixon replied that he was sending up four more battalions and that four
more could be sent if Aylmer sent back the ships to fetch them, ending
with one of the platitudinous exhortations which tended to emanate
from senior officers: 'I must leave the matter to your decision. Am
confident that you and the fine troops you command will achieve your
object.' At that time Aylmer had 10,000 infantry, 1,500 cavalry and forty-
six guns, and Townshend in Kut 8,500. The Turks, forward of Baghdad,
probably had about the same. Khalil did not go all the way back to Es
Sinn, but only seven miles to a position based on the River Wadi, which
flowed into the Tigris from the north. It was three and a half miles east
of Hanna where the Suwaikiyeh Marsh came within two miles of the
north bank of the Tigris. Aylmer's plan was for Kimball's 28th Brigade
to 'hold' the Turks by advancing directly towards them close to the
north bank, while the cavalry, 19th, 21st and 35th Brigades made a wide
turning movement on his right which would bring them over the River

Wadi: they would then turn southwards behind the enemy positions to the Hanna Gap, thus encircling them.

All these brigades were due to move from the assembly areas they had reached late on 12 January at dawn on the 13th; but an early morning mist led to postponement. By 09.00 the cavalry were over the Wadi and the infantry followed, 21st Brigade leading. At 11.00 they came under fire, causing all but the leading Gurkha battalion to veer off to the right. This caused 19th Brigade, who were due to come in on their right, to do the same. It was not until 13.00 that their supporting artillery was over the Wadi, and at 13.30 19th and 21st Brigades launched their attack on the Turks facing them, whom they had hoped to outflank. Fighting was fierce but partially successful, so that Younghusband decided that 35th Brigade could be slipped round the right flank of the 19th and reach the Hanna Gap without difficulty. But they also met Turkish defences and were still held up when darkness fell. The cavalry brigade's attempt to get through to the gap on their right was not pressed. As before, the Turks withdrew unmolested during the night, Aylmer's force having suffered 1,600 casualties of whom 218 had been killed. Lieutenant Hugh Northcote of the 41st Dogras in 19th Brigade wrote an account of the battle to his father on 15 January:

On 10th and 11th we rested but on the night of the 11th we made a night march and dug ourselves in. On the 12th nothing happened except that a few bodies of the enemy were seen in the distance. On the night of the 12th we made a long march round to a flank and arrived at our starting point about 2 a.m. We slept just as we arrived with our great coats on the ground till dawn and it was beastly cold. The next morning we started out to the attack. The enemy were much further off than we expected, so we had a long march across perfectly flat and in some cases marshy country before getting into touch. After some time the enemy began shelling us, but we kept on, the men advancing splendidly as on parade. Then came rifle bullets pretty thick. I was right in front with our C.O.,* to whom I was attached to take orders for my guns. The C.O. was absolutely fearless for himself and really was much too much in front. When we could advance no further we lay down and advanced a bit by rushes towards one of their guns which we nearly captured. The enemy who

* Lieutenant Colonel C. W. Tribe.

I hear were officered by Germans made a very strong resistance. Shortly after that I was sent back to bring up my guns and more ammunition, and I had a very long trek all over the field after them. Finally I found the ammunition and brought it up to the firing line; the men carried the boxes up magnificently though the bullets and shrapnel were pretty thick. When I got back I found the C.O. had been killed, and 3 other Bas* wounded though in the confusion we could not make out much of what was happening except that we were holding our own. The last 200 yards up to the firing line was rather nasty but I got through all right with Major Colson who had taken command. We then tried another advance but we had not enough Bas to lead the men. I managed to get a few on a bit but then we had to dig ourselves in as the enemy were close by sniping us heavily. When dark fell I went over the line with the Adjutant and to our great grief found one of the finest fellows in the regiment was killed. We now had only five Bas left and I had to take command of the whole of the left wing who had a very bad time. I made my dispositions for the night and then returned to report to the Major who came along in the moonlight to have a look. I had to defend a large gap in the line with machine guns and a very few men, and as we were crossing from one bit to another the Major was hit. It was an awful moment. I dragged him with the help of others into a trench and bound him up as best I could and then had to go on with the work – the enemy even then within 100 yards and sniping heavily. I afterwards went back to our headquarters to arrange for stretcher bearers and get orders from our next C.O. In the night the enemy withdrew and the next morning was peaceful; as we marched very tired to a new camp. Hardly had we got there when the enemy began shelling us again and we had to shift. To-day has been peaceful except for a few odd shells, and I have had a shave and washed my hands and face for the first time for 4 days. If ever I talk of discomforts in the future just remind me of this last week. I sleep in a hole in the ground with sometimes not even a blanket. Last night it poured with rain and everything was soaked. I do my best to wash my feet when possible but I have not taken off my clothes for about 10 days. I am now in command of the remains of 2 double companies as well as my own guns.

---

* British officers.

Major T. C. Catty of the 69th Punjabis was Deputy Assistant Adjutant General at the headquarters of the 3rd Indian Division. In his diary for 14 January he wrote:

I have talked to various Regt. Officers who were on the show & they all say that the turning movement wasn't nearly wide eno'. The Corps staff seem (from the accounts one hears) to have lost its nerve just at the critical moment & instead of permitting the outflanking columns to move properly round interfered with the man on the spot & tried to direct things from where they couldn't see.

We landed just in time to send off some medical personnel with 7th Bde that was going out to make good the ground on the right bank opposite the Turkish position. This was done successfully with only some 30–40 casualties & our guns established in positions from wh. it is hoped the Turkish position can be enfiladed. Crossing is very slow business as the boat bridge made by the S & M* broke & sank. It was not to be wondered at as the boats used were rotten little things that didn't stand a chance in a strong current. The usual cheap & nasty Indian way.

The tales of the wounded at Shaikh Sa'ad & the Wadi are really awful & if one wasn't on the spot they would be unbelievable. There were no MOs to dress them properly & not 20% of the proper number of stretcher bearers. Men were left out for 2–3 days before being picked up & we had won the battle – Some poor devils with fractured legs crawled in 4 or 5 miles. The whole expedition apparently started off with ¼ of their proper Medical Establishment – why no one knows, perhaps they thought that there wouldn't be so many casualties or that time was so important that they couldn't wait any longer for the Hosp'tls. Anyhow the result has been a disgraceful waste of life.

The arrangements for taking down the wounded to Basra & Amara are just as bad. There are no hosp'tl ships equipped as such – boats bring troops up river, sick & wounded are shoved on board under a M.O. & a few personnel & back it starts on its downward journey. There are no beds or bedding, no conservancy† and no cooking arrangements. Men with fractured thighs are shoved along-

* Sappers and Miners.
† Sanitary arrangements.

side dysentry cases & there they lie till they get to Basra. They're lucky if their wounds are dressed once during the voyage. It is a wicked shame as river transport on a river like the Tigris is the easiest form known. Half a dozen steamers properly equipped & all would be simple. I fear that many poor devils will died [sic] – of wounds officially – really of neglect.

Khalil had withdrawn, not to Es Sinn, but to the Hanna Gap itself, defending a front of only a mile between the marsh and the river on the north bank. Aylmer foresaw a hard slogging match all the way to Es Sinn if he tried to advance on that bank. He was also apprehensive about the arrival of further Turkish divisions to reinforce Khalil. He thought that his progress towards Kut would continue to be slow, and only two weeks remained of the two months for which Townshend had said he had food. He proposed to Nixon that he should use Major General H. D'Urban Keary's 3rd Indian Division, which had now reached the forward area, to 'enfilade' Khalil from the south bank while Townshend broke out of Kut and marched round to join him south of the Es Sinn position. He pointed out that Townshend had said that he had fifty local boats (*muhailas*) with which he could cross the river. Nixon sent a sharp rejoinder, saying, among other things: 'The course you now propose for Townshend ... would be disastrous from every point of view to Townshend, to your force, to the whole force in Mesopotamia and to the Empire, and I can NOT sanction it.' This was followed by a triangular exchange of signals between Nixon, Aylmer and Townshend about the practicality of a breakout, Nixon insisting that, when Aylmer approached Kut, Townshend's force was to stay there. He pressed Aylmer to renew his advance.

Meanwhile the weather was deteriorating, delaying the arrival of reinforcements, and Aylmer's only bridge had been destroyed in an accident with a steamer. Younghusband was then ordered to attack Khalil's position at Hanna, with the support of forty-six guns and those of the gunboats *Crane* and *Dragonfly*.* 21st Brigade had been temporarily disbanded and some of its battalions distributed to the 19th and 35th. The former was to attack on the right with 41st and 37th Dogras, the latter on the left with 2nd Black Watch and 6th Jat Light Infantry.

* Each carried one 4in gun, one 12pdr, one 6pdr and one 2pdr pom-pom.

The Black Watch mustered only 300 rifles, the Jats only 170. There was no opportunity for or attempt at surprise. On 20 January the leading troops closed up to within 600 yards of the Turkish front line, which had been subjected to one hour's bombardment. The assault was timed for dawn on the 21st after a ten-minute artillery programme; but it was delayed again by mist to give the gunners time to register after it had lifted. For all the good they did, it might have been dispensed with. After advancing 200 yards, the Black Watch and Jats met murderous fire and were slaughtered, only two officers and fifteen men of the Black Watch surviving the fight, reducing the whole battalion's strength after the battle to 120. The Dogras of 19th Brigade fared no better, and when the Seaforth joined in, they too were cut to pieces.

Hugh Northcote was wounded and sent a postcard to his father on the 23rd, saying:

> I am all right though slightly hit in the forearm. My regiment was selected to make an attack in front of all. We advanced under cover of night to within 300 yards of the enemy's trench and the next morning tried to charge them out with the bayonet, but they held their position strongly. I got to within about 50 yards when I was knocked down. I managed to roll into a ditch, where I found our C.O. also hit. There was no one in front but the enemy. I managed to crawl down the ditch, which was full of wounded and dead. Every time I raised my head they potted at me, but by luck I got through. It was pelting with rain, and I was soaked and frozen. At night I luckily struck a hospital ship, where I now am quite comfortable. I hope to get back to Basra and shall no doubt be fit again in a fortnight. All this was on January 21 – a nice birthday present!! But when I think of the murderous fire I can only congratulate myself on my extraordinary luck and sympathise with the poor fellows who are so much worse off. Another bullet went through my shirt by my stomach, but for some wonderful reason did not enter my body. Don't worry about me.

Shellfire, mud and general confusion led to a near-total breakdown of communications and, as a consequence, of organization. To cap it all, it poured with rain. When he eventually realized the situation, Aylmer urged Younghusband to renew the attack, but it was just not possible. As it was, the evacuation and treatment of casualties had been over-whelmed, many of them just lying in the mud, and those evacuated by one means or another to the *Julnar* not faring much better. The situation was so distressing that Aylmer asked Khalil for a six-hour truce to bury the dead and collect wounded, many of whom were being robbed and some killed by marauding Arabs, the Turks cooperating in chasing them away.

Major General Arthur Money was Chief of Nixon's General Staff. In a letter to his wife in England, he wrote:

> Aylmer has made a pretty good mess of his relief operations I'm afraid. All previous fighting that we've had here has been fairly expensive in casualties as its [sic] bound to be attacking over open ground without any cover, but its generally had very decisive results on the enemy whereas Aylmer's operations have been more expensive & far less decisive. The weather has been absolutely apalling [sic] too, the rain & storm & yesterday snow. The Tigris is as high as it ever was in the highest part of the flood season (March–July) last year. We have 10,000 troops on the march up absolutely stuck in various places, some columns surrounded entirely by water. They'll just have to wait there till the floods subside & the road gets practicable.

Nixon had been a sick man for some weeks and was succeeded at this moment by the sixty-year-old Lieutenant General Sir Percy Lake, who had been chief of staff to the Commander-in-Chief in India. Money was not entirely sorry to see him go, although, when Nixon had succeeded Barrett, he had written glowingly about him:

> Part of my job is to keep all worry about details from Sir John; he's an excellent man to work with in that he trusts one entirely, & leaves one to run one's own show. He's always thinking and pondering & weighing things himself, though, for he has a very active mind; & often asks me 'What about so & so?' or 'Have you considered the following?' I can generally tell him that what he asks has already been considered and settled.

In a letter sent at the time of Lake's arrival, he wrote: 'He is of course a much nicer personality than Nixon, though not so strong, & without the quickness of military instinct that the latter had.'

Before Lake sailed up the Tigris on 24 January, he learned that, in a signal to Aylmer, Townshend had posed three options: to break out, leaving his sick and wounded behind and spiking his guns: stay where he was, which blocked Turkish use of the river past Kut; or negotiate surrender. Initially he favoured the first, as did Aylmer, who painted a pessimistic picture of his chances of effecting a relief; but, after Lake had signalled that he hoped to relieve him and that therefore the other options were 'unnecessary', Townshend changed his mind and decided 'irrespective of what orders he might get' to 'stay and fight it out in Kut'. As he reported this, he revealed that he had discovered a new source of barley and that, with it and by killing his animals, he could last out for another eighty-four days. Lake received this signal as he set off up river on 24 January to meet Aylmer three days later.

Lake found Aylmer in pessimistic mood. His corps numbered 14,000, still supported by only forty-six guns. Khalil was estimated to have about 10,000 men below Kut with 11,000 above it. It was rumoured that another 36,000 had left the Dardanelles en route for Baghdad. Lake made it clear to Aylmer that he must continue to try and relieve Townshend, and then set off back on 29 January to Basra, where he appointed Gorringe as his chief of staff. There he received the good news that Major General Stanley Maude's 13th Division, the last to leave Gallipoli, was on its way to join him. At the same time the War Office in London announced its intention to take over responsibility for the campaign from the Indian Government.

One matter for decision was whether or not to await the division's arrival before renewing the relief attempt. Townshend's eighty-four days would end in the middle of April and Maude's division was due to start arriving at Basra early in March. Aylmer wanted to wait until the whole division reached him, which would be towards the end of the month; but Lake, anxious about the effect on its move of the annual flooding, gave Aylmer 15 March as the latest date for him to start another attempt. By that time part of the division would be in the process of arriving in the forward area.

Rain poured down for most of February, turning much of the area into a sea of mud and the marshes wetter than ever. Apart from bombarding the Turkish lines at Hanna, no operations were embarked upon. Captain Spackman described conditions inside Kut at that time in his diary entry for 28 February.

We have had rather a trying month with stores running a bit short horse & mule to eat, not so bad as expected; camel one day! We also

shoot rooks & starlings & sparrows for pies – no 'sporting shots'
allowed. You wait till the birds settle at dusk, and then you may get
5 or 6 rooks with one cartridge! Ration is – Fresh meat (horse or
mule) 1lb. Bread 12 oz. Dates 2 oz. Cheese 2 oz. Jam 1 oz. a little tea
salt & ginger as well. The Indian troops are beginning to get Scurvy
& the British Beri-Beri. I go daily into the town to work in the
General Hospital who are short-handed. We got heavily bombarded
one day & had some very narrow escapes an adjacent dug-out was
hit by a 50lb shell & 4 men killed in it. I have many times been
nearly hit. Yesterday my leg was missed by 6 in. & to-day my head
by a bare foot, by casual bullets, but I fancy we shall be relieved soon
now. We have heard their guns for nearly two months & are very
tired of siege conditions.

Aylmer's plan was to move south of the river in an attempt to
outflank the Es Sinn position, attacking and capturing what was believed
to be its most southerly point, the Dujaila Redoubt on the edge of a
depression of that name which extended south from there. Once round
that flank, his forward troops would be only seven miles east of Kut,
from which he expected Townshend, at that juncture, to effect a sortie.

Younghusband, with 19th and 21st Brigades and one regiment of
cavalry, the 16th, was to keep the Turks at Hanna on the north bank
occupied, while Keary, with the 7th and 8th Brigades of his 3rd Indian
Division, supported by thirty-two guns and known as Column C, headed
south-west for thirteen miles to attack the Dujaila Redoubt, and Kimball
with two columns, A (commanded by Brigadier General G. Christian,
consisting of the newly arrived 36th and 37th Indian Infantry Brigades
and 9th Brigade from the 3rd Indian Division, 22,000 men supported by
only 6 guns) and B (commanded by himself, consisting of his own 28th
Brigade with twenty-four guns), moved on the left of C, intending to
pass south of the redoubt and attack the southern tip of the defences.
6th Cavalry Brigade, now commanded by Brigadier General R. C.
Stephens, with four regiments and four guns, would move wider still.
Column B was regarded as corps reserve and would follow A. The
thirteen- to fifteen-mile move south from Hanna to the Dujaila
depression was to take place at night.

Aylmer had intended the operation to start on 6 March, but bad
weather caused him to postpone it for twenty-four hours. There were

more delays in assembling the force and it was not until 21.30 that the night march proper began. It was slow going over unreconnoitred ground with frequent halts to check compass bearings, distance being measured by a surveyor's bicycle wheel, as well as by sergeant majors with pace-sticks. However, the columns had closed up to the Turkish defences by dawn, to find them only lightly occupied, the redoubt itself apparently undefended. Aylmer's plan had stipulated that an artillery bombardment should precede the attack, and, incredibly, as the guns were not yet in position, Kimball asked Aylmer what to do and received the order 'Stick to the programme'. It was not till 10.00 that Column A finally launched its assault after the artillery had caught up, registered its targets and then fired its planned programme. Some guns had arrived earlier and Aylmer ordered them to open fire at 07.00, on the grounds that surprise had already been forfeited. By that time, 10.00, surprise had certainly been lost and Khalil had rushed reinforcements from his reserve position behind Es Sinn to strengthen the defences in and south of the redoubt. The plan had also stipulated that Keary's Column C should wait to attack until Column A showed signs of succeeding. Far from doing so, it met intense fire at short range and suffered heavy casualties. Keary's column, which Aylmer and Gorringe were accompanying, had already been delayed. Aylmer waited for news of success from Kimball, but waited in vain as successive attacks failed at mounting cost. As a last gambler's throw, after all Kimball's effort had been spent, he ordered Keary to launch a direct attack on the redoubt, which was two miles away over open ground. Nevertheless the 1st Manchesters and 59th Royal Scinde Rifles gained a foothold, but were driven out by a fierce counter-attack. Losses were heavy, 8th Brigade losing 1,127 men out of 2,300. Captain C. D. Noyes was serving with the 2nd Rajputs in the brigade and described the action in a letter to his regimental colonel in India, F. A. Smith:

> After a very wearying night march and a day's digging we were sent in to attack the Dijailah redoubt on the Sinn position (6 miles from KUT). Two Brigades before ours had already attacked the Redoubt in the early afternoon and failed to get near it. At 4–30 p.m. we were sent at it to take it at all costs. The Manchesters and 59th were put in the front attacking line – we were in support and the 47th in Brigade Reserve. The ground was a perfect billiard table with no

cover at all for 2 miles. We started off in Artillery formation behind the Manchesters and immediately got heavily shelled and began losing men straight away. After advancing about 100 yards we deployed into line – the men working just like clockwork. We never halted or fired a round during the advance and the men were being knocked over like ninepins from shrapnel, maxims and rifle fire. When we got to within 800 yards of the position we started a steady double – the men cheering like blazes though they were sadly depleted in numbers. We were soon all mixed up with the Manchesters and by the time the Redoubt was reached I don't think there were more than 100 of them and 50 of ours who got into the Turkish Trenches. The turks fled as we got there and there was a little bayonet work when we got into the 2nd Line (to which I did not get). The Turks quickly counter attacked but were killed almost to a man – they then bombed up the communication trenches and we hadn't a Bomb between us. All the members of the Manchesters had been killed or wounded – we never had any. There was no resistance we could put up and they were simply killing us in detail and it was finally decided to retire when it was seen that big preparations were being made for another counter attack. It was just before dark that we retired about 50–100 yards back with the few remaining men – among whom was the Colonel of the Manchesters. I think all of our fellows except myself, Raitt, and Stuart were hit before getting into the Trenches but I have not been able to find out for certain – 10 of us went into action – 6 were killed and 4 wounded. Poor old Landale was hit first in the stomach then twice in the legs – he died next morning after much pain. Skinner suffered terribly too with a stomach wound and died on the retreat next day. The rest I hope died instantaneously, though it is not easy to find out definite details at present. Sispal, Mehrwan, Chatar, Pahal, Shinsihai, Ram Lal, Hira, Shiuji all killed – Indar, Digambar, Puran, Reghubir wounded.* Every man behaved like a hero and I think we've made good for the sins of others – but at what a cost. I am extraordinary lucky to be alive and got only a bayonet wound in the foot from a man in the Manchesters who fell beside me. It is nearly all right. I have just had a bullet taken out of my neck and they had to cut rather deep to get it out. I shall be out in a few days and hope to get back very soon. Shaw was not

* Viceroy's Commissioned Officers.

in action as he was Qr Mr so I suppose now Commands . . . Griffith hit right buttock and left-hand is here doing well, stopping with his brother.

Casualties in the whole force totalled almost 3,500. The cavalry brigade does not appear to have affected the battle in any way and the two weak brigades which Townshend planned to cross the river if Aylmer's men drew near did not budge. That night Kimball's and Keary's men withdrew to where they had been at dawn and trudged their weary way back to south of Hanna next day, harassed by hostile Arabs. The shattered Aylmer was replaced by Gorringe a few days later. Inside Kut, Melliss wrote to his wife on 9 March.

Aylmer has failed allright & has withdrawn to the place on the river where he started from. He reports his casualties heavy & also that the Turks suffered very severe losses getting repeatedly counterattacked & were repulsed. It is sad to think of our poor fellows lives thrown away in a vain effort & that we could not help them. Aylmer says he will try again & hopes to relieve us at an early date. I had a talk with Townsend [sic] & urged him to tell Aylmer not to attempt it again until he had got up every man & gun that there is in the country and to tell him that we are prepared to starve to give him all the time it was possible. I hope he has done so & means to stick to it. Anyhow now the order has gone out to kill all our horses & mules at once except those kept to supply the British & Gurkhas with meat. Our loaf of bread is now 10 oz & the native soldiers rations is 10 oz of barley meal & 4 oz of barley grain for to parch [?] The Chief Doctor says this is his bedrock & we cant go below this. I am not too sure & am going to urge Townshend to look into the matter. On this reduced rations we can last out until 7th April and must then surrender. But I feel we could do on less food than this & so perhaps save another week of *time*. I hate to think of our poor fellows having to attack again until they can do so in great strength & there is most of the English Division & one Indian Division already at Basra & pushing up the river. We must hang on all we can since by starving is the only way we can help them. It is comforting to know that the Turks suffered very heavily.

The new Tigris Corps commander decided to revert to the northern bank for the next attempt, and planned to attack the Turkish position at

Hanna with Maude's 13th Division on 5 April, while the 3rd Division threatened them from the south bank. As Maude launched his attack, the Turks withdrew to their next position at Fallaliyeh, three and a half miles further back. This was attacked by 38th and 39th Brigades soon after dark on the same day, and again the Turks withdrew, but not until they had inflicted significant casualties, a total of 2,000 there and at Hanna. Younghusband's 7th Division was then to pass through the 13th and attack the next position, four miles on, at Sannaiyat in the early hours of 7 April. They were late in starting so that it was full daylight when the leading wave was 800 yards from the Turks, who opened up a murderous fire which brought the attack to a halt at a cost of 1,200 casualties, some of whom were drowned when a strong wind blew water off the marsh to where they fell. Lake and Money narrowly escaped, as the latter described in a letter to his wife on 9 April:

> I was jolly nearly drowned this afternoon, with Sir Percy Lake, his Mil.Sec., A.D.C. & 2 or 3 others. We were trying to cross the river – about 500* [500 yards] wide here – in the motor launch & about ½ way across got into trouble, a heavy southerly wind meeting the strong current was putting up quite big waves. We were eventually carried downstream, dashed into the bridge of boats, through which the water was rushing like a mill stream; the launch swamped & sank, & we all fortunately managed to hold on to ropes hanging from the bridge & crawled up with the assistance of some sepoys on the bridge. It was a merciful escape as no one in his clothes could have swum in the river as it was this afternoon. I was the first up, as I stood over the side of the launch just before it sank & by jumping just managed to reach the side of one of the boats on the bridge – big native boats rather like the large sailing boats on the Hugli. I pulled myself up with the assistance of a sepoy & then pulled Sir Percy & Williams who were hanging on to the same rope that I had got hold of.

Lieutenant Gallup in Kut had heard the gunfire of Gorringe's attack. In his diary he wrote:

> *April 4th.* 122nd day of the siege, so we had now beaten Ladysmith; we hear that rations can only last out until the 15th, another eleven days, and relief seemed as far off as ever.
> *April 5th.* Awakened at dawn by hearing heavy and continuous

gun fire, and later on heard that Gorringe had captured the first five lines of the 'Hannah' position, and everyone was warned to keep handy to their quarters so as to sally forth and lend a hand if necessary: this time our job was to shell the right bank of the river and cover the operation of throwing a bridge across to the south side. The 86th tried to shell the Turkish bridge across the 'Shatt-el-Hai', and by destroying it to prevent the Turks from retreating by that route, but the range was over 10000 and it was also rather windy and they did not achieve much success. On a previous occasion an attempt was made to destroy this bridge by floating a mine down the river from Kut; it was an ingenious concern, and it was expected that the current would carry it down the Hai on to the bridge and so blow it up, but the current played a dirty trick on it and washed it into the bank close to Kut where it blew up with a terrific crash; the only consolation about the whole thing was that there was a Turkish sniper's post just where the accident occurred, and the whole outfit must have gone to glory.

In the previous week Gallup had written:

On March 27th, Tozer came out of hospital where he had been since Dec. 24th. and rejoined us: Flux and I having been alone in the battery since that date. Capt. Dorling now came and took command: this sudden influx of arrivals completely upset our commissariat: we had been saving up, and had quite a decent little store of flour etc, put by in an old ammunition box which should have kept us going fairly well to the end of April: of course these two new arrivals brought nothing with them but a pot of jam which they eat, and we had to divide our store among the four, and it didn't go far: we thus kept our consciences clear but absolutely broke our hearts. I can't tell you how beastly it is to make your breakfast off a plate of indifferent horse or mule and a diminutive piece of bread, and then spend the better part of the morning on the roof of a dilapidated old house in a hot sun watching some rotten guns, and then get back to one's dugout about 2 p.m. finding it cram full of flies, and have another piece of old mule: no tea: and dinner, roast or minced horse and the balance of your piece of bread, and for pudding a very small 'Kabob' made of flour and fried in horse fat: as to the 'Kabobs', I can certainly say that the only fault with them was their size. At times I used to simply long for a piece of chocolate or a tinned apple pudding, and used to sleep at night planning how, when I got home, I would always keep a store of tinned food and chocolate in a cupboard in my smoking room so as to be able to help myself when ever I was hungry. Especially 'Horlick's Milk Tablets', these I vowed should always stand on my desk. It is extraordinary how the idea of food absolutely obsesses one when you can't get any. But I suppose I am a greedy devil.

Gorringe decided to try again with the 13th Division at dawn on the 9th. They succeeded in gaining the first line of the defences, but counter-attacks, in which the Turks made great use of hand grenades, drove the British soldiers out, inflicting 1,600 casualties on them, five of whom were awarded Victoria Crosses.

Gorringe's freedom of action was now seriously restricted by flooding. He decided to switch his effort to the south bank, using the 3rd Division to capture the next position, Bait Aisa. At first they were successful, but counter-attacks led to fierce fighting at close quarters, and they were driven out, having lost 1,150 men, but having inflicted, it was believed, about 4,000 on the Turks.

Major Catty described this operation in his diary for 22 April:

On 19th we woke up to find that the Turks had abandoned the Chahela position & our patrols occupied their trenches without opposition. Strong patrols were pushed forward to the Sinn line & fired on them from the Sinn Aftar redoubt. As the Turks were evidently going the Corps Comd. ordered 3rd Div: to concentrate & with Cav: Bde & 36th Bde to make a reconnaissance in force against the Dujaila. The concentration was completed by 10 pm & at 5 am 20th the advance started. It was found that the Dujailah was unoc-cupied so leaving a Bde there (9th Bde) the rest of the Div: pushed forward to Imam al Mansur tomb 6 miles further on. The advanced guard got in about 2 pm but the last of the transport did not arrive till nearly midnight.

It was a blazing hot day – 107 degrees by the river was official temperature – & no water was found en route. With their heavy full marching order, the men felt the heat terribly – up to Dujailah only a few fell out but the second half of the march – done during the hottest part of the day – was disasterous [sic]. The road was strewn with men in the last stages of exhaustion. Approximately 600 fell out

& the rest were so bad that they couldn't have done anything had we been attacked. It is reported that 500 Turks were in Sinn Aftar when we advanced but fled without firing a shot.

On arrival at Imam al Mansur the wells were found to be dry & the river 5 miles off. All water bottles and pakhals* were of course dry & men were offering 2 Rs for a glass of water. Animals were sent down to the river & motor lorries with a certain amount of water arrived. The River stunt soon broke down tho' as the Turks started shelling & hit a few people & animals.

Nothing happened that night altho' we fully expected to be sniped & next morning early we all marched to the river at Magasis & took up a line West of Es Sinn from Magasis fort to Dujailah Redoubt. 3 Bdes in the front line & one in Reserve was the distribution. What the reason for the long & exhausting march to Imam al Mansur on 20th was I dont know. It achieved nothing & so knocked up the division that for days after it wasn't worth a damn. Had we left the Cav: to push on to the Hai R when we found Dujailah empty & turned N up the position all would have been well as we should have avoided the night without water. I shan't forget that march for a long time, its one of the worst I've ever done. As a military operation it was a fiasco as it achieved nothing but as a test of endurance it was pretty severe. It cost I should think at least 20 lives.

As is usually the case in this country our advance was rushed & so nearly all the bundobust [sic: see glossary] broke down. A lot of men started with half empty water bottles & the food supply arrangements were incomplete, consequently on 21st there was no grain for animals & as the convoy did not arrive till 22nd morning, the poor beasts had nothing for 24 hours. All bad bundobust. It's the same everytime.

Gorringe now decided to switch back to the north bank, ordering the 7th Division, reinforced by 35th and 36th Brigades, to renew the attack on Sannaiyat on 20 April. Again filthy weather forced a forty-eight-hour postponement, but the weather was no better when the attack was launched at 07.00 on the 22nd after a half-hour artillery programme. The assaulting troops were from 19th and 21st Brigades, the former bearing the brunt as the latter reported that, owing to the waterlogged

---

* Canvas water bags.

ground, they could not move. The leading battalion of 19th Brigade was the 1st Seaforth, who fought fiercely in the mud, suffering heavily, especially when they were driven back by counter-attacks. The attack petered out after the brigade had lost 1,300 men. That was the last attempt to get through to Kut, except for a gallant but desperate attempt by Lieutenant H. O. B. Firman RN and Lieutenant Commander Cowley in the paddle steamer *Julnar*, carrying 270 tons of supplies. Armour-plated and sandbagged, they forced their way upstream through the Es Sinn position, but were stopped at Magasis, four miles below Kut, by a steel hawser stretched across the river. Most of the crew were either killed or wounded, the survivors being taken prisoner. Cowley was summarily shot.

Two days before that, Townshend had suggested to Lake that negotiations should be opened with the Turks for an honourable capitulation of his garrison, and that Lake should negotiate it with Khalil. He envisaged the garrison marching out with colours flying on condition that those who did so would not fight the Turks again as long as the war lasted. Lake agreed to obtain the permission of the Indian Government, but ruled that it should be Townshend, not himself, who negotiated it. Accordingly the latter asked Khalil on 26 April for a six-day armistice and for Gorringe to be allowed to send in ten days' supply of food for the garrison while surrender terms were negotiated. Khalil courteously agreed and met Townshend on a launch one and a half miles upstream of Kut, where he demanded unconditional surrender. Townshend tried to bargain, offering a large sum in gold in return for more lenient terms. Khalil rejected that, but suggested that some compromise might be possible. Townshend consulted Lake, who suggested that he offer his guns as well as money and an exchange of prisoners as the price of the garrison being allowed to go to India. Accordingly Townshend offered £1m sterling, fifty undamaged guns and an assurance that none of the garrison would fight the Turks again. According to the Germans, Khalil was prepared to accept that, but Enver demanded nothing less than unconditional surrender, although, in exchange for the guns and money, he was prepared to let Townshend himself go free. That naturally was rejected. The garrison then started to dump ammunition in the river and destroy all the equipment and stores that they could.

Lieutenant Gallup described this:

When these orders arrived I was at once sent off down to the horse lines to see that all the saddlery, harness etc., was destroyed this being done I took a fatigue party of drivers armed with axes or any old thing and went round to the walled enclosure where the various batteries kept their first line ammunition wagons and G.S. wagons during the siege; we set to to work on our own wagons and damaged them as much as possible by breaking the spokes of the wheels etc, eventually lighting fires and pushing them on to them, so there wasn't much left of them by the time we had finished ... This job being satisfactorily accomplished I returned to the battery and arrived there just as Flux had returned from the R.E. Field Park with the charges of gun cotton for destroying the guns; Dorling then cleared all the gunners out of the nullah and made them take cover in the communication trench running at right angles up to the Kiln and then set about the work in hand: he started on my left hand gun, and when he had inserted the gun cotton and lit the fuze we at once hid in the adjacent trench, and in about a minute it went off with a nice dignified bang and split the outer jacket; however as this was not deemed sufficient another charge was inserted and the gun was blown in half. No 3 was then taken in hand which happened to be loaded with lyddite: the charge of gun cotton being inserted and the fuze lit we again most carefully hid ourselves, a bit more carefully than before and a bit further off, as we were not certain how the lyddite and the gun cotton would agree; we seemed to wait for quite a long time while the fuze was burning down, but when it *did* go off the mixture was apparently alright, and it made a most heavenly crash which must have been heard many miles away; we remained in the trench for quite an appreciable time while bits of gun were whirring about in the air and then went down to the pit to see what had happened. There was not a vestige of the gun left; the breech block had been blown into the parados and the rest had gone to glory in bits, wheels and everything, only a small piece of the trail remaining. We heard later on that the larger part of one of the guns had been blown clean over the town.

The actual surrender took place on 29 April, Brigadier General Delamain having to preside over it as the two officers senior to him, Major Generals Townshend and Melliss, were both sick. The latter wrote to his wife on the 29th:

T sent in his formal surrender of Kut this morning. We have been destroying our guns & rifles ammunition etc even my old revolver. We are to be moved on to camp some 5 miles upstream & evacuate Kut but this to be done in steamers – we couldn't walk besides are shut in by floods. T is allowed on parole to Constantinople & hopes to get to London on parole & work on ransom. Lucky beggar anyhow to get out of this – of course I succeed him but am at present too seedy – the jaundice is still on me I feel so rotten but am on the mend. It is so wretched to be ill at such a time. I feel I want to be up & at T's elbow urging & advising though there is after all nothing to be done now – we are 'in the soup'! I sent you a wireless last night which I hope you will get Charley little K to help cheer you up. My cloud has its silver lining – things perhaps may mend for me. Anyhow Khalil is a gentleman & says we shall be treated as their 'most sincere & precious guests' as the Russians treated Osman Pasha after his glorious stand at Plevna. I hope I shall be able to get this letter to you somehow darling girl. I have tried to get to Baghdad 3 times! It looks as if I were going to get there this time allright!!

Captain Cardew was greatly upset at having to burn his precious belongings, as he described:

Everything of any value at all was thrown onto this fire. And last of all, with much sadness of heart. I had to throw onto the fire my valuable 12 power Goertz Field Glasses given to me by my mother in 1903. I also had to burn my new telescope, a beauty which I bought from Aitchisons in London with a top draw by means of which magnifications of 25, 30, 35 & 40 diameters could be obtained. This telescope had been invaluable to me during the whole campaign & especially during the siege. I also had to burn all my War Diaries & Maps I had made, my own compass, saddlery & my revolver. I often wonder now if I shall ever get the full value of these things out of the Indian Government. I only hope so. We had been told that our swords would be returned to us – a minor Turkish promise – of course they weren't, & I was a mug to hand mine in, instead of putting it where I'd put my field glasses.

13,309 men gave themselves up, 3,248 being Indian non-combatants. Of the 10,061 combatants, 277 were British and 204 Indian officers, 2,592 British and 6,988 Indian other ranks. 1,456 were sick: of these

1,136 were exchanged and sent down to Basra by boat: 345 others went by boat to Baghdad, from where they were sent to Basra by boat three months later. All the rest had to march to Baghdad, and from there faced a grim journey all the way to Anatolia, where they suffered two and half years of cruelty and neglect in disgraceful conditions of imprisonment. 209 of the British prisoners were exchanged and 1,700 died or were never traced. Of the Indians, 1,300 died and 1,100–1,200 were exchanged or escaped. The remainder were repatriated at the end of the war or were presumed dead. Townshend himself was treated as an honoured guest. In Baghdad he stayed in the house of von der Goltz, who had died there four days previously, and travelled by road and rail, in comparative comfort, accompanying the general in his coffin, to Constantinople, where he was met by a high-ranking reception party and accommodated in the former British Consul's summer residence. The officers were treated better than the men both on the march and when they reached their final destination. The first leg, from Baghdad to Samarra, was done by rail, as Captain Cardew related:

We were put into 3rd Class Carriages, about 8 to a compartment. The Generals were given 1st Class carriages, the Colonels & Majors 2nd Class. We were able to buy bread & types of 'fancy bread' off Arabs who brought it to the train on flat baskets. The orderlies were seated on open wagons. In the brake of our train was the body of General Von-der-Goltz who had died in Bagdad a few days previously from 'spotted fever'.

After Samarra they had to march, their kit being loaded on to donkeys. Lieutenant Gallup described his experience:

It is quite unnecessary to go into the details of every march, they were all much the same; some longer than others, but all very weary-some. Our marches were always done for a few hours after daybreak, from 5 to about 10 a.m., averaging about 3 miles an hour; a ten minute halt being made at the end of every hour to avoid straggling; and then a most dreary, ghastly *rest* during the heat of the day, and then we would go on again at 5 in the evening for another 3 or 4 hours, and then sleep, and then on again at the following dawn: once or twice we bought a piece of sheep from Arabs and stewed it: we might just as well have stewed my valise straps as far as eating it went; but it made jolly good broth: we also got plenty of eggs and sour cream, and chupratties and things of that sort, so we fed quite well, but for all the evilly disposed things that were ever invented to add to the trials of suffering humanity, commend to me a plateful of semiboiled rice before starting on a long march: the infernal stuff swells and swells and goes on swelling, and one soon begins to wear the preoccupied and agonised look of a poisoned pup: perfectly awful.

He described arriving at Mosul on 25 May:

We were marched to the barracks, a large stone building in the form of a quadrangle, much similar to those at Baghdad, only there appeared to be less discipline and many more fleas; I need hardly say that there is no furniture of any sort whatever in these various barracks, nor any water laid on, but at Mosul we were each given a reed mat, which makes a stone floor much more comfortable, and if by any chance you wanted a wash, you could get a bucket of water from a well in the courtyard and please yourself: except for shelter from the sun during the day these abodes are not much catch, and I far preferred the nights slept out in the open by the wayside, where peace and quiet always reigned, and a stream gave one a chance of a decent wash: of course, if there *wasn't* a stream, and only a nasty dirty waterhole to even get drinking water from it was rather a nuisance, but these trivial matters have to be overlooked at times. On several occasions during a night's march we used to try and listen for the sound of frogs croaking, because although it probably meant swamp, it also meant water.

On our arrival at Mosul we lunched on the large store of provisions we always carried in our haversacks; much the same arrangements for our feeding were made with a cross-eyed contractor, as at Baghdad and the food turned up in the evening, at least, a small quantity did, but it was such a generally hopeless scramble, and all round almighty failure that the next day we were taken out in batches under a guard and might feed at either one of two little restaurants close by; we were also allowed out in a similar manner in the bazaar, and bought odds and ends for our next march, such as raisins, figs, gram [chick peas] etc. A supply of tea and rice and flour were sent to our quarters, of which we could purchase sufficient for our wants in the immediate future.

During the short stay here we received a visit from Enver Pasha who was on a tour of inspection: he made us a speech of welcome and trusted that we should bear no malice, but rather that we should consider ourselves as the precious guests of Turkey. We felt like it . . . Flux and I had been travelling together and sharing donkeys.

The next stage of the march was 210 miles from Mosul to Rees-al-Ain, the railhead, from which they went by train to their final destination of Yozgat, a hundred miles east of Ankara. Gallup's account continues:

We now left the Tigris and travelled in a more westerly direction, this stage of our journey being done in carts, one of which was allotted to every six officers; these carts had no spring or brakes and were merely light four wheeled wagons drawn by two skinny ponies and driven by government drivers: they just held our kits, and three of us perched on the top; Flux and I here joined in with the four officers of the V.A.B [Volunteer Artillery Battery], and shared a cart with them, and as we each had an orderly, we were twelve to a cart: this meant that we could get a lift for three miles out of every twelve, but then marches were not nearly so long or tiring as on the previous stage, and we seldom did more than four hours at a stretch, night and morning: the track was good walking, but we seemed to come down into somewhat lower ground, and the days were very hot. As soon as we halted at the end of a march the carts were all packed in two rows, and everybody at once rigged up any sort of shelter from the sun with sticks and a blanket, or tied a rug on to the side of their cart, the orderlies boiling tea and eggs or anything we had, sometimes that evil rice, and the amount of almonds and raisins and hard boiled eggs consumed was perfectly appalling.

They reached Yozgat on 30 June, Gallup recording in his diary:

On our arrival, the twenty three senior officers were put into one house, and the fifty two juniors into another, the two houses being separated by a narrow lane; no furniture of any sort; mattresses and resais [counterpanes] and pillows, mostly unclean, were supplied to us at our own cost; the water supply consisted of a trickle of water from a pipe in the yard, and this was all there was for washing, cooking, and drinking purposes. For lunch we were taken under guard to the senior officers house and fed in two batches, on onion soup, goat and apricots, and much the same for dinner; our daily breakfast consisted of a small loaf of bread, two eggs, and a small glass of milk and water; a fairly stiff payment was deducted for these meals from our pay when it arrived on Sept. 8th. extras, such as honey, butter, fruit, wine could be purchased from the contractor. Except for going from one house to the other for meals, we were strictly confined until July 19th when we were *all* allowed to walk up and down the narrow passage for an hour! our houses were guarded by some ancient old sportsman [sic] in uniform with still more ancient rifles.

8

Kut Avenged

Whatever the failures and disappointments of the operations to relieve Kut, some credit must go to Lake for having got to grips with the chaos at the logistic base round Basra. Matters were beginning to improve just as the operations ignominiously petered out. One of the most important steps was the appointment on 15 April 1916 of Major General G. F. MacMunn as Inspector-General of Communications. Other changes among senior officers followed. On 16 July Lake ordered Gorringe, who was showing signs of strain, to go to England for a rest, Maude taking over Tigris Corps and being replaced in command of 13th Division by Major General W. de S. Cayley. A month later Lake himself was replaced by Maude, Lieutenant General Sir Alexander Cobbe VC taking over the corps, renamed 1st Indian Army Corps. Within it, the 36th and 37th Brigades joined the 35th (which had been in 7th Division) to form 14th Indian Division, commanded by Major General R. G. Egerton.

Maude's directive from Robertson at the War Office, cabled to him on 16 September, read:

> The Mission of the Mesopotamia Expeditionary Force is to protect Oil Fields and Pipe Lines in the vicinity of the Karun river, to maintain our occupation and control of the Basra Vilayet, and to deny hostile access to the Persian gulf and southern Persia. At present no fresh advance to Baghdad can be contemplated, but it is the desire of His Majesty's Government, if and when possible, to establish British influence in the Baghdad Vilayet. This further advance should not be undertaken unless and until sanction for it is given ... No further reinforcements for the force must be expected. On the contrary it may become necessary to withdraw the 13th Division which was sent to Mesopotamia in order to assist in the attempted relief of Kut-el-Amara.

However, Maude was not content that, with 150,000 men, about half of whom were in the forward area, he should remain totally passive. In

November he moved his headquarters up to join the corps, intent on at least forcing the Turks out of Kut. For this operation he divided the force into two corps: the 1st Indian Army Corps, commanded by Cobbe, responsible for all troops facing the Sannaiyat position on the north bank, most of them in the 7th Division, now commanded by Major General Sir Vere Fane; and, south of the river, the 3rd Indian Army Corps, commanded by Lieutenant General W. M. Marshall, who had commanded 87th Brigade in 29th Division at Gallipoli. He would have under command Cayley's 13th and Egerton's 14th Divisions and a cavalry division of two brigades (6th and 7th), commanded by Major General S. F. Crocker. This corps would move widely round south of the Es Sinn position, to cross the Shatt-al-Hai and attack Kut from the west, or at least force the withdrawal of all the Turks in Kut and east of it. One of his problems was that the rainy season was imminent, which would flood most of the area. By this time Khalil Pasha had handed over command of the Turkish troops in Kut and to the east of it, thought to number about 10,000, to Kiazim Karabekir, while he himself, back at Baghdad, entertained grand ideas of an offensive through Persia to the Gulf, brushing aside the Russian corps under General Baratoff, which had been stuck for some time between Kermanshah and Jebel Hamrin, the mountains on the Persian border, where it faced a Turkish corps commanded by the able Ali Ihsam Bey.

While Cobbe's artillery pounded the Turks at Sannaiyat, Marshall's corps set off on the night of 13/14 December, reaching the Shatt-al-Hai a few miles south of the Turkish defences on that side of the Tigris without incident, the cavalry and the leading brigade of 13th Division, Brigadier General A. C. Lewin's 40th, crossing it at dawn, while its 38th and 39th Brigades turned north on the east side of the Shatt. While 40th Brigade turned north also, the cavalry continued to the loop of the river at Shurman, four miles ahead and some seven upstream of the town of Kut. But, having got within a few hundred yards of a Turkish pontoon bridge, Crocker decided that his horses needed watering, and he trotted all the way back to the Shatt. Over the next few days 38th and 39th Brigades closed up to the Turkish defences south of the river and gradually nibbled away at them. On 20 December 35th Brigade from the 14th Division joined 40th Brigade and the cavalry, escorting a bridging train to a site on the west side of the Shurman loop, but did not make a serious attempt to erect it against opposition in pouring rain. Two days later 3rd Indian Division, with its 8th and 9th Brigades, launched an attack against the Turkish defences east of the Shatt below Kut, but did not make any progress, resuming it on 7 January.

Major Catty described their attack in his diary of 16 January:

Things have moved a bit in the last fortnight & the old 3rd Div: have been very much in the lime light. Having failed to cross the river GHQ decided to take on the Turks in the ABDUL HASSAN bend & told off 3rd Div: for the job. The 8th & 9th Bde started sapping up towards the first line early in the new year & by 8th were within 250 yds of the Turkish front line. It was by no means an easy job as the country was open & the enemy on the qui vive [alert]; before assaulting distance was reached the Div: had nearly 400 casualties.

9th was fixed for the assault & in order to divert the Turks attention the 7th Div: made a raid at 5 am at Sannayat. At 9.15 am the attack was launched the plan being to seize the Western half of the enemy's front line & consolidate inside it. All went splendidly, 1st Gurkhas & 105 MLI [Mahrattas] of 9th Bde & Manchesters of 8th Bde got in with little opposition & proceeded to consolidate & bomb onwards. 100 odd prisoners were taken & all seemed well. It was a very misty day & hard to see more than 100–150 yds. Under cover of the mist the Turks massed for a counter attack & launched it about an hour or so after the assault. It struck the line midway between 8 & 9 Bdes & at first forced it back a bit. The 59th Rifles were thrown in against it & after a bit the enemy were forced back but not before severe hand to hand fighting & close range bombing had taken place. A Company of 59th Rifles dont seem to have done very well tho' exactly what happened is hard to say – anyhow their S.M. [Subadar Major] was put under arrest by the C.O. (Stirling) on the battle field & the whole Regt had to be put in to restore the fight. During it Stirling their C.O. was killed – a great loss to the Battn. As a result of the counterattack some parties of Manchesters got cut off & it was not till late in the afternoon that the situation was properly cleared up.

The result of the day was most satisfactory we had taken half the Turks front line & were established well inside it. 500 dead Turks were counted whilst 2 Trench Mortars & 3 Machine guns were captured. Our losses were 700 all in. Next day 10th our bombing parties pushed on whilst on the right the whole of the enemy's first line was seized & consolidated. There was comparatively little fighting

& our casualties were only 50 odd. On the 11th we again pushed forward & everything seemed to be going tophole. The Turks appeared to be penned up in a small space & at midday it was reported that only a few disorganized men remained. The operation seemed over, 13th Div: Gunner Liaison Officer went back & Div: left the clearing up to Col Anderson with 9th Bde. A fatal mistake as the Turks during the night had ferried across a fresh Regt. (43rd) & relieved the old 142nd who had only 200 men left. They evidently contemplated a counter attack as guns were massed on either side of the bend. It was a typical case of being caught bending. At 2.30 pm the final assault by H.L.I. [Highland Light Infantry] was launched & at once ran into a very heavy Artillery enfilade fire. It got into the Turkish Trench but never had a chance as it was counterattacked by vastly superior force & driven back to its starting point in confusion. The price too was very heavy 15 Officers & 200 odd men – a high proportion of Officers.

On their right 2/124th Baluchs Inf advanced & met with a similar fate. The Mahomedans of this Unit don't appear to have done well & some are said to have thrown down their arms. However the Turks weren't taking prisoners & bayonetted the lot. It was a real bad show as the enemy scored all round – the one bright spot was that the Turks on the right ran into a strongpoint held by 47th Sikhs with 2 machine guns and took it in the neck. Our guns also got into them as they retired. The losses during the day were about 650 whilst it is doubtful if the Turks lost as many. A real bad show wh: might have been avoided.

Maude was anxious to prevent Turkish forces further down the river from returning to reinforce Kut, and ordered Cobbe to 'raid' Sannaiyat. It proved a total waste of life, almost all the raiding parties being lost and achieving nothing. Attacks by 13th Division east of the Shatt and 14th west of it continued for the rest of January and up to 15 February, by which time the Turks had been driven out of all their defences at Kut south of the river. Lance-Sergeant J. W. Farnol was commanding 12 Platoon of C Company of the 1/5th Buffs in 35th Brigade of 13th Division and was watching the attack of 39th Brigade to his right on 25 January. He wrote an account later following his return to India after contracting malaria:

The Turks realizing the damage done by our little trench Howitzers just in rear of our trench & seeing where the bombs were coming from, had opened fire on us with shrapnel. Most of these shells were timed to burst in the air & timed accurately at that & we were peppered with balls about the size of a marble, & in consequence sustained a number of casualties. One little fellow – the wit of the platoon – I remember, stopped one of these right on the top of the head & had a real nasty head wound. Poor little chap, he heeded not the painful wound but grabbed his haversack & a dirty piece of bread and rushed down the trench shouting 'Cheerio boys I'm off for a long rest' the blood streaming down his face alarmingly. About this time our own gun fire had almost died right down though Turkoman was still busy. Our bombers could be seen working their way up the trenches placing little red & yellow flags here & there to mark their progress for the artillery observers to mark in case of accident. Our casualties must have been frightful but the Turks must have suffered even worse owing to the intensity of the barrage. We viewed all this from a distance of 200 yards, no more, perhaps less. We had no doubt but that we had sprung a complete surprise on the enemy...

About 2 p.m. we were alarmed by the machine gun officer rushing past us & looking greatly agitated. 'How are things going, sir' I said 'My God, they are bombing our fellows out' was his reply as he dashed away. A series of dull reports could then be heard & which we knew to be those of bursting bombs. On jumping on the fire step I saw to my horror the enemy bombers making a determined assault on our chaps. The attackers seemed to resemble very devils as they hurled their bombs & I saw the havoc they were playing. Our chaps were being blown sky high! & were retiring for their lives as rapidly as possible. When I say retiring for their lives I must say also that I don't think it was fear in fact am assured that this was not the case. It was quite evident that instead of having bombed up the whole system of trenches they had left various communication trenches unsearched & were in danger of being cut off. The enemy observers on seeing the plight of the 39th brigade & that they were retiring, caused a curtain of heavy H.E. shells to be raised between our line & theirs to catch the retiring waves. It was a cruel awful sight. Our fellows went down like ninepins as they passed through it. At this moment I heard a groan from the next fire bay & on going round the traverse saw the O.C. machine Gun Coy lying flat with blood streaming from his head, a pair of binoculars hanging round his head with the left hand lens smashed completely. He had been observing for his guns & had been shot straight through the left eye as he had his glasses up, the bullet having passed right through the right [substituted for 'left', crossed out] lens, His case was hopeless of course as the bullet went clean through the brain & yet he was living and groaning pitifully. He was a Boer & had fought against us in S. Africa but was a jolly old chap & a brave one. This had a most disheartening effect on us one & all. We had entirely evacuated the position, &, after all our sacrifices. We were then informed that the 36th Brigade of our own division (the 14th) was to attack at dusk that evening & attempt to recover the lost position, but finally it was postponed to take place next morning.

Also in 1/5th Buffs was Lieutenant K. R. Scarr, who wrote to his mother from hospital at Amara on 17 February:

Of course you will have heard some time ago that I have been 'wounded slightly'. Besides, I sent a cable yesterday. By the time you get this, I expect I shall be with the Buffs in the line again, as it really is a 'cushy' one. A sniper in the trees around Kut-el-Amara got me through the fleshy part of the right thigh as I was strolling along the top of a trench on Thursday morning [later in the letter he writes Tuesday, i.e. 13 February]. The bullet went through my lower tunic pocket, through some letters and a photo (enclosed) and down through the inside of my thigh. Luckily I had my right leg forward or I might have had both legs hit. Looking at it all round, you must agree it was a very lucky one.

I needn't tell you what a relief it is to get out of it for a bit. You don't realise what a strain it is until you get out of it, though I must say, I don't like having to leave some of the fellows with whom I have spent such good – and bad – times. The few days before I was hit were some of the most exciting I've ever had and that's saying something.

To begin with, Friday Feb. 9th we moved out of rest camp for the trenches and that night we heard we were going to attack next morning and our company (C) was to lead. Harry Filmer of ours was to take the first platoon over and I was to take the second (my own platoon of course) with the bombers. Perhaps I had better explain more fully. Two companies were to go over at first and they were to go, a platoon at a time, 50 yards behind one another i.e. in 8 lines, so I had the honour of taking the second line in. We were to 'hop the parapet' at 8.34 a.m. to the tick – or rather Filmer was to and I was to follow 50 yards behind and so on.

Can you imagine our thoughts that night? We had already assisted in four attacks, but had never been the first 'over' and knew only too well what it was like. It was a very cold night and our coats and blankets had been left behind so that we could go in lightly equipped. However, I managed to pinch a dead Punjabi's coat and slept like a top from the time I came off watch, 1.15 a.m. till 5.15 a.m., when 'Daddy' Howell, our company commander, woke me. I think that was perhaps the worst time, that waking up on the fire step and realising where we were. Strange to say; from then right up to the time we went over, I hardly gave a thought to the 'nasty side'. I had no time to, what with issuing bombs and giving final instructions and getting the men into position. At 8.30 the 'intense bombardment' began and we were all ready. It is no use trying to describe an 'intense bombardment', but those four minutes were awful. Then at last I saw old Filmer up and his men after him, walking mind you, we were not to run till the last bit. Ten – twenty – thirty yards they went and still no one had gone down and there seemed to be hardly any fire against us. Forty – fifty yards – 'Come on No. 12!' I yelled and over we went! Oh my word! Those first few moments in the open! We soon shook out into a good line and went walking on, expecting every moment to hear the 'swish, swish, swish' of the bullets. But no! There were the Turk trenches 400 yards in the front, simply one mass of leaping earth. I looked round and saw wave after wave of our boys coming on as though on a ceremonial parade. I was on the left of my line with the bombers. I looked along occasionally and their dressing was perfect! And so we went on until Filmer reached within fifty yards of the Turk trenches, when we clutched our rifles and bayonets a little harder and went 'all out'.

As you have probably guessed by now, we found only a few Turks who surrendered at once. The rest had cleared out during the night, a favourite trick of theirs. My job had only just begun though, as I had taken the bombers along to the flank to get in touch with the brigade on our left. However we managed that just as easily, finding only one dead Turk 'en route'. The Lancashires congratulated us on the way we 'went over'. 'Jolly fine. It was like a parade step,' they said, whereat our tails went up at least 20 degrees more. We lost only six men and an officer wounded. He is in hospital here now. The

Ghurkas on our right were equally lucky. But for all that, *we* didn't know we weren't going to find anyone waiting for us and we should have 'gone over' in just the same style. Of that I am sure ... Then on Tuesday morning [13 February] I 'got it' and to tell the truth I was very glad. I was a 'wee bit tired' and was very pleased at the thought of a rest.

Maude now decided to have another go at Sannaiyat, actuated primarily, perhaps, by a desire to open up the river. He had intended it to be synchronized with an attack across the river above Kut, but flooding prevented that and he decided that Cobbe's attack at Sannaiyat should go ahead on 17 February. The ground was only too familiar to 7th Division's 21st Brigade, two of whose battalions were to launch it, and to 19th Brigade, which was to follow through. It followed a familiar pattern. The initial attack was successful, but a counter-attack, inflicting 500 casualties, threw the troops back to their start line. Maude now decided to do what one might have expected him to do in the first place: to make a serious attempt to cross the river from south to north above Kut at the obvious place, the Shurman loop. He planned that Marshall should attempt this on 23 February, while Cobbe once again attacked Sannaiyat. 14th Division was chosen for the crossing, Brigadier General O. W. Carey's 37th Indian Brigade to carry out the assault, supported by all the artillery available, and Brigadier General L. B. Walton's 36th Brigade to follow through.

Marshall wanted the crossing to be made by night, but Egerton persuaded him that half an hour before first light was preferable. Cobbe's attack at Sannaiyat was launched six hours before that. As before, it was initially successful and then counter-attacked, but, after a ding-dong battle, 21st and 28th Brigades held their ground. 37th Brigade's first pontoons entered the water on the Shurman bend, where the river was 400 yards wide, at 05.15 at three different sites, 2nd Norfolks at No. 1, 2/9th Gurkhas at No. 2 and 1/2nd Gurkhas at No. 3. In the face of considerable small arms and artillery fire, all were eventually successful, and by 16.00 a pontoon bridge had been completed. Lieutenant R. B. Woakes of 13 Company of the 2nd Queen Victoria's Own Sappers and Miners was involved in the bridging operation, as his diary records:

February 22nd. [19]17. Early morning orders came to say show is for tonight with the original scheme of 3 ferries. Spent the morning distributing extra pontoons. General 'pow-wow' with Pemberton & all concerned. Marched off company at 3.30 PM with 1st line transport only & pontoons. Halted at Q13–Q15 road where 1/9th Gurkhas, Hants rowing parties & 15 Coy S & M detachment joined us. Started off in column of route at 6 PM. a Turk plane came over & we all thought the show must have been spotted – halted twice & finally reached M29 where Pemberton Maunsell & self went forward to reconnoitre. Goepel & Todd brought up the company & pontoons later. We had some trouble in finding telephone line to Ferry Master's dug-out. Unloaded at end of sunken road & got the pontoons carried out onto the beach – all quite quiet so decided to carry the pontoons down at once to within 10 yds of the water – this accomplished by 1 AM without incident – very hard work for our men & they are all pretty done ... I got about an hour's sleep but damnably cold. Opposite bank looks a very long way off in this light & the river is making a lot of noise – Turks evidently not spotted us at all.

February 23rd –17. Woke up about 5 AM, woke up our men & got the Gurkhas & Hants out & at 5.30 AM to the tick started launching pontoons – this took a little longer than I expected but by 5.45 AM had pushed off all 13 boats. No shots fired until about two-thirds of the way across – then pretty heavy rifle fire & bombs – however fire seemed rather erratic as most of the bullets seemed to come over us. Maunsell killed early in the morning & Mainwaring wounded about the same time. Hell of a morning, bullets flying freely all the time & we were shelled continuously. Saw a lot of our pontoons drifting downstream – & one hit fair by a shell which disappeared completely – one machine gun in particular did us in badly. Very few pontoons came back to this bank & we were finally held up by having empty pontoons on the opposite bank with no one to row them back & no pontoons on this side – at the last I was loading up pontoons with extra rowers instead of reinforcements for the infantry. The Hants rowers were splendid & Hamilton & Jetson in charge of them did magnificent work. Finally decided to move our ferrying back to No 1 Ferry where things were now much quieter & accordingly towed down what pontoons we had to there & restarted work. Soon got the empty pontoons back from opposite bank & more ferrying hard all afternoon & we got over all the remainder of the 1/2nd Gurkhas & 1/9th Gurkhas & the whole of the 67th Punjabis by 4.30 PM at which time the bridge which was started at 8AM was

open for traffic – ferrying consequently ceased. Turks crumped us at
the bridge head all the evening but failed to hit the bridge. Conran
who had been sick in bed & who came out to see how things were
going was badly hit by one of these – I was also told that Pemberton
was badly hit by the same shell but this was a false alarm. Finally we
all collected & made a sort of camp in a nullah. Absolutely dead tired
& slept like a log all night in spite of no blankets & a battery of 18
pdrs in action just behind us. Our casualties to-day were 30, 13 Coy
about 27 & the Hants 100.

By this time Kiazim Karabekir had decided to withdraw. By the end
of the day 7th Division found that the Turks had also done so from
Sannaiyat. At Shurman it was a race to see if 14th Division and the
cavalry could cut the Turkish line of retreat from Kut before the enemy
got away. By the end of the 24th its leading troops were close to the
road, where Kiazim Karabekir's rearguard successfully held them off
until he had got all his men in Kut and to the east of it away. The
cavalry were sent over the bridge at 09.00 on the 24th to head them off,
but signally failed to do so, either on their own or in cooperation with
Cayley's 13th Division, which was sent across to follow up the withdrawal. But it was not all easy going. Farnol, promoted full sergeant and
transferred to command 16 Platoon in D Company of the 1/5th Buffs,
described his day:

I was watching the effect of the enemy shells which were following a
group of ammunition mules which group was gradually closing in
on us & as it did so the shells followed so close to me now that I
thought the next 4 would just about put the finishing touch on 16
Platoon for good & myself as well. But just then a perfect hail of
bullets suddenly greeted us & we knew that we hadn't got much
further to go before we would be at hand grips with the enemy. The
rifle fire at this juncture became so hot that it was found advisable to
make short sharp rushes of about 50 yds. We made a kind of detour
to the left heading for some small buildings on the bank of the river.
I really thought, about this time, that my last hour had come. The
lads were dropping on all sides. By this time our lines had ceased to
be lines. We were by no means demoralized but the fire was so thick
that we gave orders for every man to look after himself, to advance
singly to a certain nullah in front, taking as much cover as possible

en route. This was done by rapid dives from one building to another. When this nullah was reached we reassembled for another advance. It was in this nullah that old 'Posh' (a corpl in 14 platoon) accidently fired his rifle, the bullet passing through the knee of a certain Sergt. We thought by the agony he was in that he had sustained far more serious injuries. 'Posh' thought he'd killed him.

By this time we had got so used to the fire that none of us were the least concerned when the order came to go over again. We advanced by platoons with machine guns & rifles raking our lines at point blank range. In one of these rushes I saw poor young Ward of my late platoon down. He was rescued as soon as we had taken up a new position, by my Company Commander – Captain H. who went back after the kid under a withering fire & brought him up to us. The poor fellow seemed in awful agony. I examined him & found he had a bullet wound in the shoulder. I said 'Why Wardie, you've a "cushy" one'. 'Just a mere flesh wound!'. He looked up at me gratefully but with agonized eyes. The bullet had penetrated his intestines having swerved downwards on touching the bone & he was a dying man, How pitifully he cried for water which I gave him. He was got away about an hour after & died that night.

Poor old 'C' troop was having a rough time up in front. My old Sergt. Major Wickens was shot stone dead & also another Sergt. of my late company got about 9 bullets into him at once. Another old chum, Sergt Tom Corrigan, dropped for the last time. I still wear his numerals. Many a poor old Buff finished his career in this little strafe among the Turkish stables (for that's what these little buildings had been). Our 1st line & the Ghurkhas were now within bombing distance of the Turks & the Ghurkhas let them have it hot with 'Mills's' very best. My platoon was about 50 yds in rear behind a building & looking just a trifle tired & anxious. 'Zoggie' kept on repeating, half to himself, 'Yes, by Gum. Baghdad to day week'. (He wasn't far out either).

We remained here all afternoon. We were to go over again after a bombardment at 5 p.m. but this was cancelled for some reason or other. At dusk we were sent out to the right & ordered to dig in. Eventually the fire ceased altogether but not until after it had reached hurricane pitch. Johnny was retiring & rapidly.

We got poor old Captain H. my late company commander, in soon after dusk. He was shot through the thigh & was in awful

agony, I hardly recognized his voice. The stretcher bearers had gone
out for him once but both had been shot whilst carrying him in so
they had to leave him there in the open all afternoon.

The navy joined in the pursuit. The three gunboats at Sheikh Sa'aad,
Tarantula, *Mantis*, and *Moth*, made their way upriver to Kut and, under
the impression that Marshall's men were further forward than they were,
dashed on upriver until they ran into the Turkish rearguard, which shot
them up, holing but not sinking them. However they continued on,
shooting up Turkish transport and sinking three of their gunboats,
including one, the *Firefly*, which the Turks had captured in the retreat
from Ctesiphon.

In all these operations Maude had often been unsatisfied with the
performance of the cavalry. In a letter to his wife on 4 February Money
had written:

> The Cavalry are out (I was going to say on the loose but very far
> from it poor devils). Maude never leaves them alone from the time
> they start till they return but fires off wireless messages at them about
> every half hour. He knows nothing about cavalry to start with & his
> natural predilection for interfering wont let him leave them alone to
> do the job they've been sent out to do in their own way. If one didn't
> see the humour of it (Probably the wretched Cavalry Commander
> doesn't!) it would get on one's nerves rather. We call them our
> 'spoon fed cavalry'.

A fortnight later, as the battle to turn the Turks out of Kut progressed,
his comments on Maude were more favourable:

> Maude's been quite good & is certainly good at shoving people along,
> of which we had one or two instances today. In Lake's time I had to
> do all the shoving myself, which in the case of Commanders senior
> to myself was not always easy.

But at a later stage, he reverted to his original theme:

> We've moved about a mile upstream, alongside an old ruined fort
> where Cobbe has his Hd Qrs. I went over after lunch & had a long
> talk with him. Maude can't stand him. I like him personally, &
> always get on well with him. Knox had a row with Maude yesterday,
> & sent in his resignation for the 3rd time! He *will* not leave fellows

alone, & Knox is a very capable fellow if he's only allowed to run his own show in his own way.

Money was happier with the service provided by the Royal Flying Corps, which he described in a letter on 10 February:

I've just had my evening visit from Tennant (Major Scots Guards) who commands the Flying Corps out here, & works under my orders. Its about the last job I have to do in the day – to give orders to the Flying Corps, after the Corps and the Cavalry have received their orders for the next days operations. Each send in to say what they want from the Flying Corps – to me – Artillery observation, reconnaissance, photography, or what. I also find out if the Army Commander & Intelligence want any particular reconnaissance done & arrange with Tennant up to the capacity of the available machines. One can take absolutely accurate photos from the air of enemys trenches on a cinema camera, & so fill in the detail of maps. Of course the Turks try & interrupt by attacking our machines while photographing, but we have an escort hovering above them – a fast fighting machine – who keeps off intruders. One of our photographing machines was attacked the other day by 2 Turkish ones, but downed them both, & then went on with its job, We've got an extraordinarily keen lot of boys, who always reckon they can deal with any 2 Turkish or German machines. Today has been a very bad flying day – wind 45 miles an hour.

Telegrams now flashed to and fro between Maude, Delhi and London as to whether he should run the risk of trying to continue to Baghdad. As the Turks made no stand at Aziziyeh, he was allowed to go on. One factor behind that permission was anxiety that the Russian General Baratoff might get there before him. The first serious resistance was met where the River Diyala flowed into the Tigris, fourteen miles south of Baghdad, when Brigadier General J. W. O'Dowd's 38th Brigade reached the river on 9 March. He tried to cross in moonlight that night, but the 6th King's Own lost fifty men in an unsuccessful attempt. While the cavalry were sent north next day to find the enemy's northern flank, Brigadier General W. M. Thomson's 35th Brigade had crossed the Tigris near Ctesiphon by a rapidly constructed pontoon bridge and moved up the west bank beyond its confluence with the Diyala, from where it

could enfilade the Turks holding up O'Dowd. Sergeant Farnol described
the part 1/5th Buffs played in this:

A staff officer then came up to the head of our column & exchanged
a few words with our Colonel & the Brigade Major. We knew then
that we were for it. The order came down the line 'Lewis guns off
the carts', 'stretcher bearers get their stretchers', 'Signallers report to
HQ at once', 'Companies will advance in the following order with
distance & interval'. It was then about 2 p.m. Rifle & machine gun
fire had followed the fusilade of artillery & had increased in vehe-
mence & was now at its highest pitch. This was to our left front. Our
rear guard was being shelled, & heavily, from the rear & other side
of the river evidently from the Diala positions, which we were in
advance of. The Brigade was soon in battle formation of platoons in
column of fours with 50 paces interval between platoons. As we
advanced I looked around at the scene behind. It was immense. The
whole of the desert in rear was swarming with troops with regular
intervals in the same formation as our selves. Where they had come
from was beyond my ken. It must have been an awful sight for Abdul
in his trenches in front. Our force seemed to be an overwhelming
one. I well remember looking back just in time to see one of those
dirty black 5.9s burst right in the centre of a platoon. It was too
sickening to watch the effect which must have been awful. At this
juncture that wicked raking sound of rifle fire came from the front &
we soon had the sand spurting up all around us. Owing to the thick
fire we found it advisable to make short rushes & in consequence
suffered no casualties whatsoever, so rapid were our rushes & the
cover which we sought & found, so suitable.

We made a kind of right wheel & soon were right in the front &
heading for the river bank which we soon gained & on arriving there
found a beautiful nullah running out from it about 50 yards beyond
where we stood. To gain this it meant a bolt over the bank & would
present an excellent target to the enemy. We made a rush & had
about 2 wounded en route, but once there we found excellent cover.
We were now about 70 paces from the enemy. A rifle duel of about
2 hours duration ensued. We were plonking away at one another
point blank. A company of Ghurkhas reinforced us & entered into
the spirit of the thing with much gusto.

The shelling had almost ceased by now, but the rifle fire was deafening. My ears sang for days after. During this rifle duel we sustained a good many casualties. The Ghurkha at my left elbow was shot stone dead, a bullet having caught him straight between his eyes. As he dropped the Ghurkha on my right turned around as though he intended seeing to his dead comrade but dropped as he turned. We examined him & found that he had 'stopped' an Arab dum-dum bullet in his side which inflicted a frightful wound. We bandaged him up as well as we could. He was still alive when we went forward that evening & actually singing a little nepalese song. A chum of mine a couple from me, said, 'I'm going to have a rest, sergt – I've fired very nearly all my ammunition & my barrel is beginning to bulge.' 'Alright get down' said I. He laid his rifle with fixed bayonet across the parapet. No sooner than he had got down a bullet struck his bayonet & blew the remnants full in the face of the man next to him who was just up at the aim. He was 'out' of course. Somebody yelled down the line to Zoggie – 'Valentine & Baker have just stopped it & we have another fellow up here'. 'Alright says 'Zog' get him away and no 16! man the parapet & let 'em have a couple of rounds rapid & work to my word of command'. 'Now get loaded'. The Turks were being reinforced in front & they were presenting lovely targets. Every one of our fellows had his rifle to the aim, all that was left of the platoon at least. 'Now then 3 rounds rapid!!' Our rifles cracked with the word & did considerable damage I think. Anyway the boys gained superiority of fire for the Turks realizing that their parapets were being swept started firing wildly, up in the air. Just the muzzles of their rifles could be seen point upward. There were one or two braver than the rest. The Adjutant & a lieut. were approaching us from the rear. On nearing us Lieut. J. dropped with a bullet through his brains. One of our fellows, a jolly brave old chap, named George Pile, had been sent back for ammunition & could be seen with the box struggling along with it forward. The bullets were striking all round. Every moment we expected him to drop but he managed to reach us, laughing like a 'dood wallah'. 'They very nearly put "paid" to your name that time Uncle' some wag shouted. 'I don't think there's a bullet made for me' says George. There wasn't, for poor old 'Uncle' died a natural death at Amarah this summer, after many more narrow escapes of this nature.

That night we were ordered forward to occupy a nullah a few yds in front of this one we were in, which was much deeper. Our dead &

wounded were left behind but were cleared before morning or rather most of them for I fear there was many a corpse left for the vultures on this one occasion. This nullah was quite comfortable & we were able to stretch our limbs a bit. I think this March 1917 was almost the 'hottest shop' I've ever been in. I shan't forget it anyway. I fired, as did we all, till our bolts were so stiff that they could not be opened except with a bayonet.

Maude now decided to send the cavalry and the 7th Division over to follow 35th Brigade. On the night of 9 March Cayley tried again to cross the Diyala with 37th Brigade and the 36th north of it, but both failed. Next day the cavalry came up against Turkish defences ten miles higher up the river, which allowed them, first, to leave 28th Brigade, following them, to face the Turks, and then to go back to the river below the Diyala to water their horses. During the night the enemy started to withdraw on both banks. By 09.00 on 11 March, O'Dowd's brigade was over the Diyala: on the other side the cavalry, followed by 7th Division, was moving round to the south-west of Baghdad, when a dust storm blew up, obscuring everything. By this time both men and horses were short of food and drink and the men tired after a long march. Maude decided to wait rather than get involved in assaulting the defences and fighting in the city itself in the dark. At the same time argument was raging in the opposing camp. A German officer on Khalil's staff urged him to order an attack on the troops, the dust of whose movement they could see, although unable to decide whether they were cavalry or infantry; but Kiazim persuaded him that his men were not capable of attack, and, at 20.00, the order was given for a general withdrawal to a position nineteen miles to the north. 7th Division's patrols shortly after midnight found the Turkish defences opposite them abandoned, and by 06.00 the Black Watch of 21st Brigade were collecting souvenirs in the main railway station from which the last train had left a few hours before. Three battalions of 35th Brigade, 1/5th Buffs, 37th Dogras and 102nd Grenadiers, crossed the river in local boats, raised the Union Jack over the citadel, and set about trying to restore order, which had broken down with the departure of the Turks. Lieutenant Woakes was with them and tells the story in his diary:

> *March 11th 17.* Woke up with our eyes literally glued together with dust. Paraded 5.30 AM in the dark & felt thoroughly uncomfortable

& miserable as we could not raise a fire to make some hot tea. Moved forward with battery to main road which was absolutely packed with 7th Div: & we all moved forward in a wild rush to BAGDAD – however preference given on road to 35th Brigade so that we got ahead of everyone else & after passing IRON BRIDGE and coming out onto an open maidan in sight of the walls of BAGDAD we struck the 35th Brigade staff who had just decided to march into the town. We accordingly took our place in the column & took part in the triumphal march into BAGDAD. The streets on this side were narrow & dirty & packed with Arabs. The bridge was found to have been burnt by the Turks so General Thompson* & the Buffs ferried across in boats to hoist the flag on the citadel.

Our company & the battery moved back a bit & bivouacked in a garden on the outskirts of the city – a very nice place all green grass vegetables & palm trees. Managed to get from Arabs some eggs, a chicken, & oranges all of which are badly needed as no rations issued to-day & anyhow have been pretty bad for weeks now. Had a clean-up then went out with Pemberton & Goepel to try & send a cable home but could not do so . . . Our 2nd line transport arrived & went to bed on a mustard and cress bed in the garden after best dinner for a long time. We all feel very contented with life.

One of his first tasks after arrival was to construct a gallows on which General Thomson wished to hang some 15 Arabs and Kurds for looting. He included a design of it in his diary. Sergeant Farnol also described their entry:

On reaching the main road that led to the city, we formed up in column of route, did our buttons up & were ordered to march to attention as we marched in. On nearing the gates, we were met by crowd of children who clappped their hands & shouted for joy. Some said in very good English 'Good morning, how are you?' repeatedly, having evidently been tutored to it. They knew no more of our language. Every one seemed hugely delighted at seeing us. My company led the Brigade & I think I can safely say that I was in the 1st 25 to enter the city as our battalion has been mentioned as the first in officially. On nearing the river the mob became dense & we had to use a little force to get through. When we reached the old

---

* Brigadier-General W. M. Thomson, commander of 35th Indian Brigade.

bridge head we found the Turks had blown the pontoons up as we
of course fully expected. Whilst waiting for boats to convey us to the
other side, proclamations were read to the inhabitants who seemed
delighted. These were of course read in Arabic. Rifle shots could now
be heard, how they did rattle through these narrow arcades. Looters,
mostly Arabs, were being rounded up. They had been hard at it since
the Turks had evacuated early that morning. A great deal of damage
had been done in the bazaars though of little military consequence.
The scene was a novel one, the costumes of the money changers &
shop keepers absolutely unique. The whole scene reminded me of
biblical pictures one sees of Palestine in sunday school as children.

Maude issued a long, pompous declaration, maintaining that Britain
had long been a friend of the Arab people, mentioning favourably Sherif
Hussein's Arab Revolt in the Hejaz, in which T. E. Lawrence was so
deeply involved, and ending:

> Therefore I am commanded to invite you, through your Nobles,
> Elders and Representatives, to participate in the management of your
> own civil affairs in collaboration with the political representatives of
> Great Britain who accompany the British army, so that you may be
> united with your kinsmen in North, East, South and West in realizing
> the aspirations of your Race.

This received criticism at home, where the Speaker of the House of
Commons described it as: 'A document containing a great deal of
oriental and flowery language not suited to our western climate'. It had
been drafted by the Arab Bureau in Cairo and hotly contested by the
Indian government.

Maude now found himself in a classic strategic situation. Having
advanced to Baghdad to keep the Turks away from Kut, just as Nixon
had sent Townshend to Kut to protect Basra and the oilfield, he now
had to send forces further forward to ensure that he could stay safely at
Baghdad. He had hoped for help from the Russians – from General
Chernuzubov's 7th Caucasus Corps in Persian Kurdistan, a potential
threat to Kirkuk and Mosul, and nearer at hand from Baratoff, 120 miles
to the north-east – but a combination of factors, including snow in the
mountains and the outbreak of the Bolshevik revolution, meant that he
got no help from them.

As Baratoff was obviously not going to do anything, Maude was concerned to prevent Ali Ihsam from joining forces with Khalil, in whose Sixth Army Kiazim's corps was now commanded by Shefket Pasha. While Fane's 7th Division followed Shefket up the Tigris, D'Urban Keary's 3rd was sent up the Diyala to secure Baquba and from there prevent Ali Ihsam joining Shefket. By 20 March, joined by the 7th Cavalry Brigade, now commanded by Brigadier General R. A. Cassels, he was at Baquba and continued on to the foothills of the Jebel Hamrin at Shahraban, where he came up against Ali Ihsam's force, which he attacked with his 8th and 9th Brigades on the 25th. The terrain demanded very different tactics to those employed in the flat plains of Mesopotamia, ones which should have been familiar to the Indian Army from the North-West frontier, but in which, by this time, most of those who were serving in Mesopotamia had not been trained. It was a costly failure, the brigades withdrawing after having lost 1,200 men. Ali Ihsam moved off, as he had intended, across the Diyala towards Shefket on the Tigris. This left the road over the Jebel Hamrin open, along which Cassels's brigade rode unopposed to join hands with Baratoff's force, which numbered only 3,000 by this time. The 47th Sikhs were ordered to occupy the Khanikin Pass where the road crossed the Jebel, as Captain F. T. Birdwood recorded:

> After a short halt, we inclined over towards the Kahanakin Road, and moved along it towards the pass. It was a very hot day, rendered worse by the heat and glare reflected up by the stony ground over which we were travelling. At one place, I saw a number of bright scarlet anemones. Presently the road began to ascend at a steepish gradient, and here it was, on a high hill to the left of the road that Hd Qrs first established itself. This hill had been formerly a Turkish picquet, as indeed had all the hills to either side of us. Standing in the little niche that had been scraped in the reverse side at the summit, one could look far and wide over the whole expanse of country that was spread out like a panorama in front of one. After a while, the Colonel* called me and gave me a message to take forward to Francis, who, with his company, was posted a short distance in front. The message was tantamount to ordering him to advance 2,000x [yards], so I queried it, but was assured that it was correct. Francis, too, queried it, so I came back to make quite certain. It was,

* Lieutenant Colonel S. R. Davidson

of course, wrong. He was only to advance 200x *towards* the ridge that
was 2000x away. Once again, I went back to Francis to give him the
amended message, but before Francis had time to move off, the
Colonel came up, and after profusely apologizing to Francis on my
account, remarked in a loud voice that it was just what he would
have expected from me. Almost immediately after, he wanted me to
ride over to the left flank to the flank-guard, which was about a mile
a way, to tell them to come in closer. My horse had not come up, so
I volunteered to take it on foot. I reached the flank-guard absolutely
out of breath and done to the world, gave my message, and after
sitting down for a few minutes, I started back to find Hd Qrs again.
How I got there, I don't know, for I felt literally certain that at any
moment my heart might break under the awful strain of climbing up
and down those cruel hills. However, presently, we halted on an
eminence on one of the hills, where the 59th had halted and taken
up a line the morning before, and at 6 P.M. we established our line.
At 10.30 P.M. Francis went forward with 'A' coy and took up
position on the last line of hills – those immediately overlooking
Kezil Robat. We kept careful guard all night; my own watch lasted
from midnight till 2 A.M., and I spent the time walking along in the
moonlight from post to post – backwards and forwards; to and fro –
and in wondering whether those at home could ever in ever the
wildest flights of imagination see me as I then was.

After that, Keary's division was withdrawn to Baghdad, while Cassels
tried to keep track of Ali Ihsam.

On the way to deal with Shefket, Fane's advanced guard met the
first defences at Mushahadiya station, twenty-five miles upriver from
Baghdad. In a brisk but expensive action, involving all three brigades
and incurring 600 casualties, the Turks were driven back, 21st Brigade
remaining in the field while 19th and 28th returned to Baghdad.
Maude's other concern was that a Turkish force in the area of Falluja,
thirty-five miles to the west of Baghdad on the Euphrates, might breach
the dam which controlled the flow of water into the Sukhlawiya Canal,
thus flooding Baghdad. 7th Brigade of 3rd Indian Division was sent
there to find that the dam had already been breached by the Turks,
who, on their approach, withdrew upstream to Ramadi. Fortunately the
low level of water that year meant that the consequences were not
serious. Maude was still anxious to prevent the junction of Ali Ihsam's

corps with that of Shefket. To prevent this, he despatched Cayley's 13th
Division up the Tigris and sent the rest of the cavalry division, now
commanded by Major General L. C. Jones, to join Cassels, ordering
him to operate against Ali Ihsam, the two divisions being under command of Marshall's 3rd Corps. They met Shefket's troops at Sindiya,
halfway between Baghdad and Samarra in what was known as 'The
Battle of the Marl Plain'. After a stiff fight, in which the 5th Wiltshires
in 40th Brigade suffered heavily, 39th Brigade had more success and
Shefket's men withdrew twelve miles to where the Shatt-al-Adhaim
joined the Tigris from the north. 7th Division now came up to join the
13th and both advanced to the Adhaim, the 13th on the east, the 7th
on the west bank of the Tigris. Marshall planned to cross the Adhaim
on the night of 11 April, but on the 10th Jones reported that his cavalry
were withdrawing in front of Ali Ihsam, who was approaching from the
east. Marshall sent Cayley's 39th and 40th Brigades across to help him
and postponed his attack on the Adhaim. After a twenty-mile night
march, the brigades found themselves threatened by an enemy encirclement, but the presence of mind of their supporting gunners, the 55th
Brigade Royal Field Artillery, and the quick reaction of the 8th Cheshires and 8th Royal Welch Fusiliers in 40th Brigade drove them off, Ali
Ihsam's troops withdrawing into the hills. Having thus removed this
threat to his flank, Marshall faced the Adhaim again, on the far side of
which some 2,000 Turks held prepared defences. In a skilfully executed
night attack the Lancastrians* of O'Dowd's 38th Brigade crossed the
wide but shallow Adhaim and drove the Turks away with little difficulty, capturing 1,200 of them at a cost of only 73 casualties. Fane's
men then advanced on the other bank to within five miles of Istabulat
station, eight miles from Samarra, the terminus of the railway. There
on 16 April they came up against a Turkish position based on an
ancient ruined wall, known as the Median Wall, thirty feet high, its
north-eastern end resting on a canal close to the river. Cobbe's corps
headquarters had been brought up to command operations on this side
of the river, 7th Division providing the troops for the attack. 21st
Brigade was to lead an assault between the river and the canal, and the
19th south of the latter, while, a short time before, 28th Brigade would

---

* 6th East Lancashires, 6th Loyals (North Lancashire), 6th Prince of Wales's Volunteers
  (South Lancashire).

attack the defences south-west of Istabulat station, well round the left flank. The attack started at 06.00 on 21 April and led to fierce fighting with counter-attack after counter-attack continuing for most of the day; but in the early hours of the following day it was discovered that the Turks had withdrawn to another position covering Samarra station, four and a half miles further back.

This was attacked by 28th Brigade at 01.30. Initial success led to some over-optimism, especially in 2nd Leicesters, who were swept away by a fierce counter-attack, which hit them hard. The situation was saved by the 56th Punjabi Rifles and 136 Company of the Machine Gun Corps. Major Catty described this action in his diary for 28 April:

16th to 20th we reconnoitred the Turkish position just behind Istabulat Station & on morning 21st attacked, 21st Bde on left bank & 19th Bde on right of Dujail Canal. The position was in some high ground near the canal & then across the Rly with its flank well refused some 1000 yds beyond the line. The Turks had dug various cleverly sited trenches & built several redoubts so what was originally a young fortress had been turned into an almost impregnable position. Numerous MG commanded every approach & each trench had a covered approach.

Our advance started at 5 am with 21st Bde they rushed the advanced position in no time & by surrounding No 1 redoubt took it & 150 prisoners very easily. Further on however they ran into a real stout opposition from the hill overlooking the canal & got held up. Here the fighting was very fierce & the ground taken & retaken several times. Eventually our advance was finally hung up & by 10 am it could get no further. During the last part of the advance 9th Bhopals ran into fire of 3 M.Gs & lost 200 Men in 2 minutes. Directly 21st Bde had got the first position the 19th Bde was pushed in & managed to establish themselves in the front line for 700 yds. They blocked the Communication trenches & made themselves safe but had a very bad time from accurate shell fire. However they stuck it & even managed to push on a bit. By nightfall we were firmly established in the front line tho' every one was exhausted by the heat & want of water. 28th Bde hadn't been used & weak 8th Bde was also ready to support if necessary. During the night arrangements were made to resume the offensive next morning but the Turks didn't wait. Daylight found the position abandoned & we shoved on after them instead of assaulting. Their casualties must have been very heavy as apart from what they took away we buried 500 of them.

28th Bde being the fresh troops pushed ahead & caught up their rear guard 4 miles further on in another prepared position. An attack was at once ordered but it was 4 pm before the bombardment started. At 4.20 pm the attack went in & very soon got the front line. Pushing on ahead the Leicesters got 7 guns including 2, 5.9″. This however was more than Mr Turko could stand & he counter attacked in force. Owing to the pace they'd gone the Leicesters were far ahead of their supports so sad to say were driven back & the guns lost. By the time reinforcements got up it was dark & as the Turks were still counter attacking it was too risky (so they said) to try for the guns again.

At 8 pm the firing died down & the night was absolutely quiet. Next morning at daybreak we found them, gone again & entered Samarra without firing a shot. Here we got all the rolling stock – 16 engines & 250 trucks – the former damaged but not as badly as might be. Barring that there was nothing as there is only the Station Village – a walled place of 3000 souls is on left bank. In it we found 20 sick Turks who were added to our bag of prisoners, which since leaving Bagdad totalled 29 Officers & over 11000 men. Prisoners told us that the Turks were done & so it seemed if 7600 let themselves be beat by 7000 in a place like Istabulat.

While this was going on, Cassels' cavalry were drawing close to Samarra station, the 32nd Lancers rashly charging and paying dearly for it. At the same time the artillery with 35th Brigade on the other side of the river was joining in. At this point Shefket decided to withdraw and pull back to Tekrik, abandoning Samarra, although Ali Ihsam was on his way down the Adhaim to his rescue. This two-day battle had cost Cobbe 2,000 casualties, the Turks leaving 500 dead on the field and 259 behind as prisoners of war.

When Marshall received news from Arab sources of Ali Ihsam's move, he set off with O'Dowd's 38th Brigade in that direction at 21.00 on 23 March, telling Cayley to send Lewin's 40th Brigade and as much of 14th Division's artillery as Egerton could spare to follow him. At dawn next morning Marshall found himself close to Ali Ihsam's troops, who withdrew behind the Adhaim. Following them up, Marshall found them holding a position called Band-i-Adhaim, the Boot of Adhaim, at the head of the river in the foothills. This he attacked at dawn on 30 April, the 6th Cheshires and 6th South Wales Borderers of 38th Brigade being heavily counter-attacked and only saved by the intervention of 40th Brigade. Ali Ihsam then disappeared with his force into the mountains, leaving Maude's men to swelter in the heat of a Baghdad summer, even hotter than usual, the temperature in July rising to 123 degrees Fahrenheit. This brought fighting to an end until the autumn, except for an expedition in July with a mobile force from 7th Brigade to Ramadi, intended to evict the Turks from there. It was too weak to do so and suffered 560 casualties, 321 due to heat.

The attention of both London and Constantinople had by then switched from Mesopotamia to Palestine, where General Sir Edmund Allenby had taken over command of the British forces on 27 June. The relegation of the Mesopotamian campaign to secondary priority was emphasized by the sudden death of Maude from cholera on 18 November. There were rumours that he had been poisoned, and one explanation was that he had been infected by taking untreated milk in his coffee at a performance of *Hamlet* in Arabic, organized by the Alliance Israelite of Baghdad. Although his doctor maintained that it could not have been the cause, the Jewish contractor who had provided the milk was deported as an undesirable by Marshall, who stepped into Maude's shoes.

Shortly before this, Marshall's corps had been engaged in operations to capture Tikrit further north on the Tigris. C. A. Milward, recovered from his Gallipoli wound and now a major on Marshall's intelligence staff, wrote in his diary:

November 5th. We started in our cars at 3.30 a.m. to follow up the Inf. This time we could show no lights for fear of giving the alarm. Again we got out on to the perfect going of the plateau and again we lost the column and wandered about looking for tracks and not finding any. At dawn we saw some Cav. coming towards us, Corps Cav., and shortly after heard an awful noise and saw the whole force retiring with the tractors rattling like tin cans, dragging their heavy guns as fast as they could towards the rear: the whole force had stumbled too close to the enemy's position in the dark and at dawn had been shelled and was getting its distances. It was a most laughable sight.

Milward had begun to take an interest in conducting his intelligence work from the air, and on 3 December wrote:

> Went up in the kite Balloon, the first time I have ever done so. Did not find it at all terrifying. I carefully asked all about jumping out with the parachute and what I was to do if a hostile aeroplane came over or if we were bombed or the cable breaks. One has the equipment of the parachute strapped round one all the time, ready to jump. The C.O. who took me up said he had had to jump 4 times in France and had been very lucky as he hadn't even broken his ankle in landing. One swings tremendously and the parachute does not open until one has dropped 300–400 ft.
>
> We had not been up 5 minutes before they telephoned up that a hostile aeroplane was overhead. The Corps Commander who happened to have ridden up ordered us down although the Balloon man said it was the last thing he would have been allowed to do in France. When he said 'By now in France we should have jumped out', I began to think. So we came down and the H.A. went off. It was a most interesting experience and I shall do it again.

But his next flight was in an aeroplane, as he recorded on 18 December:

> Have had another chance lately of getting command of a Battalion. The 7th. Div. have left the Corps and country, but before they did so they again asked that I should be made Commander of the 28th Punjabis, I am sick to death about it. I loathe and detest this job and am far too senior for it after having had a show of my own. Gen Fane did his best to get me but G.H.Q. after almost agreeing refused, p.s.c. I suppose.*
>
> Had my first flight in an aeroplane this afternoon. Everidge took me up for half-an-hour and we went all round the defences over there. The view is extraordinary – one sees every ditch and path. The first few turns made me feel very giddy, especially when we banked right over to the vertical and one saw the horizon standing up vertical too. One felt also very lonely far up in a fragile machine and not a little frightened at first. But this all wore off quickly and when we

---

* p.s.c. – passed staff college. He presumably assumes that because of a shortage of fully qualified staff officers in Mesopotamia they would not free him to command a battalion.

came down in a straight spiral above the Camp with the tip of our plane keeping motionless and the machine cork-screwing round it I did not mind. The rush of wind in one's face is tremendous all the time and one cannot look ahead without glasses at all. I enjoyed it very much.

Another staff officer was not so fortunate on an unauthorized flight: he was Major P. C. S. Hobart, Brigade Major of 8th Indian Brigade in the 7th Division. A Royal Engineer, he was later to gain fame as one the most notable pioneers of armoured warfare, ending his career as a major general. When an attack on the Turkish garrison of Khan Baghdadi on the Euphrates was about to take place in March 1918, he persuaded the commanding officer of the Royal Flying Corps, Lieutenant Colonel J. E. Tennant, to take him up on a reconnaissance. They were shot down and captured by the Turks. After the capture of Khan Baghdadi, Lieutenant C. R. A. Hammond of the Army Service Corps provided the armoured car sent to try and rescue them, as he recorded in his diary:

From here [Auah] an Armoured car went on to Alona about 70 miles to see if they could re-capture Colonel Tennant, a cousin of Asquith's, who is chief of the flying Corps in Mesopotamia & had we were told written instructions not to fly over the Turkish lines, which however he not only ignored but took with him a Brigade Major from the Tigris front & flew over the Turkish lines at under 1000 feet & got a rifle bullet in his radiator & was forced to come down in their lines & were captured, & serve them jolly well right. Lieut. Todd was in charge of this Armoured car which went to rescue them & took enough petrol for 100 miles out & 50 back & a reserve was sent after him 50 miles. However when about 70 miles up they came round a bend on a hilly & rocky road & saw Tennant & Major Hobart & a Tartar guard about 50 yards off. They opened fire on both sides at the guard who were so surprised they fled. The car then drove alongside the trotting camels & Tennant & Hobart slipped off into the turret of the Armoured car which at once turned round for home before the surprised guard had sufficiently recovered to resist or to realize what had happened. They met their reserve of petrol all right & got back to Khan Baghdadi without any mishap.

I am glad to say Todd got the DSO for this. Tennant who should have got the sack & would have if he had not been related to Asquith, was sent to India to a bigger job & married the governor's of some state, or G.O.C's or some other big wig's daughter. A scandalous affair & we all wished our little general had not taken the trouble to get him back.

Although further operations were engaged in, notably in October and November 1918, coordinated with Allenby's advance to Aleppo, there were none on the scale of previous ones. One fruitless one was the expedition of Major General L. C. Dunsterville's* mobile force on a wild-goose chase to the Caspian in an attempt to contact the Caucasian people, the Azerbaijanis, Armenians and Georgians, and counter a suspected Turko-German plot to build up a force there which might threaten British Indian interests in that part of the world.

The total casualties of the Mesopotamian campaign from beginning to end were 92,501, of whom 14,814 were killed or died of wounds. 51,386 were wounded. 12,807 died of disease and 13,494 were taken prisoner or reported missing.

---

*   The original of Rudyard Kipling's Stalky.

9

To the Gates of Gaza

While fighting at Gallipoli was in progress, neither the Turks nor the British had anything to spare for greater efforts in Sinai. General Sir John Maxwell in Egypt maintained a static defence on the west bank of the Suez Canal, against which Kress von Kressenstein launched an occasional pinprick raid, which had no effect on the use of the canal by shipping. But the security of the canal was not Maxwell's only cause for concern. He had to pay attention to the attempt by the Turks to suborn the Bedouin Arabs of the Senussi sect in Egypt's Western Desert, led by Said Idris Ahmed. He had been friendlily disposed towards the British in Egypt, but the adherence to the Entente in May 1915 of Italy, who in 1911 had seized Libya, where many of his followers lived, provided an opportunity for the Turks to persuade him to foment trouble from the oases of the desert west of the Nile. A party of German and Turkish officers, led by Enver's half-brother, Nuri Bey, and an Arab from Baghdad, Jaafar Pasha, made their way by submarine to the coast and joined him at the oasis of Siwa, bringing a few mountain guns and machine guns. There they formed a force of 5,000 Arabs with which they intended to capture the small ports on the north coast of Egypt, Sollum, Mersa Matruh and Da'aba, while others occupied the oases further south, Bahariya, Far-afra, Dakhla and Kharga, and from them raided the towns of Upper Egypt. This threat began to develop in November 1915, when Jaafar occupied Sollum. In response, Maxwell sent a force under Major General A. Wallace to Mersa Matruh, consisting of one mounted and one infantry brigade. Some inconclusive engagements took place near Mersa Matruh in December and January, and in February 1916 Major General W. E. Peyton, who had succeeded Wallace, set off to recapture Sollum. He met Jaafar's force and defeated it near Sidi Barrani on 26 February, the Dorset Yeomanry losing fifty-eight men, of whom thirty-two were killed, in a gallant charge which led to the capture of Jaafar

51. As a ship steams past, Indian troops, encouraged by their vernacular band, dig defences along the Suez Canal

52. 'The struggle on the Suez Canal', a fanciful German postcard of 1915. Enver Pasha was the Turkish War Minister

53. Captured Senussi tribesmen under guard, Mersa Matruh

60. Camel carrying water tanks

61. Turkish troops leave Jerusalem . . .

62. . . . and British troops arrive

63. German prisoners being taken
through Jerusalem

64. British
artillery,
Transjordania

65. German
artillery

66. Brigadier
General C. F. Cox
of the 1st Light
Horse Brigade and
Major General Sir
E. W. C. Chaytor,
GOC Anzac
Mounted Division

67. 7th Black Watch at Arsuf, June 1918

68. Bivouac in the Jordan Valley

69. Australian Light Horseman

70. In the reserve trenches at El Kefr

71. General Sir Edmund Allenby presenting medals to the Anzac Mounted Division, Torbau Valley, August 1918

72. Concealing horses of the Middlesex Yeomanry from aerial observation in the orange groves of Sarona, 18 September 1918

73. Middlesex Yeomanry pack horse with Hotchkiss machine gun crossing the Jordan River, 24 September 1918

74. Yeomanry in the streets of Es Salt

75. Light car patrol near Aleppo

himself.* Sollum was retaken on 14 March. Lieutenant W. B. Bowyer served with the Royal Buckinghamshire Hussars (usually known as the Bucks Yeomanry) in this short campaign and described an action near Mersa Matruh on Christmas Day 1915:

> Reveille before 2 in the morning, our first experience of saddling up in the dark, getting feeds, rations etc., and we form up about 2.30. Our Colonel† wishes us a happy Christmas and we move away into the night, passing other bodies of troops moving off, with artillery rumbling along, irons clanking, and all the familiar sounds of a night march. We ride off to the west of Matruh, the Australian Light Horse riding round in a big circling movement to the east driving the Senussi towards us. We creep along in the dark, all unknown country, and waiting for the sun to shoot up. Immediately after sunrise 'A' Sq. are in action on our right. We pull off the road and the guns gallop into action in the open, firing over the Sikhs who had got into position during the night about a mile in front of us. Soon after this, a British gunboat cruising off the coast joins in, shelling the ravines and wadys with H.E. It was all a fine setting for our baptism of fire, more like the Boer War fighting, plenty of rifle fire, and everybody in the open.
>
> As the day wore on curiously enough we seemed to have a cessation mid-day for our Christmas dinner, Bully & biscuits. We keep working round their flanks like a horseshoe, with our artillery and infantry in the curved part. Darkness fell about 5 o'clock and saved them today from a decisive smashing, but they will not again worry Matruh as they retreat towards Shamash leaving about 400 dead. Our casualties are reported about 250. We start back for Matruh, a 15 mile ride, about 5 o'clock. About 7 it comes on to rain, a steady downpour, soon all are wet through. The ride seems interminable, but eventually we get back to the beach at Matruh, feed, and have some very salt tea given out to us, which with biscuits forms our supper.

---

* He escaped from prison in the Citadel in Cairo by letting himself down on a rope made of army blankets, but, under his considerable weight, it broke. He fractured his ankle and was recaptured. Later he joined the Arab Revolt, commanding Feisal's regular force; he was made a CMG at the end of the war, and in the 1920s was War Minister and then Prime Minister of the British mandated territory of Iraq.

† Lieutenant Colonel Cecil Grenfell.

Towards the middle of January the weather improved, and as our aeroplane reports the Senussi encamped at some wells about 10 miles away, we make preparations to get after them. Leaving camp about Jan. 21. our troop did the flank guard to the column and we bivouac down for a few hours before setting off for the scrap early Sunday morning – our favourite fighting day! It was a bitterly cold morning and we got some way from our resting place before running into the enemy. The cavalry open out to let the Sikhs through to the attack. I should say that today the Senussi put up their best fight, as, very fleet of foot, and supported by a few trained Turks, they were continually trying to outflank us. We race out to the left flank, quite exhilarating, though several come purlers through bullets and also boggy ground. Soon we dismount for action and fighting becomes pretty hot, we laying firing until the enemy are about 400 yards away, when we race for our horses, and away, while the artillery opens on the Senussi in the open. Our wounded, poor fellows, have a rough ride, there being a limber full of them with broken limbs, and all laying on top of each other. Crocker Bulteel, our squadron leader, shows his worth, giving his horse over to a wounded man, and running for some time on foot.

I am a section leader now, and Densfield brings our horses up in a terrible tangle. Croxford's mount gets bowled over, and Dover's little mare won't stand but we get away full cry. Dover, very good company in a scrap, and we blaze away quite enjoying it. Our friendship, started in this troop at Matruh in 1915, was only broken by his death in Palestine in 1917. We form up again to cover the artillery but the Senussi counter attack clears away and late in the afternoon we are left masters of the field, but far from our transport with the rations and necessities for the wounded. Our loss, about 270. Senussi's unknown.

Meanwhile the threat of Said Ahmed's raiding parties forced Maxwell to send the 53rd (Welsh) Division and several brigades of dismounted Yeomanry to garrison the towns of Upper Egypt. In October 1916 a force of camel-mounted troops and motor vehicles reoccupied the southern oases, and in February 1917 Brigadier General H. W. Hodgson led a squadron of armoured cars to defeat Said Ahmed himself at Siwa. After that the Western Desert remained quiet.

The evacuation from Gallipoli increased the force in Egypt to a strength of twelve infantry divisions and two Indian infantry brigades, with several Yeomanry brigades, mounted and dismounted. Initially it was feared that Turkish formations released from Gallipoli might all be sent to reinforce Djemal Pasha in Syria and Palestine, but the Russian Grand Duke Michael's offensive against Enver in the Caucasus, which brought his forces to Erzerum in February 1916, posed a greater threat to Turkey itself and to Enver personally than did British forces in Mesopotamia and Egypt. When Kitchener had visited Egypt after Gallipoli in November 1915, he had severely criticized Maxwell's Suez Canal defences on the west bank, and in December sent Lieutenant General Sir Henry Horne to plan a new line east of the canal, at the same time appointing Lieutenant General Sir Archibald Murray as overall commander of all troops in Egypt, now known as the Egypt Expeditionary Force (EEF). Murray rejected Horne's plan as needlessly extravagant and decided that it would be better to move forward into Sinai and bar the only route by which any sizeable force could advance against the canal, that is along the coast. The lack of water elsewhere imposed strict limits on the force which could be employed by either side. Even along the coast it posed a problem. Murray planned to occupy the area of Katia, twenty-five miles east of the northern section of the canal, and send a light mobile force forward another fifty miles to El Arish. Robertson approved his plan to move to Katia, but withheld authority to send a force as far forward as El Arish. In that month work was started to construct a standard-gauge railway from Kantara to Romani, near Katia, protected by the 5th Mounted Brigade, which consisted of the Gloucestershire Hussars, the Warwickshire and the Worcestershire Yeomanry.

Meanwhile the Germans were pressing the Turks to mount another offensive against the canal to prevent divisions being sent from Egypt to France. In mid-April Kress von Kressenstein set off to attack the rail construction with 3,500 men, almost all of the 32nd Regiment, with a camel-mounted regiment of Arabs, six guns and four machine guns. Approaching by a night march on 22 April, he found the 5th Mounted Brigade widely dispersed and drove them out of Katia, after which he withdrew to Bir el Abd, while the 2nd Australian Light Horse Brigade reoccupied Katia and Romani. For the next three months Kress did nothing, while he waited for the Germans to send him 'Pasha I', a collection of supporting arms including artillery of various kinds, aircraft and transportation units. In that period the infantry divisions in the EEF were reduced in number from twelve to seven, and three more left by the end of June; but the Australian and New Zealand Mounted Division was formed, consisting of the 1st, 2nd and 3rd Australian Light Horse and New Zealand Mounted Rifle Brigades, commanded by Major General H. G. Chauvel, and took over protection of the forward area. When the railway was completed to Romani in mid-May, 52nd (Lowland) Division moved up and occupied a defensive position south of Romani, known as Wellington Ridge, its southern flank facing a tangle of sand dunes through which movement of any kind was difficult.

By July Kress had received his 'Pasha I' and his numbers had been brought up to 16,000 with thirty guns and the same number of machine guns. His force set off from Shellal, between Gaza and Beersheba, on the 9th and, marching mainly by night, reached Bir el Abd, where its presence was detected, on the 19th. Lieutenant General H. A. Lawrence was responsible for No. 3 sector of the canal defences, having 52nd Division, with one brigade from the 53rd, supported by thirty-six guns including four 60pdrs, at Romani. The A&NZ Mounted Division was under his command, to which the 5th Mounted Brigade was added, and on 24 July, 42nd Division, in reserve along the line of the railway from Kantara, was also placed under his command. Murray's plan was to let Kress expend his effort on an attack through the dunes south of Wellington Ridge, while the cavalry, followed by the 42nd Division, swept round his left flank, encircling his whole force. Initially Kress showed no sign of playing his game. Ten miles from Romani he halted and stayed there for ten days. On 3 August, having noted that the Australian Light Horse came out to observe him by day and withdrew in the evening, he followed them closely that evening, and in the early hours of 4 August tried to drive in that flank, while his infantry struggled through the dunes towards Wellington Ridge. None of these attacks was successful, and all the conditions were favourable for the success of Murray's plan; but he himself was back at Kantara, the 42nd Division was late arriving, the 52nd reluctant to leave their defences and the cavalry found the going slow among the sand dunes. An opportunity was lost and Kress was allowed to withdraw to El Arish, having left behind 3,000 prisoners, four guns and a few machine guns. His casualties, including these prisoners, were estimated at 9,000, half his force, almost certainly an overestimate.* Private Robert Bethel was serving in the Army Service Corps in support of the 42nd Division in this action. He described his part in it:

Aug. 4th 1916. Received orders to pack up & the same afternoon was attached to 125 Bde H.Qs, then at 4.30 in the afternoon our Camel caravan moved off, & it was a huge affair, hundreds of camels loaded with stores and fantassies† of water, & pack mules loaded with ammunition. I was riding a camel. Passed Kilbain at about 6 p.m. & landed at Pelusium at 12.15. I was right fagged out, having walked the last two miles to ease my back, so I had a bite of food (the last for 12 hours) & went to sleep. About 3–45 we were all wakened up & told to prepare for off, so all filled water bottles and had something to eat & about 5 o'clock (this is Aug 5th) we all set off, infantry, artillery H.Qs & myself. I had been instructed to stay with 125 H.Q, but to report to my officer in the morning. I was unable to find him so of course I went with the rest, thinking that I would see something exciting, never dreaming of the horrors to go through. I marched with the rest & all went well while the morning was cool, but as soon as the sun got up, & beat down on us it was awful, & still we marched on mile after mile. Each man had only a water bottle full, & about 9–30 or ten am a lot of them had drunk it all, then the trouble began. As we marched men were dropping down right & left, absolutely exhausted, & as we passed, bringing up the rear, they would keep asking for water; the poor devils looked pitiful, lying there unable to walk & not a drop of water to wet their lips, there was no R.A.M.C. to follow & pick up the bad cases or give them a drink, all that I saw were two small Ambulance wagons about 3 miles from Pelusium, & two stretcher camels. It was awful, nothing to see but sand & scrub to right & left & the sun getting hotter & hotter every minute, & not a bit of cover or shade anywhere, & still we advanced. Then we came upon the place where the battle had been yesterday, & it was a sight. There were two dead turks lying there, & ammunition & rifles and bags & kits lying all around & some dead camels & 5 wounded Turks in a little bivouac waiting to be taken

---

* A post-war German account stated that Kress von Kressenstein lost one third of his force, i.e. 5,500–6,000.
† Oblong metal water tanks, holding about 20 gallons, carried one on each side of a camel: also known as 'camel tanks'.

away, but the poor devils could hardly move, they were covered with blood & as we went to look round they asked us for water. We couldn't spare them any because our bottles were nearly empty & we still had a long march before us, so we left & followed the troops & as we went along we passed empty shells ammunition & equipment that the turks had dropped in their retreat. (While at Pelusium 500 prisoners came in). At last we halted about 11–30 & our party filled our bottles, and as we were doing so stragglers were coming & asking, nay almost crying for water, but the officer in charge couldn't give them any, & told them to find their own unit & draw water from them, but the men were lost, didn't know where their battalions were & were hardly strong enough to pull one leg after the other, so they stood watching the water being issued, & looking half mad, seeing the water trickling into the bottles & being unable to have a drink. It was awful. The native camel-drivers were in a similar positon, they had no water, and no food & were continually asking for it. Then I had a long drink & it was delicious. I could have gone on drinking for ever. Then had something to eat, the first bite since 4-am. I was absolutely wearied to death, tired of everything, & yet the sun beat down unmercifully. When I sat down, the sand seemed to burn through my trousers, there was no shade, no cover of any kind, but I lay down in the open & went to sleep. About 5 minutes after I woke up & my body seemed to be burning all over, I stood up & my knees trembled & my hand shook. I didn't know what was the matter with me, but I longed to drink, drink & drink. My God, it was awful. I've been in a few places since I left England where water has been scarce, but I've never experienced thirst like that day in all my life.

1916 saw the development of the Arab Revolt, which was to have a significant effect on Djemal Pasha's command. This was an attempt to support anti-Turkish feeling among the Ottoman Empire's Arab subjects. A leader in this field was the Sherif Emir of Mecca, Hussein bin Ali. He was the hereditary guardian of the holy places there and at Medina. In the previous century the Sultan in Constantinople, the Caliph, had been jealous of the Sherif's position, but, as Mecca was distant and difficult to get at, he saved his face by confirming the hereditary Sherif as Emir; but once the Suez Canal was open, access was easier and Sultan Abdul Hamid removed most of the Emir's family to Constantinople, where Hussein was held prisoner for eighteen years, until released, sent back to

Mecca, and confirmed as Emir by the Young Turks. He set about restoring the authority of the Emirate, sending his four sons, including the future kings of Transjordan and Iraq, Abdullah and Feisal, to Constantinople to be educated and keep in touch with those in power. By then the Hejaz railway from Damascus had been built to Medina, and at the outbreak of war in 1914 the Turks stationed a division in the Hejaz, one in Asir, to the south, and two in the Yemen. The Turks put pressure on Hussein to support them actively, and, when he showed reluctance to do so, cut off supplies to him. As the war had also severely reduced his income from the annual pilgrimage, the Haj, he and his people were in dire straits and he appealed to the British for help, which they were only too keen to give, channelling it through the Governor and Sirdar of the Sudan, Sir Reginald Wingate. Active operations against the Turks opened at Mecca on 15 June 1915, and by September the garrison there and at Jedda had surrendered. Medina proved a harder nut to crack, and, as successive Arab attacks there failed, support for the Revolt began to fade. At that point the arrival of an unorthodox captain from Wingate's Arab Bureau, T. E. Lawrence, transformed its fortunes. He realized that attacking the Turks directly was counterproductive. Their garrisons could be turned from assets to liabilities by indirect attacks on the railway by which they were supplied, the success of which would both raise the morale of the Arabs locally and impress the anti-Turkish Arab movements in Syria and elsewhere, who had expressed their support for Hussein. Feisal, who with his brothers had returned to the Hejaz at the outbreak of war, advised by Lawrence, collected, led and moved a body of some 10,000 Bedouin 250 miles north between the coast and the railway, periodically raiding the latter and blowing up the rails, as far as Wejh, by this preventing the Turks from sending a force from Medina to reoccupy Mecca. Murray had proposed to send an Indian brigade to prevent that, landing it at Rabegh, but had been dissuaded by Wingate, who supported Lawrence's strategy. When Feisal's force reached Wejh, it was reinforced by Arabs who had been serving in the Turkish army and been taken prisoner, released from their camps. Jaafar Pasha was released to command them. From Wejh, Lawrence set off with a small body of Arabs, and riding by camel as far as Baalbek, north of Damascus, recruited a further force of 500 with which, in July 1917, he attacked Aqaba, at the head of the Red Sea, and captured it. Jaafar's force was then shipped round there from Wejh.

After the successful action at Romani in August 1916, the War Council's policy for the EEF remained strictly defensive. Hopes of success on both the Western Front in France and the Eastern in the Ukraine were still alive; but by the end of the year they had faded on both fronts. When David Lloyd George succeeded Asquith as Prime Minister on 7 December 1916, he looked elsewhere for a ray of hope and directed the War Office to tell Murray that a success was needed on his front. The latter told Robertson that he would need five infantry divisions and five mounted brigades to reach El Arish: although he had six of the latter, he only had four of the former. If he were to advance from El Arish into Palestine, he would need six. He was told that no reinforcements could be spared from the Western Front: that he was to remain on the defensive, but be as aggressive as he could with what he had. By then Murray had moved his headquarters back to Cairo and placed Lieutenant General Sir Charles Dobell in command of the troops east of the canal, known as Eastern Force. He also set in hand a methodical development of its logistical support, extending the railway beyond Romani towards El Arish and laying alongside a pipeline bringing water all the way from the Sweet Water Canal at Ismailia. This extension was protected by the Desert Column, commanded by Lieutenant General Sir Philip Chetwode, consisting of Chauvel's A & NZ Mounted Division, reinforced by the Imperial Camel Corps Brigade,* and the 42nd and 52nd Divisions. As they approached El Arish on 20 December, the Turks withdrew, partly to Rafa, thirty miles on, where the frontier joined the coast, partly to El Maghdaba, the same distance to the south. Chetwode sent Chauvel to attack the latter which, after a night march, he did successfully on 23 December, capturing 1,282 Turkish soldiers and four guns. The railway reached El Arish on 4 January 1917.

CQMS Harry Hopwood was back with the 6th Manchesters in 42nd Division celebrating Christmas, as reported in a letter on New Year's Eve:

> We have been a good way up and you would see from the papers of about a week back that Johnny Turk has been forced back from El

---

* Eighteen companies (ten Australian, two New Zealand and six British) of camel-mounted troops, organized into four battalions, supported by an Indian Army mountain battery of six guns and a machine-gun company of eight Vickers MGs. They were self-contained with food, water and ammunition for five days.

Arish. Well we were not in the fighting, it fell on the mounted troops and they were able to do it without any assistance from us. We only got within sight of the stronghold and were like Moses viewing the 'promised land' from afar. We are not that far from it now although we have come back some few miles and even if we don't get into it we can at least say that we have seen some thing of it. It is our second Christmas over here and the food they managed to get up for us was marvellous. We even had three turkeys for the company. These were raffled for between the sections so I did not sample them this time at all. The sergeants had dinner altogether at six p.m. on a table made out of empty boxes and odd boards with a sprinkling of candles to light up. Unfortunately it rained and was very cold and windy, but we carried on and with the addition of a pint of beer for everybody it was quite a cheerful gathering. Afterwards there was a concert and this finished off a very nice day indeed. For breakfast we had porridge, sausage and bacon: mid day, tinned salmon, tinned pears and tea, dinner was a special stew for the men, roast beef for the 'serges' and plum pudding (also tinned but very good) for everybody. When you think that everything has to come up on camels, you can imagine it was no small order. Even the barrels of beer are loaded up, one on each side of a camel.

His first Christmas in Egypt, in 1914, had been spent in Alexandria, about which he wrote in a letter of 3 January 1915:

We have had quite a good Christmas and New Year, including turkey for the Sergeants Christmas dinner. The turkeys were given by a Mr Carver who lives at San Stefano close by. He is a partner I understand in the firm of Carver Bros of Manchester.*

Five days later, after another night march, Chauvel's division, with the Camel Brigade, attacked the position at El Magruntein, covering Rafa. After an inconclusive day-long struggle, Chetwode had just given the order to withdraw when the New Zealand Mounted and the Camel Corps Brigades, on their feet, cleared the central keep, forcing the surrender of the Turkish garrison of 1,635 who had lost 200 killed. Chauvel's casualties were 71 killed and 415 wounded.

---

* Almost certainly the author's uncle. In 1916 the author's father was an officer in the Camel Transport Corps, perhaps bringing up the barrels of beer.

Two days later Murray received a telegram from London, informing him that 'large scale operations' on his front would be deferred until late in the year while a major offensive was launched on the Western Front, for which he had to contribute a division. He was to make his preparations during the summer for an offensive into Palestine in the autumn of 1917. The 42nd Division left for France at the end of the month, replaced at El Arish by the 53rd, released from garrisoning the towns of Upper Egypt by the defeat of the Senussi, and the 54th was brought up from manning defences in the southern sector of the canal. The 74th Division was formed from dismounted Yeomanry. The cavalry was reorganized into two divisions, Chauvel's Australian and New Zealand Division keeping the 1st and 2nd Australian Light Horse and the New Zealand Brigades, and receiving the 22nd Mounted (Yeomanry) Brigade, while a new division, the Imperial Mounted, commanded by Major General H. W. Hodgson, was formed from the 3rd Australian Light Horse and the 5th and 6th Mounted (Yeomanry) Brigades. These divisions were both in Chetwode's Desert Column with Major General A. G. Dallas's 53rd Division and two Light Car patrols.

Murray decided that, as a preliminary to the planned offensive, he should acquire as a start line at least the Wadi Ghuzze south of Gaza and, if possible, Gaza and Beersheba themselves, from which roads led northwards into Palestine. Down the ages Gaza had been the gatepost of southern Palestine, with its plentiful supply of water and its rugged hills facing the desert to the south. Beersheba, twenty-five miles to the southeast, formed the other gatepost, also providing water and marking the southern tip of the hills of Judaea. The town of Gaza was ringed by small plots surrounded by cactus hedges, and was protected on the east side by several ridges, the one nearest the town known as the Ali Muntar Ridge. During February Kress von Kressenstein was reinforced by two infantry divisions and one weak cavalry division, with which he held a position covering the Wadi Ghuzze; but, when he saw that Dobell was making preparations for an advance, including extending the railway forward, he withdrew from that to Gaza and Beersheba, but kept the bulk of his force in reserve further back. Gaza itself was held by 3,500 men, supported by about twenty guns in five batteries, two Austrian, two Turkish and one German, both German and Turkish machine-gun companies and a strong German aircraft squadron. Dobell believed that, as at El Arish and Rafa, and on the Wadi Ghuzze, Kress might withdraw again, given a push, and Murray agreed that he should launch an attack. On 25 March Dobell assembled his force south of the Wadi Ghuzze. Chetwode's Desert Column was to command all the formations taking part in the attack. The mounted troops would lead the way at dawn on 26 March across the wadi and spread out to the east and north-east, and eventually north of the town, to hold off any reinforcements that might be sent from that direction, while the 53rd Division, following them across the wadi, would attack the Es Sire and Ali Muntar Ridges, which protected Gaza from the south and east. Dobell would keep under his own hand Major General S. W. Hare's 54th Division, which would hold one brigade ready to reinforce the 53rd, while the rest supported the mounted troops by occupying the Sheikh Abbas Ridge five miles south-east of Gaza, overlooking the road to Beersheba. He held the 52nd in general reserve. Chetwode's and Dobell's headquarters were sited together at In Seirat three miles west of the wadi.

The first setback on the 26th was a dense sea fog which lasted until 07.00. Although it delayed the infantry attack, it provided concealment to the mounted troops, the leading A & NZ squadrons almost completing the encirclement of Gaza by 10.30 and in the process capturing the commander and staff of the 53rd Turkish Division which Kress had ordered to move to the front. By this time the Imperial Mounted Division and the Camel Brigade were also in position. Chetwode, a cavalryman, became increasingly impatient with Dallas's deliberate preparation for his attack. Although the latter's leading brigades had assembled within 6,000 yards of their objectives by 08.00, their attacks did not start until nearly midday. They then advanced resolutely against intense fire, 160th Brigade against Es Sire and 158th against Ali Muntar, getting to within a few hundred yards of the latter, where they came up against the cactus hedges. The 159th then came into action on their right. Chetwode meanwhile had decided to hasten a decision by ordering Chauvel to attack the northern outskirts of the town, while Hodgson's division extended its left to cover the gap between them that this would open up. The Anzacs launched their assault at 16.00 and made steady progress. 161st Brigade of 54th Division joined the 53rd at 15.00 and Dallas directed them between the 158th and 160th to attack Green Hill, from which 158th Brigade on Ali Muntar was being enfiladed. By 18.00 53rd Division had secured all its objectives and the 2nd Australian Light Horse and the New Zealand Brigade were into the northern outskirts of the town.

Victory seemed assured, but Dobell and Chetwode were taking counsel of their fears. They had decided that if Gaza had not been captured in daylight, they would break off the fight, concerned about water supply, especially for the horses, and at the vulnerability of their forces to the reinforcements which Kress was moving towards them. These had been reported by the mounted screen which was coming under pressure from them. As a first precaution Dobell ordered the 54th Division to withdraw from Sheikh Abbas to bring them closer to the 53rd. Soon after 18.00 Dobell, after consulting Chetwode, ordered the withdrawal of the mounted screen, whose horses had had no water all day, back to the Wadi Ghuzze. This left the 53rd Division's flank exposed and Chetwode told Dallas to withdraw 159th Brigade to bring it into contact with 54th Division. Dallas, who had not been informed of the latter's withdrawal from Sheikh Abbas, protested strongly, but was overruled. He then withdrew from the Ali Muntar Ridge back to the Wadi Ghuzze, abandoning all his gains except the Es Sire Ridge. Chetwode was not aware of this until 05.00 on the 27th. On that morning the two divisions found themselves back to back, the 53rd on the Es Sire Ridge facing west, the 54th on the Mansura facing east, the Turks having reoccupied Ali Muntar in greater strength than before, while another force, which had come along the Beersheba road, was occupying Sheikh Abbas, from where it could bring fire to bear on the Es Sire Ridge. It was a hopeless situation, and Dobell withdrew all the forces behind the wadi, having lost 400 killed, 2,900 wounded and 200 missing. Murray reported Turkish casualties to the War Office as 6–7,000, later increasing it to 8,000, whereas the actual figure was much less – 300 killed, 1,085 wounded and 1,061 missing, 900 of whom were confirmed as having been captured. When the attack was launched, Kress had ordered three Turkish divisions, the 3rd, 16th and 53rd, to move towards Gaza, but none had entered the battle when darkness fell on 26 March. Having no confidence in their ability to launch a night attack, he stopped, intending to launch a major counter-attack on the following day in the hope of inflicting a decisive defeat on Dobell; but Djemal Pasha countermanded it. Nevertheless Kress could claim a defensive victory.

Lieutenant Bowyer was with the Bucks Yeomanry in the 6th Mounted Brigade in the Imperial Mounted Division. He recounted his part in the battle:

The division at this time all massed in together, halts just across the Beersheba Road, the New Zealand Mounted Rifles are in touch with the enemy from Beersheba and about a mile away a battery of our guns is firing steadily in that direction. A few odd high explosives come our way but we seem to be unnoticed, and everybody is talking of being right through on the Jerusalem Road by the morrow. A good deal of rifle fire is going on back towards Gaza but we understand the day is going well. About two o'clock we push on and go forward about six miles, Gaza now well behind us, and we are just unsaddling to rest our horses for night work when some news comes in. Saddle up immediately and away! Still forward, – it is reinforcements marching on Gaza from Hebron and Megdel. The division lines a long range of heights, and rifle, machine gun and artillery fire becomes common all along the line.

The head of the column is annihilated. This is the position when darkness comes on us. Unfortunately, Gaza has not fallen: however we start to dig in, knowing that on the next day the position will be at least difficult. We dig away in the darkness; every now and then the machine guns rip out, and we imagine we can hear the Turks shouting; anyhow, one could hear them moving at times.

We had just got our trench dug for my section, and were thinking of an hour's sleep, when the order comes up – Get back to your horses quietly. 'C' Squadron lays out in the open while the remainder get all together and get mounted. I fancy I slept for a bit: then off into the dark and dust at a steady trot, – apparently the Turks have got round us. We ride to where a signal lamp flashes, and then on, wondering what daybreak will disclose. The Bucks Yeomanry are rear guard, 'C' Squadron the last squadron. The sun rose fine and red on our left so we were riding due south. Just at daybreak, about 5.30., our flank guard rides right into the midst of a body of about 60 Turkish infantry, rifle fire immediately breaks out along our left flank. Crocker Bulteel leads us straight up a valley towards the firing. At the end we dismount for action and scramble up the right bank, opening fire on the Turks whom we could plainly see. After perhaps five minutes blazing away word is sent up from the valley that some cavalry are approaching on the other bank. We leave the Hotchkiss guns to deal with these Turks and run back through our horses and up the other slope. Halfway up the slope I feel a tingling sensation in my left hand and a bullet kicks up the dirt at my feet. No 1. Troop following behind saw the incident with ease and tell me I used awful language for a minute or so, – I don't think so.

However, as it did not feel very bad I thought I would have a look over the top of the ridge. I was just in time to see the Turks dismounting for action, and as my two fingers now seemed to be useless and I could not hold my rifle, I thought 'This is no place for me', and retired on the horses. Here Mr Deverell kindly did my hand up and I was able to watch the scrap. Frank Clark is soon hit and brought down, ditto Slim Jim (Mr Stewart) coming back supported by Venner and Thatcher. The firing now seemed to be all round us: horses are getting hit, and it is an anxious period till all come back to the horses: we mount and strike up the valley.

I have visions of Sambrooke's horse leading the way riderless and one or two coming purlers. Claude Vize going past hanging grimly to his pack-mule with its Hotchkiss gun, Palmer is shot through the back and all is dust. We pull up behind a hill about a quarter of a mile away, to get together and allow the unfortunates to catch up. Both Sobey and Jack Abbott have their horses shot and come panting up over the hill, We hear Sambrook [sic] is hit and left behind, but nobody knows very definitely then. Actually he was left for dead but was taken badly hit by the Turks and is alive in England today although a cripple. While here, Capt. Bulteel, who was as cool as ever all through, . . . sent us wounded on to find a field ambulance, and so taking Palmer with us, Williams and I set off for what we imagine are our lines, passing Frank Clark with Marks. The squadron later got away from its position, although under considerable difficulty, and two Military Medals were won.

Bowyer eventually reached a field dressing station, where his hand was dressed and he got a good breakfast before being evacuated:

We are moved back at night, most of us on camels. I occupied a stretcher instead of a chair in order to balance a bad case. It was an awful ride for me, let alone for him, but I dozed a bit until the camel 'barracked'. This occurred every mile or so and would have thrown us off completely but for our being securely strapped on. Anyhow I lost all my belongings that I had saved.

General Murray's report to the War Office represented the outcome of this First Battle of Gaza as a temporary setback. Unfortunately this chimed in with a mood of optimism in London following Maude's capture of Baghdad. The outbreak of the Bolshevik Revolution in Russia was wrongly interpreted as heralding a greater war effort from her, and unrealistic hopes were pinned on the French General Nivelle's offensive on the Western Front. All these encouraged Lloyd George in his belief that Turkey could be eliminated from the war, providing a first step towards victory over the Central Powers. In the light of this, Murray was told on 30 March that Jerusalem was his immediate objective. This came as a shock. He pointed out that he had always maintained that he would need five divisions at full strength to secure his initial objective, the Gaza–Beersheba line, and he emphasized the logistic problems. The War Office however maintained that Kress could only field 20–25,000 men to oppose his nearly 40,000, and that he would have the same proportionate superiority in artillery. He had also been sent eight tanks* and some supplies of gas shell. With considerable misgiving Murray set about planning a Second Battle of Gaza. As the railway was confined to the area of the coast – it had reached Deir el Belah, four miles from the Wadi Ghuzze – it was not possible to consider an attack in any strength further inland.

Meanwhile the Turks were improving their defences. Their 3rd Division held Gaza itself with a string of mutually supporting defensive positions stretching from Samson's Ridge, two miles south of the town between the coast and the road, through Outpost Hill, two miles south-east of the town at the southern end of the Ali Muntar Ridge, thence east for four miles to Khashm el Bir and, two miles south of that, Khashm Sihan and what became known as Tank Redoubt, immediately north of the road to Beersheba. Down that road their 53rd Division and 79th Regiment held defences, linking up with their 16th Division on the railway at Tel es Sheria, fifteen miles from Gaza and the same distance north-west of Beersheba, which was held by two battalions. Their cavalry division was held in reserve near Huj, ten miles east of Gaza.

Dobell's plan was for a two-stage attack. In the first, the 53rd Division near the coast would close up to Samson's Ridge, while the 54th secured a start line from Es Sire to Sheikh Abbas. The artillery would then move forward to support the second stage in which the 53rd would take Samson's Ridge and attack Gaza from the west, while the 52nd passed

---

* They were in a poor mechanical state, having been used for training crews.

through the 54th, crossed the Beersheba road and attacked Ali Muntar Ridge from the east, and the 54th and the Imperial Camel Brigade attacked between Khashm el Bir and Khashm Sihan. Chetwode's mounted divisions would create a diversion further down the Beersheba road round Hareira. The 74th Division, which had no artillery, would be in reserve. To support this attack Dobell had 170 guns, but only sixteen – twelve 60pdr guns and one battery of two 8in and two 6in howitzers – were heavier than the 18pdr guns and 4.5in howitzers of the divisional artillery. Two tanks were allotted to the 53rd, two to the 54th and four to the 52nd Division. Dobell could also call on naval fire support from the French battleship *Requin* and two Royal Navy monitors.

The first stage was successfully launched on 17 April, the following day being spent in 'consolidation'. The main attack opened at 05.30 on the 19th with an artillery programme which lasted until 07.15, when 53rd Division launched their assault on Samson's Ridge. A quarter of an hour later the 52nd and 54th launched theirs. The former had secured Outpost Hill by 10.00, but could get no further. The 54th, on the right, reached Khashm Sihan and held Tank Redoubt for a time, but their left came under heavy enfilade fire from Ali Muntar. The 53rd, after several unsuccessful attempts, finally gained Samson's Ridge at 13.30, but could not advance beyond it. By the afternoon it was clear that committing any more troops would not achieve anything, and ammunition supply was running low. Dobell called off any further attacks, intending to resume them next day; but the reports he received during the night persuaded him to cancel that plan and to content himself with digging in on the ground that had been gained. Kress von Kressenstein planned a major counter-attack on the 20th, but again Djemal Pasha counter-manded it. Dobell's casualties totalled 6,600, half of them in the 54th Division, while the Turks lost just over 2,000.

Captain Hawker of the Devon Yeomanry was with the 4th Machine Gun Company in 54th Division, as he recorded in his diary:

Thursday 19th April 1917. Woken up in the night with orders to move at 8.30 across the Wadi at Sheik Neban for Tel el Ahmar. Got the men up at 5 am & soon got things going lucky I did as the G.O.C Division was not a bit pleased we were starting so late & we had orders to hurry up & cross at 8 am. Rather a lot of talk about it but we got there well on time. Marching fairly good but the halt was rather a box up & we only got about ½ our allotted time. Passed a good many batteries from 60 lbers downward some very heavy firing, judging from what I can hear this bombardment must be nearly the heaviest I have ever heard for continuity. Rather angry at the amount of stuff the men shed when they left camp every kind of thing imaginable & the dug-out rather dirty. Marshall got hold of all the corporals & gave them a telling off for leaving so much rubbish about. Got settled in about Tel el Ahmar & ½ the officers went off to have a look from the neighbouring hill. Saw troops advancing & the Turks putting any amount of shelling over them but to very little effect. Saw a tank going on in fine style but of course it was not close enough to be firing. Two other tanks seemed to be out of commission one stuck tail in rather a deep wadi & another one apparently on fire way out on our right. Had lunch quite comfortably except for a large H.E. which made the horses jump about & one broke loose to be easily caught again. Spent a good bit of the afternoon watching events & saw a Brigade go out & some of our men coming back in one place. A few casualties about, an enormous proportion seem to have grazed wounds in the leg. Frantic orders from Brig adc to get on the move & all C.O's to report forthwith to the Brig. We all quite thought we were off to the rattle of the Battle but the only thing that happened was a H.E. came along & nearly had the lot of us covering us with dirty black smoke & dust. That over I went back to the Company to get them on the move & just as I was fetching up another H.E. came along. It was a case of smiling as there was no chance to duck as I was mounted so addressed some men who were lying at the bottom of a deep wadi with 'up she comes again' luckily it went a long way over. Got a move on & after waiting ages for the Devons to get clear of a small wadi & got tucked up under the Mansura Ridge due S of Ali El Muntar. Spent most of the evening watching various things & saw quite a lot all most desperately interesting. Saw one devil running back towards our lines but don't know if he was one of ours or a Turk but someone bowled him over, he picked himself up but could not move very far & was still there at Dark. Just about Dusk some of our troops came back for some unknown reason & seemed to come through a perfect hail of bullets & I never saw any of them stop. More men went out to meet them & we finally pushed further forward than they had been before. Brig insisted in sending out a short line of outposts & succeeded in

making people thoroughly uncomfortable for no reason at all. Slept
in my clothes just under the Mansura ridge in a most uncomfortable
spot but managed to sleep allright. Mules had to be watered in two
lots which was hard lines but the poor devils had had no water all
day as we had been expecting to be on the move at any minute.
Heard that a bomb from a Hun Aeroplane had dropped right on the
place where we had lunch so it was a good job we moved. Company
stood fire very well for the first time & I don't think there is any fear
of them 'hopping it' when the time comes.

Lieutenant Colonel V. L. N. Pearson was commanding the 2/10th
Middlesex in the 53rd Division. In a letter home he wrote:

You might tell Mrs de Pass that her young nephew, Ronald, turned
out a gallant youth, & when badly wounded on 26th March, proved
himself a stout-hearted fellow, & showed a splendid example of grit
& endurance. He got rather a rotten one through the thigh, and the
exit wound may prove troublesome. I have nothing but praise for
this Battalion who have one and all played the game up to the hilt &
I am proud to command them. In the two shows we have entered,
the Battalion has carried a golden reputation & on the 19th of April
was called upon to capture a position at the point of the bayonet, a
task which called for the very highest endurance and grit. They did it
& did it well too. But alas at a cost, & now I'm left with a remnant
of a fine Battalion. I cannot quote numbers, but higher than any
other unit in any of the other Divisions, which means a lot. I have
had narrow & lucky escapes myself, but suppose shall get my turn in
due course – one can't have such constant luck all the time. I frankly
admit I've seen enough bloodshed, & hoped that they might have
proved walkover, but far from it. My losses in officers is as bad as
anything ever in France – 70%. At present we are working like mad
digging, & all are utterly exhausted with work & with heat.

Pearson did not mention that he had administered a severe rebuke to
the large number of men he had had to report as missing when his
battalion had been withdrawn into reserve, who rejoined next day,
having made their own way back, either accompanying wounded or
mixed up with other units.

Dobell himself left soon after the battle and was succeeded by
Chetwode, Chauvel taking over command of the Desert Column,

replaced in command of the Australian and New Zealand Mounted Division by the New Zealander Major General E. W. C. Chaytor. Murray stated in his report on the battle that if a further attempt to advance into Palestine was to be made, he would need two more full-strength infantry divisions and more artillery. The reaction in London, following the failure of Nivelle's offensive in France, was to continue to pin hopes on knocking Turkey out of the war, and to reinforce the EEF by withdrawing the 60th Division, two mounted brigades and some artillery from Salonika, and to form the 75th Division in Egypt from troops already there and others sent from Aden and India. Murray himself was to be replaced by General Sir Edmund Allenby, a cavalryman, whose Third Army's success at Arras in April had done something to relieve the prevalent gloom on the Western Front. He arrived in Egypt on 27 June 1917.

10

Jerusalem for Christmas

The War Cabinet's increased interest in operations by the EEF was actuated not only by their desire to find some alternative to the disappointments, frustrations and massive casualties of the Western Front, but also by reaction to Germany's plans. The latter was concerned that Turkey's enthusiasm for the Central Powers was waning. In an attempt to remedy this General Erich von Falkenhayn was sent in May 1917 to persuade Enver to organize an attempt to recapture Baghdad by assembling an army of two corps, the III and XV, near Aleppo, formed from troops who had been engaged against Romania and against the Russians in the Caucasus to which the Germans would provide a contribution 6,500 strong. The German intention was that this force, forming the Turkish Seventh Army, would join Khalil's Sixth Army in Mesopotamia under the overall command of von Falkenhayn, the operation to be known as YILDERIM, the Turkish for lightning. Mustafa Kemal was appointed to command the Seventh Army, but resigned when he found that he was dictated to by the Germans, and was replaced by Fevzi Pasha. Von Falkenhayn insisted that the Palestine front should be secure, so that there was no threat to his line of communication near Aleppo. From the point of view of Britain, it was clearly strategically more effective to frustrate YILDERIM by developing a threat in Palestine than by reinforcing Baghdad via Basra. The argument for this reinforced Lloyd George's own inclinations, with the result that when Allenby asked for more resources he received them. Signs that the EEF was being strengthened, combined with the logistic difficulties of maintaining a force the size of YILDERIM as far as Baghdad, persuaded von Falkenhayn that it should be diverted to Palestine, joining Kress von Kressenstein's Eighth Army. Djemal Pasha objected to being bypassed in this way, and a compromise was reached by which Djemal would retain responsibility for everything north of Jerusalem and east of the River Jordan and the Dead Sea. Von Falkenhayn's intention was that Fevzi's Seventh Army would be deployed to the east of Kress's Eighth, assuming responsibility for the left flank, including Beersheba. The assembly and preparation of the army took a long time, and it was not until September that the first elements left Aleppo.

Meanwhile Allenby (whose nickname was 'the Bull') charged about and infused new vigour into the EEF. Major General Money, who came from Mesopotamia to be Allenby's staff officer responsible for civil administration, described him thus:

> There were two things that always infuriated Allenby: if he thought a man was not straight, and did not give him a direct answer to a direct question, and if he found a man did not know the job with which he was entrusted. I have seen at Corps conferences the knuckles of his fist grow white with strain, when he had asked the Australian Corps Commander a question as to what his corps was to do, which the latter as usual could not answer. When once he had given an Officer his complete confidence, he was a delightful fellow to serve under, as I found; and a refreshing contrast to Maude.

On arrival Allenby had accepted the general lines of the plan which Chetwode proposed to him: to turn the Turkish defences by the capture of Beersheba and envelop them from there. Preparation for this would involve considerable logistic development, including extending a branch of the railway eastward from Rafa to the Wadi Ghuzze, much of which could not be concealed. The plan would have to include an attack on Gaza, both to deceive the Turks as to the real point of main effort and also to pin down the forces defending it and the area immediately east of it. Training in movement over and fighting in the desert would be needed, especially for newly arrived troops. The Turkish force deployed on the Gaza–Beersheba front was estimated at that time to consist of one cavalry and six infantry divisions, totalling 46,000 rifles, 2,800 sabres, 250 machine guns and 200 guns. To overcome these would call for seven infantry and three mounted divisions with appropriate support. An essential element of the plan was the rapid capture of Beersheba to ensure that the enemy did not have time to destroy or seriously damage the water supply there.

On 12 July Allenby signalled to London his requirement for additional resources, principally of artillery, so that each division would normally have its full complement of 18pdr guns and 4.5in howitzers, and that corps artillery should be able to support each with four 60pdr guns and eight 6in or 8in howitzers. He asked for and received another infantry division, the 10th being withdrawn from Salonika, and for five squadrons of aircraft and more engineer, signal and medical units. His requests were met, although not fully as far as artillery was concerned. He moved his headquarters from Cairo to near Rafa, himself assuming command of the army in the field, which was organized into three corps: the Desert Mounted Corps under Chauvel, with Chaytor's Australian and New Zealand Division,* Hodgson's Australian Division,† and Major General Sir George Barrow's Yeomanry Mounted Division.‡ In corps reserve were the 7th Mounted Brigade (Brigadier General J. T. Wigan) and the Imperial Camel Corps Brigade (Brigadier General C. L. Smith): the XX Corps (Chetwode), with 10th (Irish) Division (Major General J. R. Longley), 53rd (Welsh) Division (Major General S. F. Nott), 60th (London) Division (Major General J. S. M. Shea) and 74th Division (Major General E. S. Girdwood); and the XXI Corps (Lieutenant General Sir Edward Bulfin), with the 52nd (Lowland) Division (Major General M. G. J. Hill), 54th (East Anglian) Division (Hare) and 75th Division (Major General P. C. Palin). The artillery of the corps, in addition to divisional artillery, totalled sixteen 60pdrs, and sixteen 8in and forty 6in howitzers.

Allenby originally planned to launch his attack in September, but delays of various kinds forced him to postpone it until October, dangerously close to the rains expected in November, but fortunately just in time to pre-empt the deployment of Fevzi's Seventh Army. 31 October was set as Z (Zero) Day, and in the four preceding days, under cover of intense air activity by the Royal Flying Corps's new Bristol fighters, the Desert Mounted Corps and the XX Corps gradually side-stepped to the right, so that the former, by the evening of the 30th, was deployed thirteen miles south of Beersheba round Khalasa and Asluj. Captain Hawker had already carried out a reconnaissance for the move of his machine guns. He described it in his diary of 18 October:

> No great hurry to rise as we were not due to leave the E side of the Wadi till 9.30. Excellent breakfast the thoughtful Harvey had man-

---

* 1st and 2nd Australian Light Horse and New Zealand Mounted Rifle Brigades.
† 3rd and 4th Australian Light Horse and 5th (Yeomanry) Mounted Brigades.
‡ 6th, 8th and 22nd Mounted Brigades.

aged to get some eggs on the way over. Watered our horses in the
Wadi troughs nice & full & not too crowded. Got to El Buggar about
11 nothing much of note on the way except a dud 5.9 shell which no
one seemed to know where it came from. Had a bit of lunch there &
had to wait for the Brig who was late, when he did arrive he gave
any amount of instructions to our R.E. officer about marking
crossings etc. Managed to get Boyle to obtain permission for me to
start on my voyage of discovery saw Darrells & Shelton at El Buggar
& agreed to meet them at Dart Wadi Lowe & I went out of our way
a bit but happened on the Quarry where our Ammunition is to be
on the day of the Battle, it seemed miles into Yeomans Hill, altogether
too far back for any likelyhood of our being able to get supplies up
quickly. Got into Devon Wadi allright & rather disappointed to hear
from the officer in charge of a troop of Warwick Yeomanry we could
not go any further. Went up Dart Wadi & waited for Darrels &
Shelton after we had put our horses well under cover. Turks put over
two or three shells then about Devon Wadi but nowhere near us.
Held a council of war as soon as Darrels arrived & we decided to risk
shells & go across the open so over we went. All went well till we got
to the Abushar Wadi when some Yeomanry did a flank movement &
the bullets came over thick & fast. We lay low for a bit & then moved
up it till we were under cover of some big hills which were held by
our troops. Worked along the bottom of these for some way till we
got heavily fired on & at one time it was most unpleasant as the
bullets seemed to be coming down both slopes of the hill. Lay low
again & moved further down the hill & then along. Darrels was not
keen to go further forward but as I had seen one of the Warwicks
officers trot to the place I wanted to go to & not to be fired at I ran
for it & there was not a shot fired. By this time Lowe & I were some
5–600 yds in front of the Cavalry screen & it was impossible to do
any hill climbing as we were too near their advanced line of snipers.
As far as we could see we were quite justified in supposing that
should we get a Section so far forward we could give the S end of the
wadi line a very nasty time. Found a very nice wadi for the Section
HQrs & I think they should be very snug there. Had a good look at
the Turks line & could see them moving about freely one bay was
quite full of men & the officer was out on the top looking at us with
his glasses. There seem to be observation posts too all over the place
in most advantageous positions. The wire looks a bit skimpy nothing

very serious & the posts fairly widely distributed so they ought not to be very difficult to blow up or cut through. Took a photo of the position & returned down the Wadi Saba. Very interested in a plant I found which looked very much like a fine type of heather pulled it up but don't know if it will grow as it was in full bloom. The sentry group in the Wadi took a good deal of interest in us but did not put up his gun & make us walk with our hands above our heads. Walked straight down the Wadi Saba & decided it would not be at all a bad way for our Section to come up on the 'night of the murder'. Got back to Devon Wadi just about ready for a bite & a drink. Looked in at the Yahia well & found it had gone quite dry & someone presumably Turks have removed the wheel for firewood judging from the chips & waste lying around. Met Wall & Hunt in Devon Wadi & we all rode back together via the outpost position we are to take up at El Buggar. Saw Brig riding about at a great pace which showed he was in a bad temper so gave him a wide berth. Gave Wall, Hunt & Lowe an idea as to where the outpost line was to be & we came in down the Fara Beersheba road which seems in excellent condition now so cars go along it at quite 'turnpike speed'. Had a drink with Mackintosh at El Buggar & took his tip to clear out so waited for Leir some 200 yds further on & it was well I did so as everything was wrong when he got the car, he had a row with Genl McNeil in Devon Wadi & was apparently scored off. Rode back with Leir & we made quite a good shot for the gap in the wire. Horses awfully thirsty poor brutes & I thought mine was going to burst. Got back to Camp about 7.30 & soon got down to an excellent meal which included fried steak & tinned carrots. Turned in fairly soon afterwards & slept like a log. Brig had to give us a job to do on the way home so chits were sent round all units to reconnoitre a line at Abu Sittu with a view to taking up night outposts there. Leir took up his usual place at the bottom of my bivouac. The wind changed in the early morning & blew the smoke from the incinerator into our bivouac which was most unpleasant & woke us up.

In XX Corps, 60th Division was on the Wadi Ghuzze the same distance from the town, while the 74th was east of the wadi a few miles to the north of the 60th. The plan was that these two divisions would attack the Turkish defences about five miles south-west of the town, pinning them down while the Desert Mounted Corps made a wide detour through the hills to the east of it, cut the road to Hebron to the north-east, and attacked the town from the east. The 53rd Division, on the left of the 74th, would take part in XX Corps' attack and also face north to protect the left flank. The night moves to bring divisions up to their start lines were successfully completed by 03.00 on the 31st, a heavy bombardment of Hill 1070 in front of the 60th opening at 05.55, causing such a cloud of dust that it had to be stopped at 07.00 for the effectiveness of the fire to be observed. It was resumed at 07.45 until 08.30 when 168th Brigade successfully assaulted the hill. Guns then moved forward and the attack was taken up by 74th Division at 12.15, and later by the 53rd and one brigade of the 74th to the north. By 19.00 the objectives of all three divisions had been secured at a cost of 1,200 casualties.

In the Desert Mounted Corps, the Australian and New Zealand Mounted Division had set off from Asluj at 18.00 on the 30th, following the bed of the Wadi el Imshash to the north-east, followed by the Australian Mounted Division, for fifteen miles. The 2nd Australian Light Horse Brigade then continued in the same direction, while the rest of both divisions inclined to the left to Khashm Zanna, four miles east of Beersheba, at the edge of the hills overlooking the Wadi Saba and the Hebron road. No opposition had been met on this night ride through rugged country. By 08.00 the 2nd ALH Brigade on the right and the New Zealand Brigade on the left of the Anzac Mounted Division had reached the Wadi Saba, six miles east of the town, the start line for their attack on two hills overlooking the Hebron road, Tel es Sakaty and Tel es Saba. The Australian Mounted Division was a few miles south of them in reserve, and the 7th Mounted Brigade was six miles south of Beersheba, facing the defences on the right flank of XX Corps.

At 09.00 the 2nd ALH and NZ Brigades moved forward to the attack. The former galloped through the enemy's artillery and machine-gun fire before dismounting for the assault on Tel es Sakaty. Progress was slow, but by 13.00 the hill had been captured. The New Zealanders had a more difficult time. They dismounted about half a mile from Tel es Saba and soon came under heavy fire. At 11.00 Chaytor reinforced them with the 2nd and 3rd Regiments from his 1st ALH Brigade, who, dismounting 1,500 yards from the hill, attacked from the south, while the New Zealanders were assaulting from the east, finally reaching the summit at 15.00.

Chauvel, concerned at the time all this was taking, decided to commit the 3rd ALH Brigade from Hodgson's division also, but by the time he did so, the hill had been taken. He then ordered Chaytor, with the 1st and 3rd ALH Brigades, to close in on the northern defences of the town and decided that he must now take the risk of a mounted attack directly into it from the east. He ordered Hodgson to commit his other two brigades (Brigadier General W. Grant's 4th Australian Light Horse and the 5th (Yeomanry) Mounted) to it, at the same time ordering 7th Mounted Brigade to attack from the south. The 4th ALH Brigade was to lead. Its horses had been unsaddled and it was not until 16.30, with only an hour of daylight left, that they were ready to start. The brigade galloped into and through two lines of Turkish defences, some men, bayonet in hand, then dismounting to clear them, while others rode on into the town as the Turkish garrison fled, having failed to complete the destruction of the wells, which they had started to demolish. They left 1,400 men and fourteen guns behind, Grant's brigade losing 32 killed and the same number wounded. It was a brilliant first step on the road to victory: in concept, in preparation and in execution.

The timing of subsequent stages of the battle depended on water supply. It had been estimated that forty-eight hours would be needed to repair whatever damage might have been caused to the wells in and near Beersheba and to ensure that before XX and the Desert Mounted Corps started their attacks on the eastern end of the Turkish line as a prelude to its envelopment all their animals had been watered and there was a day's reserve in hand. XXI Corps's attack on Gaza was to precede that by twenty-four or forty-eight hours. The optimistic report Allenby received about the state of supplies at Beersheba persuaded him that Chetwode and Chauvel could launch their attacks on 3 or early 4 November and that Bulfin should therefore launch his on the night of the 1st/2nd. Bulfin's plan was for Hare's 54th Division, reinforced by 156th Brigade from the 52nd, to attack Gaza from the west, in the sand dunes between Samson's Ridge and the sea, from which the town would then be cut off. It was to be a night attack, starting with an assault on the prominent Umbrella Hill, a few hundred yards from the southern end of Samson's Ridge. After a pause of several hours, intended to persuade the Turks that this was an isolated action, the attack would be resumed along the coast for 4,000 yards to Sheikh Hasan, the site of the anchorage serving Gaza. The 7th Scottish Rifles of 156th Brigade successfully seized

Umbrella Hill by 23.30 on 1 November. The second phase, supported by six tanks, began at 03.00 and had reached Sheikh Hasan by 06.30, taking 650 prisoners, three guns and thirty machine guns at a cost of 350 killed, 2,000 wounded and 350 missing. The reaction of the enemy was affected by the reorganization in their command. Fevzi's headquarters of Seventh Army was established at Hebron on 27 October, the day that the artillery programme on Gaza started; but von Falkenhayn did not reach Jerusalem until 1 November. When the attack on Beersheba was launched, Kress von Kressenstein, in his Eighth Army, had XX Corps at Gaza, with the 3rd and 53rd Divisions, and the XXII at Tel es Sheria with the 16th, 26th and 54th. The XV Corps, with the 7th and 19th, was in reserve. Fevzi had only one corps, III, with the 24th Division at Kauwukah and the 27th and 3rd Cavalry at Beersheba. The loss of Beersheba made von Falkenhayn's staff fear that Allenby's main thrust would develop up the road to Hebron and Jerusalem. Their fears had been accentuated by the appearance of Lieutenant Colonel S. F. Newcombe and a hundred of Feisal's Arabs on the road at El Dhariyeh twenty miles south-west of Hebron. Kress sent his 19th Division to reinforce Fevzi, who, having attacked Newcombe's men with no less than six battalions, forcing their surrender, occupied a strong position on the prominent hills at Tel el Khuweilfeh and Ras al Nagb nearby. When the 7th Mounted Brigade, sent by Chauvel on 2 November to dislodge them, failed to do so, the 53rd Division and 1st ALH Brigade were given the task next day, but also failed, and inconclusive fighting continued there for the next few days.

Meanwhile water supply was proving a greater problem than antici-pated, with the result that mounted troops had to be widely dispersed, in some cases right back to the Wadi Ghuzze, to water their horses, delaying preparations for the start of the next phase. That, due to begin at dawn on 6 November, would start with an attack by XX Corps against the eastern end of the Turkish line of defences east of the railway south of Tel es Sheria by 74th Division. During this, on their left, the 60th, with one brigade from the 10th, would close up to the Kauwukah defences and bombard them in order to cut the barbed wire. When that had become effective, they would attack them and thereafter turn north to cooperate with the 74th in ensuring that the important high ground, the Tel itself, was firmly secured by the end of the day. On the following day, 7 November, the 60th would join Chauvel's Desert Mounted Corps

in its thrust north to Huj and Jemmameh, while the 10th was to deal
with defences west of Sheria round Abu Hareira.

All went according to plan. The dismounted Yeomanry of 74th
Division, moving forward at 05.00, advanced five miles and captured all
their objectives by 13.30, one and a half hours after the 60th had
launched their attack, which also was successful. By 16.30 both were
on their way to Sheria, where they intended to seize the Tel after dark;
but a huge blaze, caused by the Turks having set fire to their main
ammunition dump, caused a postponement. Meanwhile Chaytor had
been placed in command of all the troops attacking Khuweilfeh, his own
Anzac Mounted Division, the 53rd and the Imperial Camel Corps
Brigade. They made little progress, but contributed to the success of the
operation by containing the enemy there, who might otherwise have
been used to reinforce the defences elsewhere. Early on 7 November it
became clear that a general withdrawal was taking place all along the
front.

Drury of the 6th Dublin Fusiliers, now a captain, was still with the
10th Division and wrote in his diary:

Monday 5th November. We have now a great collection of guns
behind us for to-morrow, there are any amount of 18-pounders with
4.5 howitzers – 60 pounders – 6 inch howitzers and one or two 8″
howitzers. We paraded at 17.15 and moved up to the Wadi close to
the Samarra bridge. When we were moving up in the dark with the
strictest orders against showing a light or making any noise, we were
quite startled by a light suddenly rushing overhead like a very light.
It proved to be a wonderfully brilliant shooting star which shot across
the sky directly overhead from horizon to horizon. It lit up everything
and I could plainly see other columns of troops to our right and left
which I didn't know were there. We arrived in position about 22.00
and waited for the night. To-morrow's attack is to go in Echelon and
the 60th Division go first and we don't move till they get the
positions in P.15 and P.21. They then go north, while we wheel half
left, facing N.W., and then clear the Kauwukah redoubt.

Tues. 6th Nov. Had a great view of the battle. It was the most
magnificent sight and I will never bother to look at a military review
again. The 60th were the limit of stickiness and wouldn't push on
although I was positive there was nobody in the trenches opposite to
them. In fact, I was strolling about on top of a wave or undulation

in the ground and not a shot was fired at me and only a few shells dropped about. Later in the forenoon we had to go and take the place for them and we swept up the whole of the Kauwukah redoubt and reached our arranged line in the Rushdi system from 0-22-a to 0-17-b. I could see the 53rd Division through my glasses having a heavy fight away on our right in the hills. There were several heavy counter attacks which they seemed to drive off but the dust and smoke of the shells hid a good deal of what was going on. I had a great view of two batteries of 18-pounders galloping up under heavy shrapnel. They tore along at top speed over the desert and, when they got to 50 yards of where I was, they wheeled round and got the guns into action like a flash. I had the pleasure of getting them on to a Turk battery, which nobody was able to spot, which was doing a good deal of damage. I found them by a puff of dust from the crest of a rise every time one of the guns was fired. The battery was dug in behind the rise in the trench system at P-15-c-8-3 and when we reached there later, we found the battery absolutely flattened. The horses had just been hooked in to get the guns away when our shells got them. What a mess. Gunners, horses, broken guns and limbers scattered around mixed up with bivouacks, empty and full rounds. I patted my own back as nobody else seemed to think of it. I found a spare sight for one of the guns in neat steel box screwed in the trail and I got it as a souvenir. It was beautifully made by C. Zeiss with adjustable eye piece focussing. Also got an English made periscope in a beautiful leather case. There was an officers tent pitched beside the guns and it was all ripped to shreds, but the camp bed in it was perfect and looked brand new, so I got one of our transport men to take it away for me and I hope it will follow along somehow till I get a chance to use it. There seemed to be very few of our planes about during the day and none of the Bosch until about 16.00 when four of ours came over and were set on by five Bosch. Twice I thought one of ours was hit, but it was only the pilot deliberately side slipping to avoid the Bosch. One enemy plane was hit and came down slowly in their lines.

Wednesday, 7th Novr. Last night was bitterly cold and I got no sleep. Had no coat or blanket. The men were cold too but had a fair amount of digging to do reversing trenches in case of counter attack. To-day was the 'grand finale' of the Turks great Gaza–Beersheba line. We finished clearing up the Rushdi system with very little opposition and then attacked the Hareira system. Hareira is a hollow hill like a volcano about 200 feet high, round the south-eastern side of which runs the Wadi-Es-Sheria in a deep gulley. This gulley has on its southern side a lower hill or spur of the main hill. The Turk seem to have expected the attack from the south and west and also up the Wadi bed, as most of the defences were facing that way, and they had large mortars aligned on the Wadi as the most likely place for attack. However, Allenby's scheme of rolling up the Turks left allowed us to attack this redoubt from the eastward and although the Division were allotted most of the day to take the place, it was ours in a couple of hours, with a lot of prisoners and supplies, but, better still, a water supply and a clear road for the cavalry.

The 60th Division were as usual behind their time-table taking Tel-Es-Sheria. We were to move to Sheria after the 60th Division, but this was countermanded and we had nothing special to do except stroll about and see all that was going on, and to prevent any Turks doubling back into their trench systems.

The Desert Mounted Corps were waiting behind us for the word to push off and presently away they went. It was a thrilling sight, and the whole battle area was just perfect for using cavalry. They swept up the rising ground towards Sheria in a big left-handed sweep, moving in lines of sections at about 250 yards interval between the lines. The frontage was about 2 miles, and the thunder of the hoofs and the glitter of arms was a sight never to be forgotten. They rounded up prisoners and guns, a train complete, a hospital, a bakery in full blast, and many other odds and ends. I saw 4 guns brought in and 750 prisoners and got a photo of them. One prisoner said he was a doctor, educated in the American College at Constantinople. I think he was an Eurasian. He had his wife and children and carried his black bag of instruments. The little boy was greatly delighted with a piece of chocolate I gave him.

Gunner (possibly Bombardier) M. W. Winslade was serving with a 4.5in howitzer battery supporting the 60th Division. In March 1919 he gave a series of talks about his experiences in the campaign at the Wesleyan Institute in Port Said. In one he gave this account of the part his battery played in the operation:

We advanced past Irgeig Wells and one morning before daybreak took up a position about 10 miles south of Sharia Wadi. About 9 o'clock that morning I had to lay a line up a hill along the top of which the 2nd wave of infantry were lying entrenched. Jacko was just about smothering that hill with pipsqueak shrapnel and it will be one of [the] marvels of my life, how I got through without being hit. Shrapnel bullets were hitting the ground all around about 6 inches apart. If ever I've had 'pukka' wind-up it was that day. When I reached the top the C.O. galloped up and directed the fire for the first wave who were advancing across about 3 miles of plain beneath us. On they went getting smaller and smaller until at last we saw them reach the railway embankment and then a hand to hand fight ensued. Once again Jacko was licked and soon afterwards we moved forward to the railway where we stopped for the night with every gun in the brigade wheel to wheel that is 12–18 pdrs and 4–4.5″ alternated with ammo wagons. Just in front of us lay Sharia Wadi with the wells and village and the railway crossing it by a big bridge which Jacko had blown up. He was firmly entrenched on high ground beyond the wadi.

Early morning we soon got orders to advance and directly we crossed the ridge Jacko started pumping in 5–9's and pipsqueaks. 'Trot' came the order and the guns moved forward down the long slope, but this soon developed into a mad gallop and without losing any one we dropped into action close under the steep cliff and being howitzers were able to clear the cliff. The two eighteen pounder batteries were more unfortunate. One of their wagon[s] while unlimbering had the whole team killed men and all. 18 pounders have a very flat trajectory, being field guns and consequently had to stop on the higher ground behind us. Altogether our two eighteen pounder batteries had 20 casualties at Sharia.

On 6 November Allenby had ordered Chauvel to concentrate his corps in readiness for the coup de grâce of encirclement. Barrow's Yeomanry Mounted Division was already well placed on the right flank of XX Corps. Chaytor's ANZAC Mounted was to concentrate just behind it, leaving the New Zealand Brigade at Beersheba, while Hodgson's Australian Mounted, back at Karm, was to move forward behind XX Corps, leaving its 3rd ALH Brigade on the left flank of XX Corps. Shortly before midnight Allenby told Chauvel to move as rapidly as possible on the 7th, reinforced by 60th Division, to Jemmameh and Huj, the ANZAC Division via Ameidat Station, five miles up the railway from Sheria,

where the Australian Mounted would concentrate, joined by the 3rd
ALH Brigade. Progress on the 7th was disappointing. The Anzacs reached
Ameidat Station, but could not get beyond it. Although 60th Division
captured the Tel es Sheria at dawn, they were held up by Turkish
resistance a mile further north, and an attempt by the Australian
Mounted to remove it got no further either. It was not until the end of
the day that the 60th Division finally dislodged them. In contrast to this
disappointing performance, Bulfin's XXI Corps advanced rapidly on
their feet. By dark the 52nd Division's 157th Brigade had reached and
crossed the Wadi Hesi seven miles north of Gaza, which 54th Division
occupied while the Imperial Service Cavalry Brigade pushed out five
miles to the north-east to Beit Hanun, the same distance from Huj.
Progress by the Desert Mounted Corps on the 8th was again disappointing, partly due to difficulty in watering the horses. Chaytor's Anzacs did
not reach Jemmameh until after 15.00 and the 60th Division Huj later
still, after the Yeomanry of the 5th Mounted Brigade, by a gallant but
costly charge, had helped to clear the way, capturing eleven guns. Of the
158 men of the Warwickshire and Worcestershire Yeomanries who
charged, 26 were killed and 40 wounded, and 100 horses were killed.
However, no significant body of enemy had been cut off. Difficulties in
watering horses and problems of logistic supply of all kinds, made worse
by the onset of a khamsin, a hot southerly wind which stirred up clouds
of dust and sand, limited Allenby's ability to move formations forward
quickly.

By the evening of 11 November the 52nd Division in XXI Corps had
reached the river, the Nahr Sukherein, at Esdud and Beit Duras, seven
miles beyond the Wadi Hesi. XX Corps was halted, with 60th Division
at Huj and the 10th and 74th back at Karm, while the 53rd was still in
the hills north of Beersheba. In the Desert Mounted Corps, the Anzac
Mounted Division was over the Nahr Sukherein just ahead of the 52nd,
while the Yeomanry Mounted Division and the Camel Brigade were on
their way to join them. The Australian Mounted was south of them,
further inland, having reached Falluja and, on the railway, Arak el
Munshiye. The Turks were attempting to delay Allenby's advance while
they organized defences on the approaches to Jerusalem in the Judaean
Hills. The principal routes, apart from the Hebron road through Bethlehem, were the railway, which followed the course of the Wadi Surar
from Junction Station, and the road from Ramleh up the Vale of Ajalon.

On 12 November 52nd Division had a successful but costly clash with their rearguard at Burka, east of the Nahr Sukherein, which opened the way for a direct advance towards Junction Station from the west.

On the other flank, an attempt by the Australian Mounted Division to advance towards the station from the south was driven back near Tel es Safi, six miles south of it. A major attack was planned for the 13th. Hodgson was to make another attempt to reach the station from the south, while Bulfin, with the 52nd and 74th Divisions, was to press towards it from the west. Barrow's Yeomanry Mounted Division was to attack on his left, and as soon as the station and the railway running north from it were reached, the ANZAC Division and, on the coast, the Camel Brigade, were to ride north towards Jaffa, cooperating with the Yeomanry to seize Ramleh and Ludd on the way. The attacks were successful, although fighting at times was tough. When 155th Brigade of the 52nd Division were held up at El Mughar, the 6th Mounted Brigade of the Yeomanry Division came to their assistance with a gallant charge by the Buckinghamshire and Dorset Yeomanries, which led to the capture of over 1,000 prisoners, 2 guns and 14 machine guns, but cost them 16 men killed and 113 wounded, and the loss of 265 horses. 52nd Division's casualties during the day totalled about 500.

Lieutenant Bowyer took part in the action at El Mughar (which he calls El Mugheir) and tells the tale:

Hon. Neil Primrose, our squadron leader, comes up to our troop which was doing the advanced work. From the hill we are on we can see bodies of Turks moving from Katra to El Mugheir, and continually entering the cactus gardens that abound there, while from direct in front the Turks are shelling the brigade on our left from Yerbna. Capt. Primrose sends Dodger back with a report: also Lt. Alston takes Hedges and his section out to a village on our right, finding it practically unoccupied, but capturing half a dozen Turks. Meanwhile, Mr Primrose goes on himself to a higher hill in front, taking my section and self as escort. We can now overlook all the plain to Mughair village and ridge, on which there is a good deal of enemy activity. Luckily he leaves us there as a look-out, so we make ourselves snug behind boulders, and have an excellent view of the morning's attack. A Scotch Brigade of infantry are going to attack across the plain to El Mugheir, right round to the far side of Katra. We can see their supporting batteries come up and about 12 o'clock they start the attack, the infantry advancing in waves covered by their artillery. They reach a wady about half way across the plain, but after that they cannot push home the attack, the ground being open and swept by fire of all sorts from the top of the ridge. They make about four attempts, and returning wounded infantry say it is hell in the valley.

It is now about mid-day, and our post is called in to the main body. We are going to gallop out to the wady for an attack. We spread out and go a troop at a time: most of us get across safely. Keigwin, in my section, gets a bullet through the neck, luckily too, as he was feeling the strain of continuous operations. The mounted machine gun corps follow us across, and we know the Berks and Dorsets are somewhere on the flanks. Meanwhile, 'A' Sq., have attacked Yebna, galloping straight at the village, capturing it and its defenders at a comparatively slight loss. Dodger, about all that is left of my original section, comes along with the news that we are going to gallop the position. The [this] suits us better than a long tiring advance dismounted, but it seems rather an awkward finish. Anyhow we have dinner together, finishing a whole tin of jam in great style.

Soon we get our definite orders, – up on top at 3 o'clock sharp, spread out, and go for the position in lines, a squadron at a time. 'B' Sq. leading, Crocker Bulteel at their head. 'C' follow immediately. At three o'clock we scramble out all along the valley and start galloping. Johns, now in my section, is my next door neighbour and we strike over for the 1st. Troop. Immediately a great clatter of fire starts all along the top of the ridge. Old 'Owen', one of the original Bucks horses and well known before the war with Leopold de Rothschild's staghounds, is struck full in the chest, and blood is pumping out, but he galloped the whole mile and three-quarters and then dropped dead at the foot of the position. Gallant old fellow. For a moment the shell fire is heavy, as Johnny has the range of the gulleys, and an H.E. drops just between a machine gun pack horse and its fellow. A few yards in front I have a momentary vision of two horses, a man, and a lot of smoke, flying outwards as I flashed past.

Half a mile from our starting point we come on another slight wady. He also has this ranged for his guns. We cannot get down and through all along so several casualties occur here. Johns and I get through straightaway, and, after this, are up in the middle of 'B' Squadron. I can see Capt. Bulteel just in front so know we have a good 'un to follow. I believe the rifle and machine gun fire got heavier as we neared the slope. Anyhow, several horses and riders turned over in quite the approved battle picture style, and the ground was zipping and spluttering as the bullets hit it.

We seemed now to be an extraordinary few to be charging a position, but we drew our swords and 'Forward on!'. We had come through a line of infantry lying flat on the plain and not enjoying life a lot. On seeing swords come out, not flash out as a saddle with two feeds and extra bivvy sheets will now [not?] allow of this, the Turks began to crawl back over their trench. This put fresh cheer into us and our shouts redoubled, but the last hundred yards up a steep slope, horses blown and almost in a walk, with heavy enfilade fire, were trying moments.

However, now we are on top we jump the Turkish trench and sweep over the hill, down the far side, right through a mob of Turks, and swinging round and driving them into a very convenient ravine on the far side. I think there were about eight of us under Capt. Bulteel, and about 90 Turks, all shouting and gesticulating, but quite willing to lay down arms. Immediately we are through the line, the Turks sweep the top of the hill with shrapnel, and we are glad of our shelter, several of the Turks being hit with their own fire. The trouble is that we are isolated – we do not know where the remainder of the attackers have got to. I have never seen Capt. Bulteel so excited, and we have some rare shooting at bodies of the Turks running back out of the cactus gardens. Soon the firing dies down a bit and we get in touch with the remainder, who, under Capt. Primrose, had driven a wedge in, about a quarter of a mile to our right. Here, Major Evelyn Rothschild is mortally wounded at the foot of the hill, and the fire is even hotter than where we went over.

The Dorsets and Berks almost simultaneously have attacked further along the slope, and the position by dusk is finally won. This was imagined to be the Turks' next big position behind Gaza and it was a great feat of the cavalry to have taken it. I have never known our boys in such high spirits as we were that night, although our losses had been grievous. We had had what every cavalryman longs for, – and had been successful against an almost impossible position. To turn to our own squadron losses, Joey Harland was wounded, also Stroud, Spink, Sgt Revel of our immediate troop. In all, I think, we lost about 60% of our horses hit and about 40 men, killed and wounded, in our two squadrons.

75th Division, five miles to the south, fought their way forward to the line of the railway from Gaza at Kustineh, and early in the morning occupied Junction Station, from which the Turks had withdrawn during the night. On the following day, together with the Australian Mounted Division, they advanced north-eastward through the hills to Latrun on the road to Jerusalem, while the ANZAC Division occupied Ramleh and Ludd. Its New Zealand Brigade, after a successful action at Ayun Kara, west of Ludd, went on to occupy Jaffa unopposed. Between these two divisions, the Yeomanry Mounted also reached the Jerusalem road after another gallant charge by its 6th Brigade at Abu Shusheh. In the advance from Gaza and Beersheba most of the mounted troops had actually ridden some 170 miles. The infantry of 52nd Division had marched 69, fighting four major actions on the way. Over 10,000 prisoners of war and 100 guns had been captured and heavy casualties inflicted on the enemy.

Allenby had originally intended to pause at this stage and build up logistic resources to support the employment of his whole army, but the apparent disorganization of his opponents led him to decide to press on towards Jerusalem in spite of a warning from London, anxious to avoid another Kut, not to overcommit his forces. His problem, apart from the limits imposed by logistics, was that there was only one road capable of taking vehicles leading to Jerusalem, and that the rugged hilly country was ideally suited to defence. The principal part was to be taken by Bulfin's XXI Corps, 75th Division attacking up the road from Latrun, on which the Turks had carried out several demolitions. On their left the 52nd and Yeomanry Mounted Divisions would make their way up minor roads, which were little more than mule or donkey tracks, aiming to cut the road running north from Jerusalem to Nablus, by which the Turkish Seventh Army was supplied. On the right of the 75th, one brigade of the Australian Mounted Division would try to make its way up the line of the railway in the Wadi Surar. The ANZAC Mounted Division and the 54th, moved up from Gaza, would guard the left flank in the plain.

The advance began on 18 November and progress was slow, conditions being made worse for the soldiers, who were still in their tropical uniforms, by heavy rain. By 21 November both the 75th and the 52nd Divisions were within five miles of Jerusalem, 234th Brigade of the 75th having captured the important hill of Nebi Samwil, where they were thrown back by a counter-attack. The 52nd were just to the west of them and the Yeomanry, having almost reached the Nablus road, and then been driven back, were six miles to the north-west. The struggle through the hills had exhausted these divisions, and Allenby ordered a pause while he moved up XX Corps to relieve them. During this period the Turks carried out several counter-attacks, in which they suffered heavy casualties as they were repulsed. As Chetwode's corps relieved Bulfin's, the 60th Division, which had marched all the way, took the place of the 75th and 52nd, and were followed by the 74th which relieved the Yeomanry Mounted, the 10th coming into reserve. The 53rd, with the Corps Cavalry Regiment, 1st/2nd County of London Yeomanry, and a battery of 60pdrs, still on the Hebron road, came directly under Allenby's command. The Australian Mounted Division filled in the gap between the 74th and the 54th on the plain, where the ANZAC Division had advanced to the River Auja, five miles north of Jaffa, which the New Zealand Brigade crossed at its mouth.

The night of 7/8 December was set for the final attack to reach the Holy City. While 53rd Division advanced up the Hebron road to Bethlehem, the 60th, on its left, relieved by the 74th at Nebi Samwil, would attack between the Hebron–Bethlehem road and the one from Latrun, and the 10th Division came into the line on the left of the 74th. The objectives given to the 60th and 74th would bring them across the Nablus road, cutting the city off from the north. The strength of the Seventh Army opposing them was put at 15–16,000 men. As the troops moved into their final positions for the attack, it began to pour with rain which lasted all night. By daylight on the 8th both 60th and 74th Divisions had reached their intermediate objectives, but fog and rain held up the 53rd, exposing the southern flank of the 60th. In the afternoon Chetwode called off further attacks, intending to resume them next day. However Turkish morale had weakened and many of them withdrew during the night, so that all three divisions advanced without difficulty to their final objectives on the 9th, although the 60th had a fierce clash with a Turkish rearguard on the Mount of Olives. Soon after midday the Arab Mayor of Jerusalem came out with a white flag and surrendered the keys of the city to the commander of the 60th Division, Major General Shea, having previously tried to do so, first to an officers' mess cook looking for eggs, next to two sergeants, then to two gunner subalterns, then to a lieutenant colonel and finally to a brigadier, who accepted the surrender document, to Shea's fury. Allenby himself made a ceremonial entry on foot two days later. His casualties since 25 November had been 1,667, and 1,800 prisoners had been taken. Casualties in animals (horses, camels, mules and donkeys) from 31 October to the end of the year were 10,000 (11.5 per cent of the total strength), of which half were killed or died.

Allenby had given Lloyd George his Christmas present. Before settling down for the winter, he had to make his position more secure. XXI Corps took over responsibility for the coastal plain with 52nd Division on the coast, 54th in the centre and 75th in the foothills. On 20/21 December they attacked over the River Auja and forced the Turks back so that they were eight miles north of Jaffa, out of artillery range of the port, which could then be used. Before the end of the month XX Corps advanced north of Jerusalem and, fighting against stiff opposition while the Seventh Army was trying to drive them back to the Holy City, reached their final objectives of Beitin and Deir Ibzia, twelve miles north of the city, by the end of the year.

11

Mobility at Megiddo

Lloyd George, not content with his present, urged Allenby to press on, but the latter insisted that a pause was essential while the railway was extended forward, logistic resources built up and his forces rested and reorganized. In London argument was rife between 'Westerners', who wanted resources to be concentrated on that front now that with Russia out of the war Germany could concentrate all her resources on it, and 'Easterners', who believed that the Entente should adopt a defensive strategy there until American forces were deployed in strength, and that the defeat of Turkey would lead, not only to her desertion of the Central Powers, but to that of Bulgaria also, with serious effects on the attitude of Austria. To resolve the issue General Smuts was sent in February 1918 to discuss possible strategy with Allenby. It was proposed to transfer to his command three Indian divisions from Mesopotamia, one Indian cavalry division from France, perhaps two, and some artillery and aircraft.

The plan that Allenby was developing in his mind was, first of all, to secure his right flank by occupying the Jordan valley, cutting the Hejaz railway, and, by this and other means, supporting Feisal's operations against the Turks, so that Feisal in turn could support his strategy. He was impressed by the fact that all three Turkish armies, the Seventh and Eighth west of the Jordan, and the Fourth east of it, commanded by the lesser Djemal under the greater, the Pasha, were dependent on the railway from Damascus to Dera'a. There a branch split off the Hejaz line westward through the Yarmuk Gorge for thirty-five miles to Semakh at the southern tip of Lake Tiberias (the Sea of Galilee), where it turned south along the Jordan valley to Beisan, and up the valley of Jezreel to El Afule, where it split again, one line going on to Haifa, the other cutting through the long ridge between that port and Nablus to the latter, Tul Keram and Jaffa. Liman von Sanders, who had replaced von Falkenhayn on 1 March, could not afford to neglect a threat to that line, and Allenby intended, by operating in and beyond the Jordan valley and encouraging the Arab Revolt, to persuade him to devote as much effort as possible to countering it. For he himself intended to make his main effort near the coast. He proposed to concentrate infantry and artillery there to make a rapid breach in the enemy defences through which as many mounted troops as possible would immediately be passed to cross the Mount Carmel ridge into the Plain of Esdraelon, where they would seize the exits from the ridge and cut the routes by which the Seventh and Eighth Turkish armies were supplied and through which they would have to withdraw. Having reached the line from Lake Tiberias to Haifa and extended his standard-gauge railway (the Turkish one was narrow gauge) to the latter, he would continue northwards between the coast and the mountains to Beirut, extending the railway as he did so. A subsidiary force would cross the Jordan valley and advance towards Damascus east of the Golan Heights. Beyond Beirut, he would advance to Tripoli and thence inland to Homs to cut off any Turkish forces still in the area of Damascus. Smuts took the plan back to London where it was approved by the War Cabinet, except that only two Indian divisions would be sent from Mesopotamia.

Meanwhile he gave Chetwode's XX Corps the task of occupying the Jordan valley, with the 60th Division, having replaced the 53rd, descending to Jericho while the ANZAC Mounted attempted to cut the enemy garrison off by moving between the town and the river. However the Turkish commander withdrew in time to the bridge over the river at Goraniyeh, five miles to the east, and the 60th occupied the town on 21 February. Shortly before this, on 26 January, a Turkish force, 900 strong, which was occupying a group of villages at Tofileh, fifteen miles southeast of the Dead Sea, was defeated by Jaafar Pasha's Arabs, accompanied by Lawrence and a collection of local tribesmen, who captured 250 of them, 200 horses, 27 machine guns and 2 mountain guns. Many of those who fled were killed by the Arabs before they reached the safety of the railway. It was March before the Turks reoccupied the area with a brigade-sized force, including a German battalion. In order to relieve pressure on the Arabs and to increase the perceived threat to the Turkish lines of communication, Allenby ordered Chetwode to advance to Amman and cut the railway there, where it passed over a viaduct and through a tunnel. On 21 March, Major General Shea, with his 60th and the ANZAC Mounted Divisions and the Imperial Camel Brigade, crossed the Jordan at Ghoraniyeh and attempted to advance up the Wadi Nimrin to Es Salt on the plateau above the valley, fifteen miles west of Amman. It took him two days to cross the river, swollen by rain, and it was not until the evening of the 25th, after clambering up and slithering down the steep hillsides, that the 1st Australian Light Horse Brigade and 181st Brigade of the 60th Division reached Es Salt, moving to within six miles of Amman next day. By this time the enemy had received ample warning of their approach and reinforced the garrison. From 27 to 30 March the two brigades tried to take the town but failed, although the Light Horse reached the railway north of it. By this time a Turkish force had crossed the Jordan from the west and was attacking Es Salt. Shea's force withdrew the way it had come, reaching the west bank on 2 April with 1,000 prisoners, having suffered 1,350 casualties; but Feisal had been helped, as the Turks withdrew from Tofileh and moved part of the garrison of Ma'an to Amman.

Gunner Winslade's battery of 4.5in howitzers took part in this operation, as he described in one of his talks at Port Said after the war:

> Moving in a S. Easterly direction we went into action again about 2 miles west of the Jordan, and settled down for the night. At 2200 hours I was warned for F.O.P.* and carrying all our equipment 'phones etc and 2 reels of wire each, the three of us in charge of an officer made our way towards the Jordan laying our wire as we went. About 12 o'clock we arrived at a pontoon bridge which had only just been flung across. Australian Engineers in fact were just completing the cutting through the bushes on either side, and the 60th Division infantry ... had gained a slight rise about ¾ mile from the Jordan. We connected up with the infantry and waited for daylight. Early next morning the 'Aussies' came across and soon had 'Jacko' on the run. About midday The Duke of Connaught, Allenby and a few 'buckshee' generals came across and lunched off ham and egg sandwiches. *WE* had bully & biscuits and personally I was very short of biscuits because the day before my horse had got away with me while cantering up to the new position (Of course the staff always go ahead), and my ration bag, tied on my bandolier, broke loose from its moorings with 24 hours rations in it. Of course the other boys helped me out but I was none too plentifully supplied ... the day

---

* Forward Observation Post.

after we crossed the Jordan again by another bridge, and had a unique opportunity of using open sights – a very unusual thing with a 4.5 howitzer. The gunners were going dotty with excitement to see their own shells bursting behind Jacko as he made his way up into the hills. That night we camped at the foot of the hills and next day marched about 12 miles up a fearful road (All ruts and rocks) with a perpendicular wall of rocks on one side and a sheer drop of about 150 feet on the other with only just room for two wagons to pass. By this time the Australians had charged up the road and got Jacko beyond Es Salt.

Having reached Es Salt, where he had problems with Arabs stealing the telephone wire, he described the withdrawal:

At last one night the order came to withdraw and not having time to reel in, about 10 miles in all of wire at £5 a mile was left out. We came as fast as the horses could walk down the road again and next night crossed the Jordan having been very nearly cut off by Jacko's cavalry who, knowing every track in the country, had been able to work round the hills.

By then Ludendorff's offensive on the Western Front had driven Gough's Fifth Army back almost to Amiens, and Allenby was told to go over to the defensive and send two divisions, the 52nd and 74th, ten more British infantry battalions, nine Yeomanry regiments, five machine-gun companies and five and a half medium artillery batteries to France, the despatch of fourteen more infantry battalions being demanded later. Indian cavalry regiments from France would replace the Yeomanry, but the British infantry battalions would only gradually be replaced by Indian ones from India. The 7th (Meerut) Indian Division (Major General Sir Vere Fane) had already reached Egypt from Mesopotamia, the 3rd (Lahore) (Major General A. R. Hoskins) being on its way. While digesting this unwelcome news, Allenby became involved in another action east of the Jordan. The Turks had themselves taken the offensive in the valley after the abortive expedition to Amman, but had been held. Allenby planned to force them back in that area by cooperating with the Arabs in taking Es Salt and dominating the plateau around it, which would also have the advantage of reducing the number of troops who would have to spend the summer in the stifling heat of the valley. He intended to attempt this when the reorganization of his mounted divisions, due to the departure of the Yeomanry and the arrival of the Indian cavalry regiments, had been completed; but his hand was forced by an offer of cooperation from the unreliable Beni Sakhr tribe. The operation began on the night of 29/30 April with an attack by the New Zealand Mounted Brigade on the positions of the Turkish VII Corps on the northern side of the Wadi Nimrin. While the Australian Mounted Division moved up the valley, the 3rd Australian Light Horse Brigade captured Es Salt by the evening of the 29th, being joined there by the 1st and 2nd next day. Unfortunately the 4th Light Horse Brigade, left to guard the valley at the foot of the Wadi, was attacked from three directions and driven back into the foothills, endangering the route up to Es Salt. A hastily mounted counter-attack by a regiment from the New Zealand Brigade and one from the 5th Mounted saved the situation. However the attempt by the 60th Division to roll up the enemy's left flank north of the wadi failed, and the whole force had to be withdrawn to the west bank, having suffered 1,500 casualties, two-thirds of them in the infantry.

Shortly before this, the 10th Division was involved in operations to improve its position in the Judaean Hills. Captain Drury's diary records his battalion's part in them:

Week ending Saturday 16th March. We had a pow-wow at the bottom of the Wadi and settled the objectives which were the row of sangars and M.G.posts running from K-3-a-50-90 to K-4-a-60-85. Having secured this which seemed to be the key of our hill, we would stretch out right and left to get in touch with the Inniskillings and the Munsters respectively.

I'll never forget that climb. It was impossible to see over any terrace to the one above, and every moment we expected a shower of stick grenades on our heads. We pushed up in as uneven formation as possible, every man either pushing up his pal first or pulling him up from above. How the mules got up, I don't know and can't imagine, as I was away ahead of them. Anyway, we pressed on up and up, seeing no Turks but hearing their M.G's, chattering away aloft, and the bullets zipping and pingeing off the rocks. We had hardly anybody wounded, which is surprising.

At last, we got in sight of the sangars and could see German officers running backwards and forwards between them. We got everyone collected on a fair frontage and gave them a breather for five minutes, discarded our packs and haversacks and fixed bayonets. When the whistle blew, away we went with a 'screech' like only Irishmen can give (it reminded us of the 15th August, 1915 on the 'K.T.S.' ridge at Suvla Bay, Gallipoli). When the Turk saw us coming, he never waited till we were within range, but just bunged every grenade he could lay his hands on, in our direction, and even some of their rifles and FLED!! What a scene! We arrived at the sangars puffing and blowing like grampus-es (or is it grampi?) and laughing a little shamefacedly as if our little bit of sword rattling had been rather overdone. We were sure Johnny Turk would have waited for us and put up some scrap, and everyone was disgusted to find we had only to say 'Boo' and he ran away. When we got up to what we thought was the top, we found it was a only a false crest. There was a slight hollow of comparatively smooth ground about 300 yards wide and then the crest proper. This ran slightly diagonally across our front through H-33-a to H-34-c and just covering the village of Jiljilia. We could see the Turks holding this crest strongly and they seemed to have a good many M.G's going.

The Colonel allotted the attack to A and D Coys and they lay down under a terrace in shelter and sorted themselves out in proper order. The M.G's. had by this time arrived up behind us and we got them on each flank to give cross fire. The two companies were as keen as blazes to see which would get to the other crest first, as Bill Whyte in the good old style stood between them and sang out 'Are you ready A Coy?' Cheers and shouts of 'Blow the whistle, sir'. The same with D. Coy. 'Away you go' yells the C.O. and away they certainly did go 'hundred yards speed', bayonets glinting in the last rays of the sun, and no gear to hamper them. The Turks looked like sticking this time, but no, before our men got half way across, old Johnny Turk broke and ran as hard as ever he could leg it, throwing away his rifles and equipment and bombs, and just clearing out – vamoosing – for all he was worth. We bagged a few with rifle fire, but it was impossible to fire steadily after a spring like that, and to have really caught them meant following them down into the Wadi Gharib in front and this would have been the height of folly with darkness coming on fast.

We were not long arranging the line for the night and having picquets posted. I went off to examine the village of Jiljilia and we found that we had just missed capturing four 77m/m guns which had been posted just south of the village immediately behind the crest. They had cleared out in a hurry leaving everything behind except the guns, limbers and ammunition. Their tents and shelters were there with bedding and officers' clothing, food and waste of all kinds. . . . Poor old 'Woody' (Major A. H. Wodehouse) got a clip in the neck during the last dash, but the 'Doc' says it won't trouble him. We had very few casualties compared with our estimates, – one man killed and about 12 wounded.

A major reorganization of Allenby's forces was now put in hand. In the Desert Mounted Corps the Yeomanry Mounted Division, the 5th (Yeomanry) Mounted Brigade and the Imperial Camel Corps Brigade were broken up, 2,000 of the latter's camels being handed over to Feisal's Arabs. The remaining Yeomanry mounted regiments were combined in brigades, numbered 10 to 15, with Indian cavalry regiments to form the 4th (Major General Sir George Barrow) and 5th (Major General H. J. M. MacAndrew) Cavalry Divisions. The Australian battalions of the Camel Brigade were formed into two Light Horse Regiments (14th and 15th) which, with a regiment of French Spahis and Chasseurs d'Afrique, formed the 5th Australian Light Horse Brigade, replacing the 5th (Yeomanry) Mounted Brigade in the Australian Mounted Division. That division elected to exchange its rifles for sabres, but the ANZAC Division hung on to theirs. In the British infantry divisions, the 54th was unchanged, but the 10th, 53rd, 60th and 75th were reorganized on the pattern of the Indian Army, their brigades having one British and two (or three) Indian battalions.

This reorganization took time and involved a significant amount of posting of men between units and retraining. Allenby and his chief of staff, Major General Sir Louis Bols, gave high priority to a deception plan to conceal the final concentration near the coast and to create the impression that the next major effort would be on the axis of the Jerusalem–Nablus road and in and beyond the Jordan valley. In the latter an attempt by two Turkish divisions, with two German battalions, to force back the ANZAC Division on 14 July was successfully defeated by the 1st Australian Light Horse and the Imperial Service Cavalry Brigades.

Allenby faced three Turkish Armies. The Eighth, 10,000 strong, now commanded by Djemal Pasha (Kress von Kressenstein having been sent to the Caucasus), with headquarters at Tul Keram, held a line from the coast just north of Arsuf to Furkhah, twenty miles to the east, and consisted of the XXII Corps of three infantry divisions, and the Asia Corps of two, with three German battalions. East of them in the Judaean Hills was Mustafa Kemal's 7,000 strong Seventh Army (Fevzi was ill), consisting of the III and XXII Corps, each of two divisions. In the Jordan valley and east of it, the lesser Djemal's Fourth, with head-quarters at Amman, had 6,000 infantry and 2,000 cavalry in his II Corps (one cavalry and one infantry division) and the VIII of one infantry and one composite division, which included a German regi-ment. Liman von Sanders, with headquarters at Nazareth, held another division in reserve, and 6,000 Turkish soldiers were scattered along the Hejaz railway.

Allenby had almost twice that strength (57,000) in infantry and a great superiority in his 12,000 mounted troops. They were supported by 540 guns, of which 100 were heavy or medium. His plan was that Bulfin's XXI Corps would concentrate on a narrow front on the coast with four infantry divisions, the 60th, 7th Indian, 75th and 3rd Indian, which, after a brief but intense bombardment of the Turkish defences, would punch a hole through and thereafter swing to the north-east, the right directed to Messadieh Junction, the southern exit of the Dothan Pass. East of them, the 54th and a French brigade would attack between the railway and the boundary with XX Corps. The 5th Australian Light Horse Brigade, under Bulfin's command, would operate on his left flank. As the corps launched its attack at dawn on 19 September, Chauvel's Desert Mounted Corps would move from its assembly areas to immedi-ately behind the infantry, the 5th Cavalry Division behind the 60th, the 4th behind 7th Indian, the Australian Mounted Division, less its 5th ALH Brigade, being in reserve. As soon as the infantry had punched their hole, the cavalry divisions would gallop northwards, the 5th making for the track which led over Mount Carmel to Abu Shusheh, eighteen miles south-east of Haifa, from where it would make for Nazareth; the 4th for a similar track through Musmus to El Lejjun, thence on to Afule, the junction of the railway to Nablus with that to Haifa. Chetwode's XX Corps in the Judaean Hills would advance, not by the obvious route up the road from Jerusalem, but with the 10th Division on the left assaulting on the Turkish inter-army boundary five miles east of Furkhah, heading for Nablus, and the 53rd starting east of the road and following the watershed to the head of the Wadi Fara. In the Jordan valley Chaytor had his own ANZAC Mounted Division, the 20th Indian Infantry Brigade, the 38th and 39th Battalions of the Royal Fusiliers and the 1st and 2nd of the British West Indies Regiment, supported by one battery of six 18pdrs, two Indian mountain batteries of 3.7in howitzers and one heavy battery of four 60pdrs. He was to engage the enemy's attention and try and persuade them that his force was larger than it was.

On the night of 16/17 September Nuri Said, Jaafar's chief of staff, accompanied by Lawrence and other British officers, led a strong party of Feisal's regulars, effectively supported by the Royal Flying Corps, to attack the railway west, north and east of Deraa, demolishing the line in several places. In addition to the damage caused, the operation had the desired effect of causing von Sanders to despatch part of his small reserve in that direction from Afule. On the night of 18/19 September the 3rd Indian Division attacked in its sector to improve the start line for its main effort next day. These preliminary actions, including air attacks on Nablus and in the Jordan valley, were intended to divert attention from where the main blow was to fall. It fell as planned at 04.30 on 19 September and was an instant success. It was accompanied by air attacks on Seventh and Eighth Army headquarters and the important telephone exchange at Afule, aimed to interrupt communications. By 07.00 60th Division had secured a crossing over the marshy stream of the Nahr el Falik, five miles behind the enemy front line, clearing the way for the 5th Cavalry Division. By the end of the day the 60th had marched seventeen miles and captured Tul Keram, the other divisions of the corps having swung into a line running south from there, while the 5th ALH Brigade on its left had reached and cut the Messadieh–Jenin railway near the former, and the Royal Flying Corps had a field day attacking Turkish troops attempting, in a state of confusion, to escape up the Dothan Pass.

Gunner Winslade's battery was supporting the 60th Division, as he recorded:

Directly I returned to the battery, of course, I resumed my job as a staff man and also my horse which at the time was 'Nigger' a big black standing about 17h, who had a heart of gold and a mouth of iron. He would attempt any jump no matter how high and as often as not pull it off, but when once he got going you wanted your reins on the bar to stop him. Whoever had saddled him up forgot to put them there with disastrous results, as I will explain.*

About ¼ hour after the infantry had gone over we got the order to advance and away went the O.C. followed by the staff, and in the end I won. Nigger got clean away with me and I thought I was in for a dose of Constantinople or something. The country up there is very sandy and covered with a kind of sage grass and prickly bushes and Nigger took everything at a flying leap. His knees were a bit tender and he'd never go through prickles. In the end I managed to turn him in a wide circle and eventually pulled him up and made sure of the reins being in the top bar. The battery had meanwhile limbered up and after trotting forward about 2 miles dropped into action and managed to get a few shots in before Jacko was out of range again. Then we limbered up again and all moved off at a walk . . .

We trekked all that day northwards, about 3 miles inward from the sea. At 5 o'clock that night about half the battery were travelling together. The remainder were spread out over 3 or 4 miles, coming along as best they could. We had been doing a bare 2½ miles an hour so that the infantry were moving along with us. It was just getting dusk when I was sent back with a pair of Marcus traces (. . . for use in emergency by outriders) to help 'A 'subs' gun along. I was told they had stuck somewhere about 2 miles back and as the road was no longer marked and the country was very undulating I realised I was in for a good game. However I started off by doing the Red Indian stunt and followed the tracks back for some distance, but then they became confused as practically every battery and baggage column made its own track. However I took a general direction Southwards for about 3 miles and seeing nothing of A subs' gun thought it about time I returned. It was by now almost dark and I soon found myself 'in the cart'. But I had learned as far back as France to trust to my horse so I slacked the reins and off he went in a direction which I thought totally wrong. After a time I noticed a dark patch on my right and dismounting found it to be a small hole dug in the ground with about 6 inches of water in the bottom. Of course it was too stinky for me to drink, although I've drunk some awful water at times, but poor old 'Nigger' had had nothing to drink since about 8 o'clock in the morning so, with the aid of my mess-tin,

* He is referring to the bar of the bridle's bit.

I managed to give him a little at any rate, and then continued my journey. About 9 o'clock he ran me smack into the battery who had settled down for the night after turning N.W. for a bit. Next morning we had a three mile ride to water, which had to be pulled up from a 70 foot well with buckets. You can imagine what a time it took us to water 130 horses.

Both cavalry divisions were over the Nahr el Falik by 10.00. After a pause near Liktera, ten miles north-west of Tul Keram, to water and feed their horses, while armoured cars led patrols to reconnoitre the tracks over the Carmel ridge, they started off again in the early evening, crossed that range by night and were on the far side, the 5th at 02.30, the 4th at dawn on 20 September. The 5th's 13th Brigade reached Nazareth at 05.30, surprising Liman von Sanders and his staff, who, in the confused fighting in the town, managed to escape.

The 14th Brigade had moved on to Afule, where they met the leading troops of the 4th Division. The latter's 10th Brigade had had a satisfactory action on their way there, described by Captain D. S. Davison of the Indian 2nd Lancers:

As Squadrons moved off a steady fire broke out from direction of Point 193 at 05.30 hours. Leaving Capt. Vaughan to bring along the reserve I rode forward to find out what was happening, and on approaching Point 193 I received a verbal message from the O.C. 'C' Squadron to the effect that he was held up by a force estimated at 80 rifles. I found the situation to be as follows. The Turks were holding a position in the open about ½ mile East of Point 193. 'C' Squadron had dismounted 1 troop under R. M. [Risaldar Major] Mukand Singh, and their Hotchkiss Troop, and were engaging the enemy with fire at about 800 yds range, while the remainder of the Squadron was concentrating in rear with a view to moving round the enemy's flank. The 11th L.A.M. [Light Armoured Motor] Battery were in action about 300 yards in front of 'C' Squadron and were engaging the enemy with Machine Gun fire. From the high ground about Point 193, the enemy's position could be seen, and was fairly well demarcated by the dust raised by his rifle and M.G. fire, and I realised that the estimate of 80 rifles was much below the mark. The soil was black cotton, but in this particular place, was not so bad as to stop horses galloping. The enemy's flank could be distinguished and, as there seemed to be no obstacle to hold us up, I decided to turn his left flank and gallop the position.

I accordingly directed the O.C. 'D' Squadron, (Capt. Vaughan) to 'Left Shoulder', pointed out the enemy's position and ordered him to go slow for five minutes to enable me to get the Machine Guns into action, and then to turn the enemy's flank and charge. I then ordered the O.C. M.G's to come into action from the neighbourhood of Point 193. In the meantime I had despatched the Adjutant (Capt. Ranking) to get into touch with the O.C. 'A' Squadron, who at this time was on the road about halfway between LEJJUN and KHEL KHUZNEP, and order him to work round the enemy's right flank. Owing to the distance that this message had to go and to the fact that 'A' Squadron was rather scattered when the order was received, the fight was over before the order could be acted upon.

By the time I had got the M.G's into action, I could see that 'D' Squadron was well round the enemy's flank in Column of Troops, and almost immediately they wheeled Head-Left, formed Squadron and charged in open order, rolling up the Turkish Front line, capturing or killing every man. R. M. Mukand Singh, on seeing 'D' Squadron charge, mounted his troop of 'C' Squadron and charged from the front with good results. In the meantime the O.C. 'B' Squadron, seeing what was happening, decided to cooperate with 'D' Squadron on his own initiative. My original intention had been to leave 'B' Squadron out to watch the right flank but the necessary orders did not arrive in time, so, seeing what was happening, I sent a message to Jamadar Sarkjit Singh, who was commanding the troop of 'B' Squadron sent to seize TELL EL DHAHEB, to remain out at flank guard. As things turned out it was just as well that O.C. 'B' Squadron acted as he did, for the Turks were found to be holding the position in two lines one immediately behind the other and some 300 yards apart, and had 'D' Squadron been alone they might well have suffered heavy casualties from the fire of the second line. The O.C. 'B' Squadron, realising this, swung round outside 'D' Squadron and charged the Turkish support line, rolling it up. During the advance 'B' Squadron ran into a wire fence and became considerably disorganised while under heavy fire from rifles and M.G's. Ressaidar Jang Bahadur Singh however rallied his men with great coolness and reformed the Squadron in time to cooperate with 'D' Squadron.

The 4th Cavalry Division then rode on down the Vale of Jezreel to
Beisan, the Indian 19th Lancers continuing north up the Jordan valley
for twelve miles to the bridge at Jisr el Mejamie, having covered nearly a
hundred miles in thirty-six hours. By then the 5th Division's 15th
Brigade had rejoined it at Afule and the Australian Mounted Division
had also crossed the ridge north-east of Tul Keram and reached Lejjun,
sending its 3rd ALH Brigade from there to block the exit from the
Dothan Pass at Jenin. An officer of the 15th Brigade told this story:

> I myself coming along later with the guns left HUDEIRA in the early
> hours of the 20th, the 15th Brigade timing their arrival at the hills
> about dawn. So travelling as we did in daylight one was able to realize
> the difficulties the other 2 Brigades must have [had] on their march
> during the night before. On the way a man of my own Regiment
> leading a tired pack reported to me, this Sower [trooper] by name
> ABDULLAH KHAN belonged to 'A' Squadron, P Ms* from the Salt
> Range.
>
> He told me that he had broken the stock of his rifle, at which I
> reproved him for his carelessness, thereupon he launched forth into
> the following story which at first I didn't believe, but was subse-
> quently able to corroborate. After leaving HUDEIRA his pack horse
> gave out & he was told to come along as best he could. As he trekked
> along he fell in with a sowar of HODSON's horse in a similar
> position & so they joined forces, journeyed till night began to close
> in. Seeing a haystack by the side of the road, they hitched up their
> horses and lay down to sleep. During the night they were awakened
> by the noise of a motor approaching. When the car came opposite
> the stack it was stopped and a figure descending advanced towards
> them. They got up, suddenly the advancing figure opened fire on
> them from about 10 paces & emptied his revolver at them but
> fortunately missed; meantime the 2 men had picked up their rifles &
> attacked their assailant knocking him down, ABDULLAH KHAN
> breaking his rifle at the stock.
>
> While they were making up their minds as to what they were to
> do with the senseless form at their feet, they recognised in the bright
> moonlight that they had assaulted a British staff Officer, with 'wind
> fairly up' they proceeded to revive him & do what they could for

* Punjabi Mussulmans.

him. Eventually he came to & was able to continue on his way, before leaving he congratulated the 2 men on the offensive spirit which they had displayed.

This story was more or less forgotten until one day in November a bandaged officer arrived at BARRON'S Hotel in ALEPPO, he it was who was the victim of that midnight encounter & turned out to be the C.R.E.* of the Corps.

On the 21st, the 13th Brigade, which had moved to a position between Nazareth and Tiberias, was ordered back to intercept a Turkish force said to be advancing towards the former. Captain A. H. Brooke was commanding B Squadron of the 18th (K.G.O.) Lancers and wrote this report of the action which followed:

After midnight the C.O.† came round to see us & warned us of probable arrival of enemy troops from HAIFFA. In fact as he was speaking to me we heard carts moving along the HAIFFA road, in due course the shooting started on A Squadron's front, the C.O. leaving me went across to the other squadron. As soon as he had left I and my subaltern, a lad small in stature but with the heart of a lion, slipped down to the right of our line near the footpath mentioned as the squadron dividing line. Finding the machine guns near the path firing I sent him across to find out what their target was, as though we could see nothing there was a great hubbub in front of A; about 20 yards from the crest of the hill he ran into a Turkish patrol the 2 leading men of which upped with their rifles, but, closing in an instant, he seized the rifle of the nearest man & wrenching it from him knocked them both down. Meantime we had run down to his assistance, 2 more being bayonetted the remainder fled down the hill.

Thinking that the Turks might be going to develop an attack up this road I telephoned down to R H Q suggesting that it might be advisable to send up the reserve squadrons. I was holding an extended front & had actually about 12 men with whom to make a counter attack should the enemy elect to come up the path.

Major MILLS who was acting 2nd [in] Command sent up D Squadron at once & brought up C himself later and arranged a counter attack with one squadron. Forming up C Squadron along

* Commander Royal Engineers.
† Lieutenant Colonel V. A. S. Keighley.

the pathway they went in with the bayonet clearing the ground in front of A, the latter coming in from the crest. Bag 300 prisoners 7 machine guns & 40 Turks buried. D Squadron sent out at dawn followed the HAIFFA road & secured the country in it's vicinity collecting another 50 prisoners. We had one man slightly wounded.

The Gloucestershire Yeomanry were outside the area of the attack but their picquets became involved in battle with a tame bear which tried to get through them & back to NAZARETH, bear died.

In XX Corps the 10th and 53rd Divisions made slow progress through the hills against stubborn opposition, but during the night of the 20th resistance began to crumble. By midday on the 21st, 10th Division had reached Nablus as the 5th ALH Brigade did so from the west. Most of the Turkish Eighth Army had by this time surrendered, but some of its remnants and most of the Seventh were trying to escape by a road they had built down the Wadi Fara to the Jordan valley. As they did so, they were attacked by the Royal Air Force for four hours, while Chaytor's force blocked the eastern exit. Most scattered into the hills and eventually surrendered. The RAF had also effectively attacked Turkish columns trying to escape northwards through the Dothan Pass.

Gunner Winslade passed that way and commented:

All along the road were broken Turkish wagons, dead horses, bullocks, and men and whole litters of papers. As it transpired afterwards our aeroplanes had caught Jacko retreating and swooping right down had played havoc with Machine gun fire. In most cases the drivers of the wagons had attempted to get out of the way by turning off the road, but as a rule they had collapsed in the ditch. However we often had to unhook teams to pull dead bullocks & wagons off the road before we could proceed.

Lieutenant T. O. Clogstoun of the Royal Warwickshire Regiment was a pilot in the Royal Flying Corps, which had been absorbed, on 1 April 1918, into the Royal Air Force. He was serving with No. 111 Squadron, based at Ramleh, and his log book records that on 21 September he carried out two sorties in his SE5a, one at 8 a.m., the other an hour later, both at 5,000 feet. Of the first he wrote: '4 bombs dropped with good effect on troops & transport near Nablus in Hills. 200 rounds fired.' And of the second: '4 bombs dropped on head of column of transport retreating. Good results. 250 rounds fired from 200' at troops

& lorries. "Death Valley".' On the 22nd he carried out a sortie at 10 a.m. at 7,000 feet, writing in the log book: '4 bombs dropped on Infantry & Cavalry in Retreat in Desert 25 miles NE of Nablus with good effect. 450 rounds fired. Retreat stopped.' And on the 23rd at 10.a.m. at 10,000 feet: '4 bombs dropped on Bedouins & Turks in retreat with transport at Esault [sic] 200 rounds fired at transport with good effect. Country dangerous hostile arabs.'

Colonel (as he later became) H. B. Morkill was with 144 Squadron involved in the same operations, which he described in an interview in his old age:

> We used to bomb, diving down line ahead, and at Nablus we got a very warm reception indeed. The machine gun fire was very heavy. Our leader, A. H. Peck, who was a great chap, had forty bullet-holes through his machine; I had seventeen through mine, all round me. It was absolutely amazing – the petrol tank was just in front of me, and one went into the petrol tank halfway up and came out the top. It made a big hole the size of my fist at the top, but left me enough petrol to get home on . . . I was very lucky indeed.

Victory over the two armies was complete, and Allenby's attention turned to the Fourth, over the Jordan. On the 21st the New Zealand Mounted Brigade in Chaytor's force had moved north on the west bank and early on the 22nd reached the road up the Wadi Fara from Jisr ed Damieh. From there they were directed to Es Salt, which they reached on the 23rd. Allenby ordered Chaytor to take Amman and cut off Djemal's II Corps, based on Ma'an. After a brush with rearguards, Amman was occupied on the 25th, 20th Indian Brigade holding the town, the three mounted brigades deployed to the north, securing the water supply, the east and the south, from which direction the first troops of the Turkish II Corps appeared on the 28th. Having been assured by the commander of the 2nd ALH Brigade that he would protect them from the Arabs, they surrendered – 4,000 of them, bringing the total of prisoners taken by the ANZAC Mounted Division in the campaign to 11,000 with 57 guns.

While Chaytor was thus engaged, Liman von Sanders was trying to establish a defence line from Deraa down the Yarmuk Gorge to Semakh and thence along the western shore of Lake Tiberias and up the River Jordan to Lake Huleh. Hodgson's Australian Mounted Division was given the task of dealing with this, which he handed to Grant's 4th Australian Light Horse Brigade. Its 11th Light Horse Regiment rode to Semakh during the night of 24/25 September, approaching its defences in moonlight just before dawn on the 25th. Received by machine-gun fire, they charged and then dismounted, successfully overwhelming the enemy, of whom they killed 100 and captured 350, including 150 Germans, at a cost to themselves of 14 men killed and 29 wounded, and 100 horses killed. Grant's brigade then cleared the western shore of the lake and joined hands with the 3rd ALH Brigade, who had ridden from Nazareth, at Tiberias itself, thus bringing what became known as the Battle of Megiddo to a victorious conclusion.

Allenby's eyes were now on Damascus. Barrow's 4th Cavalry Division was to cross the Jordan at Jisr el Mejamie and make straight for Deraa, where he would either cut off the rest of Djemal's Fourth Army, or, if it had withdrawn, pursue it up the railway to Damascus, a total distance from Semakh of 140 miles. Hodgson was to take the direct route from south of Lake Huleh through Kuneitra over the Golan Heights, a distance of 90 miles, and was to be followed by MacAndrew's 5th Cavalry Division. Barrow started off from Beisan on 26 September and, after fighting rearguards west of Deraa on that and the following day, reached the town to find it occupied by Feisal's Arabs, who were continually harassing the retreating Fourth Army. Brigadier General W. G. K. Green, commander of the 10th Cavalry Brigade, which led the way, reported:

During the night [27/28 September] a representative of the Sherifian Army reported the arrival of some Sherifian Troops in the vicinity, but it was still unknown that DERAA was actually in their hands. Consequently at 04.30 on the 28th the 10th Cav. Bde moved out from ER REMTE and marched to the hills. Two Regiments were disposed in position to cover the assembly of the Division. DERAA Station was now seen to be in flames: the roof of the large Hospital and other buildings that were intact the previous evening had fallen in and much of the rolling stock on the railway was black and smouldering. The outposts reported having seen the red glow of fires during the night, and early morning patrols brought in information that, though the place did not appear to be held, there was a great deal of firing going on in the streets.

At 07.00 the Brigade was ordered forward to DERAA. On the Eastern edge of the hills the Brigadier met Colonel Lawrence with some of his Arab Irregulars. He stated that the Sherifian troops had entered DERAA soon after noon the previous day. He accompanied the Brigade to the Railway Station where he was shortly joined by the Divl. Comdr. about 09.30.

Words fail to describe the appalling scenes that the Station settlement presented. Many Turkish dead and wounded were lying unheeded and in agony about the roads and buildings; hordes of local Arabs were hurrying hither and thither carrying off furniture and other loot; the whole area was littered with books, papers, machinery and quantities of property wantonly destroyed and scattered abroad by the marauders. Locomotives and railway carriages had been burnt, broken up and stripped of important accessories for no other reason than sheer lust for destruction. The cruelty exhibited by irresponsible Arabs to the miserable vanquished Turks was abominable in the extreme. After the Brigade had picketed the Station and principal routes some measure of order was established and looting ceased. The enemy wounded were collected and attended to by the medical establishments and steps were taken to bury the dead. The Brigade bivouacked for the night on an open space South-West of the Station while the 12th and 11th Brigades marched direct to MEZERIB from ER REMTE and were there joined by Divl. Hd. Qrs.

During the afternoon the Brigadier received a formal visit from Col. Lawrence and the Emir Nasir accompanied by Nuri Bey, the Chief of the General Staff of the Sherifian Army, whose Irregulars were encamped in and about the Railway Station. They had in their charge some 1200 Turkish prisoners, caged in an enclosure in the station premises, the remnants that failed to escape towards DAMASCUS. The night passed quietly with the exception of some firing by the inhabitants of the old town who had amassed a goodly collection of rifles and ammunition that had been cast away by the fleeing Turks.

This was the first real nights rest that the Brigade as a whole had had since leaving BEISAN. Some of the Squadrons had only had their saddles off for two hours since starting from JISR MUJAMIA until they settled down at DERAA.

Hodgson's men set off on the 27th and met their first opposition at Jisr Benat Yakub (the Bridge of the Daughters of Jacob) south of Lake Huleh. Both the 3rd and the 5th ALH Brigades had difficulty in fording the river to outflank it, and, when they did, the Turko-German rearguard withdrew in lorries. The bridge was not repaired until the afternoon of the 28th and they did not get further on that day than Kuneitra, where both waited for their guns and other vehicles to catch up. It was not until 29 September that the advance was resumed. The intention was that the Australian Mounted Division would move west of Damascus to block the roads to Beirut and Homs, while the 5th Cavalry moved to the south of the city to cut the road from Deraa and, it was hoped, intercept the Fourth Army withdrawing in front of Barrow. After brushing aside rearguards, Hodgson's leading brigades, the 3rd and 5th ALH, were brought to a halt by the deep Barada Gorge, west of the city, through which ran the road to Beirut. Unable to cross it, they stopped the traffic on it with machine-gun fire, which inflicted very heavy casualties on the refugees, civil and military. A ban on entering the city was later lifted, and at dawn on 1 October the 3rd ALH Brigade rode through and out on to the road to Homs, on which they engaged rearguards, capturing 2,250 prisoners on that and the following day, while 12,000 Turkish soldiers had surrendered in the city itself. While the 3rd Brigade was passing through, Feisal's Arabs, led by Sherif Nasir Said of Medina, rode in, accompanied by Lawrence, who, having met Chauvel in the outskirts, found himself immediately involved in a struggle with rival Arab and Druse movements to assert Feisal's claim to be the political authority replacing the Turks. Feisal himself arrived next day by special train from Deraa to meet Allenby, who had driven from Ramleh in his grey Rolls-Royce.

Of the 100,000 or so Turkish soldiers in Syria and Palestine, only some 17,000 had escaped, and it was estimated that only 4,000 of them could form an effective fighting force. London urged Allenby to press on to Aleppo, but, as always, he had to face logistic realities. He decided that the first stage would be to move up to Beirut and Rayak, where the railway from Beirut to Damascus joined that to Homs, south of Baalbek. The 7th Indian Division, which had already marched to Haifa, set off again along the coast, reaching Beirut on 8 October, where they found the French navy in the harbour and armoured cars from both the cavalry divisions, who had met no opposition on their way from Damascus, which the Australian Mounted Division was left to occupy and where they suffered heavily from malaria and influenza, as did Barrow's 4th Cavalry. MacAndrew's 5th was therefore given the task of advancing the

275 miles from Rayak via Homs to Aleppo, supported by some of Feisal's Arabs under Sherif Nasir. The leading column, the 15th Cavalry Brigade with two of its regiments, three armoured car batteries and three light car patrols, reached Homs on 16 October, where Nasir joined them, Tripoli having been secured by XXI Corps's cavalry regiment, a composite Yeomanry regiment. On 23 October, after a minor skirmish, the leading armoured cars reached the outskirts of Aleppo and MacAndrew sent in a demand for surrender, which was refused. While waiting for the rest of 15th Brigade to arrive, reconnaissances were carried out and a plan made for a joint operation with Nasir's Arabs on the 26th; but the latter, with the help of sympathizers in the city, succeeded in entering it on the 25th and expelling the Turkish garrison, so that MacAndrew was able to drive in with the armoured cars at 10.00 next morning, after which the two cavalry regiments, the Jodhpur and the Mysore Lancers, met with a rebuff when pursuing the Turks retreating up the road to Alexandretta, to which Allenby was now urged to press forward. For this Hodgson's Australian Mounted Division was ordered forward on 27 October and was nearing Homs when an armistice with Turkey came into force on 31 October, almost exactly four years since the war with the Ottoman Empire had broken out.

Since 18 September Allenby's army had captured 360 guns and 75,000 prisoners of war, of whom 3,700 were German or Austrian, 200 of them officers, at a cost of 5,666 battle casualties, of whom 853 were killed, 4,428 wounded and 385 missing. Total battle casualties in the campaign since January 1915 had been 51,451.

Epilogue

The three campaigns described in preceding chapters resulted in 264,000 battle casualties. That may not seem a large number in comparison with the total number of casualties in the First World War: 5,200,000 dead on the Allied side, 2,300,000 of whom were Russians and 513,000 from Great Britain and Ireland. It might be considered not too high a price to pay to achieve an important strategic advantage. But what did the war against Turkey achieve? It is not an easy question to answer. It certainly kept the Suez Canal and the supply of oil from the Anglo-Persian oilfield at Ahwaz secure; but that could have been achieved with much less effort and cost in lives. The first question to ask is: could Turkey have been dissuaded from joining the Central Powers and persuaded at least to remain neutral, as she sensibly did in the Second World War? Would it not have been possible to have agreed in 1911 to the request of the new Young Turk regime for an alliance, and, if it had been agreed, could it have remained effective, given the strong German influence in the Turkish army and in the country generally? Was it wise to have seized the two Turkish battleships in 1914? Even if they had been opposed to us and had forced the Royal Navy to keep more battleships in the Mediterranean, would that have been critical to the balance of naval strength in the North Sea; and how should that have weighed in the balance against the possibility of keeping Turkey neutral? When, with the advantage of hindsight, one counts the cost, at Gallipoli, of trying to achieve the same aim – for to frighten Turkey out of its alliance with Germany was the purpose of sending a fleet into the Sea of Marmara – one is forced to the conclusion that Churchill's decision to requisition the battleships may have been a serious misjudgement.

That brings one to the whole issue of the Dardanelles affair. First, would the presence of a British fleet off Constantinople have frightened Turkey into trying to get out of her alliance with Germany? It is possible that it might; but what was the fleet to do if that did not happen, or did not happen quickly? Were they to bombard Constantinople, and would that have been effective? Is it not possible that the Turks, urged on by the Germans, might have managed to bottle the fleet up there by closing the Straits behind them? Once the landings had taken place, but had not cleared the peninsula to get the fleet through, was it sensible to persist? It would surely have been better to have cut our losses, for, even if the fleet did manage to get through later, its chances of achieving its aim were slender. The argument that to abandon the enterprise would cause a serious loss of face in the Muslim world, especially in India and Egypt, causing serious security problems which would tie down troops, weighed heavily, but was shown to be exaggerated by the lack of such a serious reaction when we did eventually leave the peninsula. The verdict on that campaign must be that it was ill-conceived and incompetently executed. Churchill, Kitchener and Fisher must bear a heavy load of blame, as must Asquith at the top and Hankey lower down. There can be no doubt that the 120,000 casualties of all kinds incurred there did not achieve any worthwhile strategic advantage.

Both in Egypt and in the Persian Gulf, the initial strategy was purely defensive, and the operations to secure the Suez Canal and the oilfield at Ahwaz and terminal at Abadan entirely successful. But in both operational theatres the familiar process of pushing forward in order to keep a potential threat at arm's length came into play, an old-fashioned version of 'mission creep'. There is no doubt that Nixon made a fatal error in encouraging, indeed forcing, Townshend to advance beyond Kut. He should then have given priority to developing his transport resources so that, if necessary, he could move forces between Basra and Kut with greater speed, in either direction, to deal with any threat that might develop. Once Kut had been recaptured, it was probably right, for both political and military reasons, to go on and occupy Baghdad.

In the case of Egypt, it was undoubtedly right of Murray to decide to defend the canal by moving forward to El Arish. The decision to go on to Gaza was less soundly based, except as a means of making it more difficult for Kress von Kressenstein to build up a force capable of posing a serious threat to the canal. However, there was something to be said for staying near El Arish and facing him with the problem of moving through Sinai's waterless desert. Both the First and Second Battles of Gaza suffered from an underestimate of the enemy's strength and fighting quality, and of a lack of adequate preparation. They proved a waste of lives and effort.

The best argument for Allenby's offensive, which started with the Third Battle of Gaza, was that an advance northwards towards Aleppo was a more economic way of preventing YILDERIM threatening our position in Mesopotamia than reinforcing the latter. Lloyd George's belief that knocking Turkey out of the war would be a decisive move towards victory over Germany and Austria does not hold water; but the capture of Jerusalem and the victory of Megiddo were welcome presents for a war-weary Britain. Allenby's victories did much to preserve the presence of horsed cavalry in the British army long after they should have been replaced by mechanized forces. It was appropriate that the one cavalry division, mostly Yeomanry, still remaining in the British army in 1939, was sent to Palestine for internal security duties on the outbreak of the Second World War.

To return to the first question raised. If we had been successful either in persuading Turkey to keep out of the war, or, by a successful passage of the Dardanelles, frightening her out of it, what would the subsequent history of the Middle East have been? Would Mustafa Kemal have had the motive or authority to convert what had been the Ottoman Empire into the secular, Western-oriented Turkey that he, as Atatürk, almost succeeded in making it? Would there have been an Arab Revolt against a post-war Turkey, and what form might it have taken? A Turkey which maintained authority over all the area which, in 1914, comprised the Ottoman Empire would have become the greatest oil-producing country in the world, potentially very powerful. What of Egypt: would it have maintained its nominal subjection to Constantinople, or Istanbul? There would have been no state of Israel. Of one thing one can be certain: the Middle East would have been as troublesome a place as, in the event, it has proved to be. The lives lost by British, Australian, New Zealand and Indian soldiers in the war against Turkey between 1914 and 1918 changed the area decisively, but whether for better or worse it is hard to say.

Select Bibliography

All books were published in London unless otherwise stated.

Official Histories

Military Operations, Egypt & Palestine, vol. I, Lieut.-Gen. Sir George Mac-munn & Capt. C. Falls, 1928; vol. II, Cyril Falls (Parts 1 & 2), 1930.

Gallipoli, Brig.-Gen. C. F. Aspinall-Oglander, vol. I, 1929; vol. II, 1932.

The Dardanelles Commission, Parts I and II, 1918.

The Campaign in Mesopotamia, 1914–1918, Brig.-Gen. F. J. Moberly, vol. I, 1923; vol. II, 1924; vol. III, 1925; vol. IV, 1927.

Barker, A. J., *The Neglected War: Mesopotamia 1914–18*, 1967.

Bird, W. D., *A Chapter of Misfortunes*, 1923.

Calwell, Sir Charles, *The Dardanelles: Lessons of the Campaign*, 1919.

Candler, Edmund, *The Long Road to Baghdad*, 1919.

Deane, Edmund, *British Campaigns in the Nearer East*, 1919.

Ensor, R. C. K., *England: 1870–1914*, Oxford, 1936.

Fromkin, David, *A Peace To End All Peace*, 1989.

Gilbert, Martin, *Winston S. Churchill*. Vol. III, *1914–1916*, 1971.

Hamilton, Sir Ian, *Gallipoli Diary*, 1920.

Hickey, Michael, *Gallipoli*, 1995.

James, Robert Rhodes, *Gallipoli*, 1965.

Kannengieser, Hans, *Gallipoli*, Berlin, 1927; tr. C. J. P. Balls as *The Campaign in Gallipoli*, 1928.

Lawrence, T. E., *The Seven Pillars of Wisdom*, 1935.

Lee, John, *A Soldier's Life: General Sir Ian Hamilton 1853–1947*, 2000.

Mango, Andrew, *Atatürk*, 1999.

Mansel, Philip, *Constantinople*, 1995.

Masefield, John, *Gallipoli*, 1916.

Massey, W. T., *Allenby's Final Triumph*, 1920.

Moorehead, Alan, *Gallipoli*, 1956.

North, John, *Gallipoli: The Fading Vision*, 1936.

Preston, R. M. P., *The Desert Mounted Corps*, 1921.

Quetta Staff College, *A Critical Study of the Campaign in Mesopotamia*, Calcutta, 1925.

Steel, Nigel, and Hart, Peter, *Defeat at Gallipoli*, 1994.

Taylor, A. J. P., *The Struggle for Mastery in Europe: 1848–1918*, Oxford, 1954.

—— *English History 1914–1945*, Oxford, 1965.

Townshend, Charles V. E., *My Campaign in Mesopotamia*, 1920.

Tuchmann, Barbara, *The Guns of August*, New York, 1962.

Wavell, A. P., *The Palestine Campaigns*, 1928.

Index of Contributors

Ranks are those which, as far as can be ascertained, the contributors held at the time that they are first mentioned. Names in round brackets which follow are those of the copyright holders, whose permission has been obtained and who in many instances have transferred copyright to the Museum. Where there is none, it has not been possible to trace the holder. In those cases, the Museum would be pleased to hear from anyone who claims to be such, or knows the address of the person they believe to be the copyright holder. The figures in square brackets are the accession numbers of the papers from which extracts have been taken.

Photographs numbered 57 and 59 were taken by Corporal Joseph Egerton, King's Shropshire Light Infantry, and reproduced by kind permission of Mr John Egerton.

General Index

FIELD MARSHAL LORD CARVER

The National Army Museum Book of

The Boer War

PAN BOOKS

A vivid military history of what was Britain's first modern war, written with original sources chosen by one of Britain's foremost soldiers and military historians. Published in cooperation with the famous National Army Museum, it quotes extensively from the museum's unpublished archive of diaries, letters and documents. The text is complemented by unpublished photos from the museum's collections, together with seven detailed maps devised by Lord Carver.

Field Marshal Lord Carver was one of the most distinguished British soldiers of our time. His previous book, *Britain's Army in the Twentieth Century*, received superb reviews: 'particularly readable' – *Sunday Telegraph*; 'masterly' – *Spectator*; 'vivid . . . masterful' – *Military Illustrated*; 'lucid' – *Soldier*.

'Sobering reading, laced with sudden infusions of raw excitement as some violent encounter comes to life in a soldier's own words'
John Spurling, *Times Literary Supplement*

JULIAN THOMPSON

The Royal Marines

From Sea Soldiers to a Special Force

PAN BOOKS

A complete and authoritative history of one of Britain's elite forces

The Royal Marines' achievement, toughness, professionalism and enterprise puts them in the same league as such other elites as the SAS and the Paras. This is the stirring story of their rise from poor pay, lack of public regard and promotional structure, to a special force, brilliantly and authoritatively told.

The Royal Marines's roles in many central military campaigns, including Northern Ireland and a decisive role in the recovery of the Falklands, are recorded in detail and brought to life with previously unpublished material from the Imperial War Museum and the Royal Marines Museum.

Major-General Julian Thompson joined the Royal Marines at the age of eighteen, serving for thirty-four years. He led the 3rd Commando Brigade in the Falklands and was in the thick of the fighting. He is now Visiting Professor in the Department of War Studies at King's College, London, and is author of four previous books and editor of *The Imperial War Museum Book of Modern Warfare*.

'Major-General Thompson did more than most men to save the Marines' very existence, and no one could have made a better job of telling their stirring story'
Max Hastings, *Evening Standard*

JULIAN THOMPSON (ed.)

The Imperial War Museum Book of

Modern Warfare

British and Commonwealth Forces at War 1945–2000

PAN BOOKS

An authoritative and readable book that fills a gap in British and Commonwealth military history

Since 1945, British and Commonwealth troops have been involved in fifteen major campaigns and conflicts, not a single year having passed in peace. The chapters (Java, Palestine, Malaya, Korea, Kenya, Cyprus, Canal Zone and Suez, Muscat and Oman, Brunei and Borneo, South Arabia/Aden, Northern Ireland, Dhofar, Falklands, Gulf, Bosnia and Kosovo) are all by an acknowledged expert and/or participant.

The Korean chapter is by General Sir Anthony Farrar-Hockley who, as a captain, was captured after the epic stand of the Glosters at the Imjin in Korea. He was a persistent escaper, but never made friendly lines, and was singled out for 'special treatment', a euphemism for torture, by the Chinese and North Korean camp guards and interrogators. The chapter on the recapture of Jebel Akhdar (in Oman) is by Tony Deane Drummond who commanded the SAS there and describes one of the most daring feats of modern warfare.

JULIAN THOMPSON

The Imperial War Museum Book of

War in Burma 1942–1945

A Vital Contribution to Victory in the Far East

PAN BOOKS

An unforgettable account of one of the greatest campaigns in British military history – the war against the Japanese in Burma

The campaign in Burma was remarkable in many ways. It was the longest and biggest ground war fought by the British and Americans against the Japanese. It was won in some of the bitterest fighting experienced by the Allies in the Second World War, and included one of the longest retreats (1000 miles) and one of the greatest Allied Victories, Kohima-Imphal. It saw the emergence of one of the greatest British commanders of all time, General Slim. The Allied forces serving in Burma were among the most multi-racial in the history of warfare.

'Julian Thompson's authoritative study of this romantic and romanticized aspect of twentieth-century warfare encompasses all the significant forces operating behind enemy lines . . . the result is both a serious contribution to our military history and a compelling read'
Alan Judd, *Sunday Times*

'Julian Thompson brings many a desperate close encounter vividly to life'
Duff Hart-Davis, *Daily Telegraph*

MALCOLM BROWN

The Imperial War Museum Book of

The Somme

PAN BOOKS

The shadow of the Somme has lain across the twentieth century. For many it is the ultimate symbol of the folly and futility of war. Others see it as a hallmark of heroic endeavour and achievement.

This book offers a remarkably fresh perspective on the bitterly fought 1916 campaign; it also describes the later battles of the Somme in the Great War's final year, 1918. Using hitherto unpublished evidence from the archives of the Imperial War Museum, it tells its powerful and dramatic story through the letters and diaries of those who were there.

Distinguished military historian Malcolm Brown has woven the many and varied accounts by well over a hundred participants – mainly British, but with not a few Germans – into a rich tapestry of experience.

'Admirable . . . If you can buy only one book on the Somme, it should be Malcolm Brown's powerful and scholarly account'
Richard Holmes, *Times Educational Supplement*

MALCOLM BROWN

The Imperial War Museum Book of
The Western Front

PAN BOOKS

The First World War was won and lost on the Western Front. Covering the whole war, from the noise of the guns of August 1914 to the sudden silence of the November 1918 Armistice, *The IWM Book of the Western Front* reveals what life was really like for the men and women involved. With first-hand accounts of off-duty entertainment, trench fatalism, and going over the top, this is an extremely important contribution to the continuing debate on the First World War. Malcolm Brown has updated this edition, introducing new evidence on sex and homosexuality, executions, the treatment or mistreatment of prisoners and shell shock.

'An unrivalled and readable introduction to the years of Trench Warfare'
Times Educational Supplement

'A blockbuster . . . as near as anyone is likely to get to the authentic life of the trenches'
Yorkshire Post